BODY LANGUAGE IN BUSINESS

Also by Adrian Furnham

Reaching for the Counter (1993)

Business Watching (1994) (with Barrie Gunter)

The Myths of Management (1996)

Corporate Culture Shock (1997)

The Psychology of Managerial Incompetence (1998)

Body Language at Work (1999)

The Hopeless, Hapless and Helpless Manager (2000)

Children and Advertising (2000)

The 3D Manager: Dangerous, Derailed and Deranged (2001)

Growing Up with Advertising (2002)

Mad, Sad and Bad Management (2003)

Binge Drinking (2003)

Management and Myths (2004)

The People Business (2005)

Dishonesty at Work (2005) (with John Taylor)

Management Mumbo-Jumbo (2006)

Head and Heart Management (2007)

Management Intelligence (2008)

Dim Sum Management (2008)

The Elephant in the Boardroom (2010)

BODY LANGUAGE IN BUSINESS

Decoding the Signals

Adrian Furnham

&

Evgeniya Petrova

palgrave
macmillan

First published 2010 by
PALGRAVE MACMILLAN

Palgrave Macmillan in the UK is an imprint of Macmillan Publishers Limited, registered in England, company number 785998, of Houndmills, Basingstoke, Hampshire RG21 6XS.

Palgrave Macmillan in the US is a division of St Martin's Press LLC, 175 Fifth Avenue, New York, NY 10010.

Palgrave Macmillan is the global academic imprint of the above companies and has companies and representatives throughout the world.

Palgrave® and Macmillan® are registered trademarks in the United States, the United Kingdom, Europe and other countries.

ISBN 978–0–230–24146–6

This book is printed on paper suitable for recycling and made from fully managed and sustained forest sources. Logging, pulping and manufacturing processes are expected to conform to the environmental regulations of the country of origin.

A catalogue record for this book is available from the British Library.

A catalog record for this book is available from the Library of Congress.

10   9   8   7   6   5   4   3   2   1
19   18   17   16   15   14   13   12   11   10

Printed and bound in Great Britain by
CPI Antony Rowe, Chippenham and Eastbourne

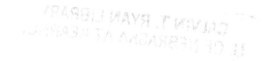

For Alison and Benedict of course (AF)

For my parents (EP)

CONTENTS

CONTENTS

LIST OF FIGURES AND TABLES

FIGURES

TABLES

PREFACE

This is a second edition of a short book on a similar topic. It sold very well but needed updating and extending, which was, overall, both an interesting and an amusing task. This now greatly expanded book contains material from the first edition and other pieces we have written on related topics. However, we have revised and integrated this material into what we hope is both a useful and exciting new book. We have attempted to write an approachable, popular, but not misleading, book.

Judging by the number of popular books we found, bought and read on this topic it appears that a great number of people are interested in body language. This is not that surprising, given its intrigue and ambiguities. We all appreciate how important it is as a medium of communication. As we point out, there is a great deal of nonsense written about body language. Academic studies have been misinterpreted; evidence-free assertions made; and exaggerated claims spread around. We have endeavoured to produce a useful and practical guide to body language which is informed by the research on the topic. Enjoy.

ADRIAN FURNHAM
EVGENIYA PETROVA

Every effort has been made to contact copyright-holders for work used in this book, but if any have been inadvertently overlooked the publishers will be pleased to make the necessary arrangements at the earliest opportunity.

1

INTRODUCTION

This book is about body language: signals we send out and receive, messages we transmit and decipher, and "statements" we make about ourselves nonverbally. Body language is the most primitive system of communication that we share with other species in the animal kingdom. We use it extensively to exchange information about our claim to territory and status, as well as our mate preferences and deepest desires. We use it in the boardroom and the saleroom, to great or little effect. We send out and decode messages of interest and concern, hope and despair, belief and disbelief in the office every day. It is the language we all speak regardless of background or upbringing. It is in our "DNA": it is a part of our human nature, the very stuff of communication.

Of course, it is not all there is to communication. Verbal, spoken language and linguistic abilities are much more complex and ubiquitous phenomena that let us articulate such concepts as space–time, religion, love and beauty. Nevertheless, some things are often easier to express by means other than, or in addition to, words and sentences. Emotions, in particular, are hard to put across verbally (or all the talking therapies would have been dead by now), as are expressions of abstract beliefs. Pain, for example, is difficult to describe, as are complex shapes without the use of gesture.

In this book we seek to clarify a few issues. First, we pose and answer the question: What does it entail to communicate via body language; what sort of information do we send, to whom and under what circumstances? Chapter by chapter we introduce and evaluate the different media of nonverbal messages. Gestures, body positions, facial expressions, vocal tones, touch, smell and even our taste in clothes convey messages about who we are and how we feel.

Second, we deal with the issues of how body language can be used and, regrettably, sometimes abused, to mis-communicate. There is

1

much confusion (and dare we say nonsense) about how to interpret nonverbal signals. Hence a delicate balance needs to be struck between reading too much or too little into small (or large) body signals. Further, while we all praise ourselves as natural "man and woman watchers", we are particularly susceptible to trusting fake body language. We include a comprehensive section on lying and how to detect it that deals with this issue.

Finally, we choose to concentrate on practical applications of these facts and observations to the world of work and business. Whether you "live to work" or "work to live", you must have had to meet, negotiate, present and sell (yourself, your ideas or products) at some point in your career. Body language is important at work, from the selection interview to the farewell speech. Awareness of, and ability to manage, one's own body language and read that of others is at the heart of business success, whatever the business. Nonverbal communication (NVC) is also the essence of political propaganda, PR, marketing and advertising, and understanding how these silent signals work can be a crucial asset to business as well as to consumers' education.

Most of our adult life is spent at work. In the words of Steve Jobs, the chief executive officer (CEO) of the Apple computer company, and the person with the most appropriate surname for this kind of quote, "Your work is going to fill a large part of your life, and the only way to be truly satisfied is to do what you believe is great work. And the only way to do great work is to love what you do". This book will not teach you how to find that dream job or rediscover your passion in life, but it will give you practical tips and advice about how to become better and more successful in business by reading the body language of others and displaying appropriate body language yourself.

WHAT IS BODY LANGUAGE?

Bodily communication is communication without words: it is anything someone does to which someone else assigns meaning. Of course, not all the "signals" a person sends are intentional and often they are not "picked up" or are misinterpreted. Nonverbal behavior, as we shall see, is complex, subtle and multichannel. It may be structured (following certain rules) but is more likely to be unstructured; it may be continuous, unlike language, which comes in disconnected units; it may be learnt, but some functions seem innate; and it may be "right-" as opposed to "left-brained".

It is no wonder that so many people are fascinated by body language. We are all "humanwatchers" and amateur psychologists, partly because we have to be. In every aspect of communication at work – the selection interview, the annual appraisal, the board meeting – we need to observe others carefully to try to understand better what they are feeling as well as what they are (really) saying. Being adults, we are all skilful deceivers; we have learnt, for myriad reasons, to present ourselves in a particular way; to manage the impression we leave; not always to say directly what we mean (perhaps to protect others' feelings); to sell products or ideas; and to explain away some undesirable behavior.

Politicians and CEOs are often trained by actors to present themselves in a particular way. They know that while they may have very clever speech writers, it is as much about *how* the speech is delivered as *what* is said. This is very important in our television age, where the camera can focus in on small beads of sweat, fingernail-biting or occasional scowls by important speakers. Experts now record speeches and analyze frame-by-frame the minute changes in facial expressions and body movements, usually to explore evidence that the speaker is being insincere. All actors know the importance of body language when portraying a character; as do comedians who mimic famous people. Often a very simple mannerism, if exaggerated, can immediately signal who it is they are attempting to impersonate.

As a result, many people believe messages conveyed by different body signals, particularly emotional states and attitudes to oneself and others, are in some way more real, more fundamental. We send and "leak" nonverbal signals, which may or may not be picked up in the communication process. The sender of the message may be aware or unaware of the signals he or she is sending. And indeed, receivers may not always be aware of the messages they are picking up. For example, most people are not aware of the dilation of their pupils; nor are observers aware that they can on specific occasions respond positively to dilated pupils (when people are sexually aroused).

There are many ways to define and delineate nonverbal behavior. One feature concerns whether it is speech-related or speech-independent. Another is in terms of its social functions. We know that nonverbal behaviors (NVBs):

- repeat, echo and emphasize what is being said;
- complement, modify and elaborate on verbal messages;
- conflict, contradict or confuse verbal messages to show ambivalence or cover up motives;

3

- substitute words;
- underline, accentuate, punctuate and moderate language; and
- regulate and coordinate language.

Body language can be subtle or blatant; it can be consciously sent and unconsciously received; it can be carefully practised and displayed but also physiologically uncontrollable; it can let you down by revealing your true beliefs and behaviors, but also (when learnt) help enormously to get across a message. Facial expressions, gestures, head and gaze movements, body contact and orientation, sheer physical proximity as well as tone of voice, clothes and body adornments send clear messages . . . and some of these are even intended!

Consider the ability of actors on the silent screen (Charlie Chaplin, Buster Keaton, Harold Lloyd, for example) to communicate. They had to be very perceptive students of expression. They used sign language (gestures to replace words, numbers and punctuation marks) to convey a bewildering array of meanings. Nonverbal communication is a more primitive and often more powerful means of communication than verbal communication. Some things may be better expressed nonverbally than verbally, partly to keep them ambiguous. Subtle and intentionally vague messages can also be sent through the imprecise channel of nonverbal communication. Cultures, as we shall see, develop specific rules about nonverbal communication, often set out in etiquette books, such as when, where and why to touch others, how to give greetings and so on.

Nonverbal communication is a rather misleading term. "Nonverbal" excludes vocal or paralinguistic cues and signals such as the emotional tone of speech, which is clearly very important. Body language also excludes vocal cues. Communication suggests, furthermore, that giver and sender (encoder and decoder) are conscious speakers of the same body language. Intentional messages may or may not be intentionally received nonverbally. Equally, unintentional messages may be unintentionally sent and received.

NATURE OR NURTURE?

Most human characteristics are the products of nature and nurture, which are difficult to separate. Certainly, we learn at school, at home and from the media the acceptability or unacceptability of various behaviors – touch, gesture, eye gaze. But is it hard-wired? Are we born with a "body language instinct"? Below is the evidence for the nature side of the debate.

- Blind children who could not have learnt behaviors such as smiling, nodding, scowling from observation, still display them.
- Newborn infants show recognizable emotions such as joy, surprise or interest, and a response to pain. They also start mimicking their mothers' facial expressions very shortly after birth.
- Identical twins separated soon after birth and raised apart show strikingly similar NVBs such as posture and head movements.
- Primates (apes and monkeys) show a whole range of emotions, particularly anger and fear, in a very similar way to humans.
- Cross-cultural studies done in various countries on all continents show that people not only express basic emotions very similarly (happiness, fear, surprise, anger, disgust, sadness), but also recognize them without hesitation.

In this book we choose to define body language quite broadly. By nonverbal communication we mean all the signs and signals relating to visual, vocal and sensory inputs as well as subtle, but pervasive, social markers such as dress, color and objects with which we surround ourselves. While such a definition might seem unconventional, it allows us to make the most comprehensive review of available material on this fascinating topic.

As such, the term 'verbal' is also used throughout the book loosely. A dictionary definition of 'verbal' is 'expressed or conveyed by speech rather than writing'. However, when using 'verbal' we refer to to the properties of words or the ability to communicate through speech and in writing using the power of words.

THE FUNCTION OF BODY LANGUAGE

Nonverbal messages are used to replace, reinforce, and occasionally (deliberately) contradict, a verbal message. Nonverbal cues can easily substitute for verbal ones: for example, "Yes/No" or "I don't know". Often nonverbal cues can stress, underline or exaggerate the meaning of the verbal message. But nonverbal cues can also negate verbal cues. A "kinetic slip" is a *contradictory* signal where words give one message, while voice and expression another: "I'm telling you I'm not angry" or "Of course it didn't upset me" can easily be said in one of two ways.

Often bodily communication *complements* speech. One can nonverbally restate a message so as, in effect, *to repeat* it. A nonverbal signal can *substitute* for a verbal message, or indeed accentuate it. Most obviously, nonverbal communication serves to *regulate* or *coordinate* daily dialogue between people. It is through nonverbal cues that we know when it is our turn to talk, and when the topic of conversation is becoming embarrassing; certain things are deliberately not said or are coded in polite body language. That is why it forms such a big part of the concept of *emotional intelligence.*

People also appear to understand nonverbal behavior metaphorically. Thus people use the *approach or distance metaphor,* which suggests that chosen location/distance is an indication of liking or closeness. Physical proximity implies mental closeness, alliance or liking, as all children instinctively know. The excitement or *arousal metaphor* suggests that facial expression, speech rate and speed of movement are indications of excitement, and that all nonverbal behavior gives some insight into how interested, involved and excited a person is. The *power metaphor* emphasizes that nonverbal communication tells us about dominance and submission in everyday communication. Powerful people are "allowed to" engage in more eye contact than less powerful people – and all children know this, too. Put simply, body language tells one about the closeness, relative excitement and status of two or more people communicating with each other. But it also tells us much more than this.

Body language has a clear *biological base* and is a product of evolutionary development. Animals are able to communicate without a need for even the most primitive linguistic system. They touch, smell, gesture and point to each other and so do we. It doesn't come as surprise, then, that, for example, standing positions that we adopt give out social rank order and mirror those of primates. Yawning, widely regarded as a sign of boredom, is an action even fish engage in. Consequently, the way we sit, hold a cigarette, smile and shake hands could also be interpreted and read into to reveal both the inner state of mind and social status.

Body language is also about *emotion.* It is quite easy to recognize and match facial expressions and underlying emotions. Some emotions appear to be innate and universal – such as fear, happiness and disgust. We can convey emotions through touch as well. Sometimes a hug sends more sympathy than carefully prepared words. What is

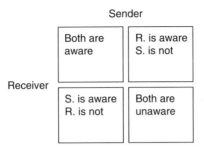

Figure 1.1 **Body language awareness**

more, people are not very good at expressing their emotions verbally, hence the very prosperous industry of psychotherapy, role play and counselling.

Sometimes the signal system of body language works very efficiently. The sender gestures, the receiver sees; and both are aware of the unspoken message. In a conversation, for example, if one person is confused or overwhelmed by what the other is saying, he or she might raise a hand to ask for clarification. This gesture lets the speaker know that they did not express themselves clearly or need to back up their argument. In this case, both people benefit from the silent cue.

Sometimes the sender is unaware of his or her own behavior–fiddling with the hair or wedding ring, moving feet up and down, darting glances to the left or right. The receiver picks this up and interprets it; but the sender remains unaware. This situation works to the advantage of those in the know, as long as the interpretation is correct.

Some "clever" people send signals by lightly touching people, copying their gestures, invading their space. Distracted by words, the recipient is unaware of the sender's often subtle but deliberate moves. Influencing through peripheral channels of attention by utilizing existing cognitive algorithms of information processing is one of the most powerful ways of persuasion, since it does not require conscious attention on the part of the receiver and does not give them an opportunity to reject the proposition. Successful political and marketing influencing regularly uses this type of communication.

Occasionally neither party is really aware – at least consciously – of what is being signalled. The sender may have dilated pupils or give off pheromonic body odours indicating sexual excitement, but neither of the parties brings the cues to conscious awareness. In romantic relationships this might cause feelings of instant, unexplainable attraction.

SENSE AND NONSENSE ABOUT BODY LANGUAGE

The first scientists to make a systematic study of body language were biologists. It is no surprise that those skilled in bird-watching were easily able to turn their skills to man-watching. Charles Darwin wrote the first acknowledged text in 1873, entitled *The Expression of the Emotions in Man and Animals*. Irenaus Eibl-Eibesfeldt wrote a scholarly popular biology book in 1971 entitled *Love and Hate: Natural History of Behavior Patterns*. But it was Desmond Morris's book, *The Naked Ape*, published in 1967, ninety-four years after Darwin – that electrified popular interest in body-watching. There are now dozens of books on this topic, as a quick internet search will reveal (see Appendix at the end of the book).

Since the early 1980s scientists from different disciplines – anthropology, psychology, sociology and zoology – have brought their methods and concepts together in order to help the understanding of bodily communication. More recently, physiologists, endocrinologists, sexologists, and even marketers and advertisers have taken a particular interest in highly specific physiological processes that have nonverbal consequences.

Despite the excellent and careful research in the area, much nonsense is still written on the topic, often by journalists and other self-appointed "experts", whose aim is to entertain (and sell) rather than to enlighten and educate. Fascination with the topic, as well as its apparent importance in business, has led many self-styled experts and gurus to make confident proclamations about nonverbal communication. Inevitably, nearly all of their "findings" and "recommendations" over-emphasize the importance and power of nonverbal communication. Often there is no evidence at all that their interpretations of literature are correct; though many exaggerate something that is based on fact.

Misleading and sometimes completely incorrect statements about body language communication seem to fall into four areas: symbolism; power; controllability; and "you can read people like a book".

Symbolism: all bodily communication is symbolic expression

People with a fondness for psychoanalytic (Freudian) ideas love to interpret explicit behaviors as manifestations of (often unconscious) desires and feelings. Thus one observer believed that Prince Charles's habit of "fiddling" with his cufflinks indicated that he felt chained by handcuffs to the monarchy. Those with a stiff and military bearing

TABLE 1.1 **Body language: alternative interpretations**

Behaviors	Psychological explanations	Alternative explanations
Hands in pockets	The person is secretive, withdrawn, possibly depressed.	It is cold; the person is searching for a small object.
Folded arms	Defensive act formed for physical reassurance. Indicator of uncertainty and lack of confidence.	It is cold; the arm rests are occupied; it is comfortable
Yawning	Faced with a difficult situation one would prefer to avoid.	Very tired; not enough oxygen.
Crossed legs	Defensive, repressed, even feeling hostile.	Women are taught to cross legs to look more feminine; men do so because it is comfortable.
Nose touching	The person is lying or covering up his or her emotions.	He or she has a cold or an itchy nose.

have "imprisoned anxiety". Numerous otherwise common behaviors such as the wetting of lips, the crossing of legs and the folding of arms are all indicators of repressed sexuality. A man talking to a pretty woman (or indeed a woman talking to a handsome man) may fiddle with his wedding ring: a psychoanalyst might claim they want to take it off and appear available to the new partner. A person describing their mother may suddenly seem to hug themselves: the symbolic explanation would state that perhaps the person is trying to recreate the warmth and affection of motherly cuddles.

The temptation among too many body language experts is that they favor "unconscious", Freudian, psychological explanations over more obvious ones. It is too easy to over-interpret incorrectly. For example, look at the table above and consider two types of explanation given for the same behavior (one innocent, the other not).

As noted earlier, people often communicate via body language without being aware of it. However, this should not encourage explanations based on unconscious drives or needs for all idiosyncratic behaviors. People acquire and internalize gestures and other behaviors from parents, teachers, even film actors. Some nonverbal cues are symbolic of unconscious desires, hopes and urges but many, probably most, are not.

Power: bodily communication is always more powerful

It is not uncommon to read statements such as: "Seventy percent of the communicative power of a message is sent nonverbally" or "It is not what you say but the way that you say it". Body communication pundits have a natural inclination to "talk up" their area of expertise, to over-emphasize its importance. Nonverbal communication can, indeed, at times be extremely powerful – sheer rage or terror are often much more efficiently communicated through facial and body expression than through words, for example. Pain or love can also be signalled by changes in facial expressions, especially by children and others who articulate their feelings via a limited vocabulary. Ability to communicate a message nonverbally is the whole point of the parlour game "Charades".

Yet words have extraordinary precision. Consider, for example, the power of poetry to move people emotionally. It is the precision of words that create sharp and clear imagery, and arouse emotional responses. Tell politicians to give up their scriptwriters and communicate by their nonverbal charm alone: only those with natural charisma and an exciting impromptu message to impart will be able to succeed. Ask all those people who advocate "talking cure" therapies to rely more on nonverbal rather than verbal cues. On the contrary, to actively acknowledge and verbalize a problem is regarded by many as a first step to recovery.

Further, if one uses gesture, for example, to communicate, it is immediately apparent that there are very few gestures compared to words. The power of bodily communication lies primarily in the fact that it often tells one about the physiological state of the individual because of changes in the central nervous system. Certainly, extreme emotions such as anger "leak out", however carefully a person tries to hide them. Sexual excitement is difficult to hide, as often is guilt. But these physiological states are nearly always an expression of emotional extremes that are not that common in everyday life.

Body language can shout and it can be subtle. But those who claim it is so powerful should try to send to a stranger the following, relatively simple messages nonverbally: "Thank you very much", "I totally disagree"; and "I feel very happy for you".

EXAGGERATION, LIES AND HALF TRUTHS

It is common to hear various claims about the power and importance of nonverbal language. To back it up, some even express it in percentages. So one is told that 93 percent of the information communicated in face-to-face meetings is nonverbal. Most of it is through face and body movements and expressions, and around a third is derived from voice quality and tone.

The lowest percentage is always applied to verbal communication: the words that people actually say. This is, of course, patent nonsense: why would anyone bother to learn a foreign language when they could be communicating nonverbally with 90 percent efficiency.

Max Atkinson (2004), in his charming book, *Lend Me Your Ears*, did the detective work behind those often repeated modern myths. The story goes like this. An American social psychologist, Albert Mehrabian, published a series of papers in the 1960s researching the types of information (visual, verbal and vocal) people give their preference for or find most useful, when presented with messages where these types of information are incongruent. The nature of the task involved participants detecting and matching the feelings and attitudes of people shown in short film clips. The presented messages were either consistent or inconsistent across three channels (the words did or did not match the nonverbal expressions). He found that when the information was incongruent, people put more trust in the nonverbal cues. Mehrabian's analysis converted the frequency of information preference into numerical values: 38 percent of total information liking came from the vocal cues; 7 percent from verbal cues; and 55 percent from facial or visual cues.

This conclusion is quite different from exaggerated claims about universal laws of general communication. It is about judging specific attitudes in the presence of incongruent information. Atkinson asked Mehrabian, the author of original research, what his thoughts were about this, and his response was dismay and discomfort about being completely misquoted.

However once this statistic was publicized and, unfortunately, misinterpreted, it has become an accepted truth repeated since in magazines, training sessions and corporate events. It makes, or should make, people very sceptical about many other claims surrounding body language and nonverbal communication.

Controllability: we can control all the messages we send

Some nonverbal behavior, such as gestures and touch, are naturally controllable; while others, such as sweating and pupil dilation, are not.

Often people want to cover up evidence of their anxiety or specific motives (such as sexual pleasure, for example) but are unable to do so. Most people in conversation are not particularly aware of others, or of their own legs and feet, which if they chose they could control. They are not aware of small changes in posture and micro-facial expressions as certain things are said.

Once these behaviors have been witnessed on a video-recording, it is surprisingly easy to see and understand their meaning. Once an "actor" becomes an "observer" of his or her own behavior, awareness of what is going on is increased.

Naturally, some people attempt to control their nonverbal behavior. Stage actors may be required to weep, rage or demonstrate fear, loathing or passion on cue. They have learnt, often with the help of make-up, to produce certain recognizable signals of those emotions. But most of us are not so gifted. Indeed, the more we try to control emotions – particularly if we try to conceal powerful emotions – the more they leak out nonverbally.

You can read people like a book: decoding nonverbal language is easy

There are many misleading aspects to this analogy. Books are passive, whereas people are not. Most observers are aware that when two people are speaking, each is attempting to "read" the other. However, this reading is often an advantageous feedback mechanism, not a deliberate attempt to outguess the other party. The curious claim of many popular books is that it is possible simultaneously to read techniques of others but hide your own – to disguise one's secret intentions by putting on a believable poker face.

True experts in the area of nonverbal communication are surprisingly diffident on this point. Research tells us that such a "double blind" show is extremely difficult to perform, if not impossible for many. Indeed, hiding one's feelings while reading the other person's mind would mean that a person is engaged in two tasks simultaneously, and people are generally very bad at dividing their attention resources. Further, experts on lying point out how tricky it is to detect it in skilful dissimulators. They all highlight how much information one needs to confirm a hypothesis that "he is lying", "she is an extrovert" or "they are not competent in this area".

Just as in learning any language, one can become more fluent, more perceptive and more skilled at reading body signals, but there is no magical solution, partly because of the subtlety of the cues but also because of the multiple meanings attached to identified behaviors.

WHY IS IT IMPORTANT IN BUSINESS?

Certainly, knowledge of nonverbal communication and body language is very helpful in business. Understanding the motives, fears and strengths of those sitting on selection committees, or opponents in bargaining situations, is a considerable asset in the business world. Observing subtle changes in body language as it accompanies speech may be one of the best ways to gain advantage. Also, a knowledge of body language can help people to improve their performance at conferences, in appraisals and even in day-to-day management. If such matters were not important, politicians, business people and diplomats would not spend so much money and time attending workshops on communication skills and body language. Poor performances on stage – at a party political conference, or an annual general meeting, say – can literally wreck whole careers, no matter how talented, productive or hardworking a person might be.

It is no surprise that social and interpersonal skills training contains so much about nonverbal behavior. These are often called "soft" skills, which are unlikely to be taught at school or university. The sudden interest in emotional intelligence, which is largely related to the recognition and management of nonverbal behavioral cues, took the world by storm. We all know talented, educated professionals with all the "hard" skills of their occupation. However, because management is a "contact sport", they fail to reach their ultimate potential because of their lack of ability to communicate with people. Dismissed as "geeks", "nerds" or "boffins", such professionals are seen as technically competent, but interpersonally incompetent. Indeed, they may have spent critical learning periods for interpersonal behaviors (usually early adolescence) avoiding and eschewing learning opportunities.

The higher the level that people reach in business, the more relevant are the soft skills. Senior management is about choosing, directing and motivating specialist teams. Often called charm or charisma, it is about sensitivity and perceptiveness, reading social cues and putting your message across well. All leaders, particularly politicians and senior executives, know the importance of communication skills. They make or break careers.

Nonverbal communication is also at the heart of political and marketing influence. Tell people to buy more of your product and they won't even notice your message. Tell people to vote for your party and they will most likely ignore you. So how do you persuade voters and consumers to act on your message? You make them identify with it, you provoke desire, you create a need. It is the clever use of nonverbal signs, such as images, sounds and colors that distinguishes a successful campaign from a runner-up.

EVOLUTIONARY APPROACHES TO BODY LANGUAGE

It is clear that we are wired to communicate with each other not only by means of verbal language but also via the reading of nonverbal signals. The way we look, stand, dress, walk and smile insinuate how we feel, experience emotions and relate to other people. It also can be indicative of general health condition, mood and energy levels. Why, one might ask, have we evolved such an ability? What is more, how much of it is applicable to the modern-age human?

The premise of evolutionary psychology is the process of natural selection. Floyd (2006) outlines the following principles governing the work of evolution:

1. *Superfecundity* – each generation usually produces more offspring than can survive or grow to maturity.
2. *Variation* – combination of traits are different among members of the same species.
3. *Heritability* – some of these differences are hereditary.
4. *Selection* – those traits that are advantageous for a particular environment in a given species will be inherited more frequently.

It is clear, then, that over time people have evolved particular traits, physique and dispositions to cope better in their natural environment. High neuroticism, for example, a personality trait that is characterized by excessive worry, susceptibility to stress, and general irritability, might have been extremely adaptive in prehistoric times, when extra vigilance meant survival. A bigger build and more muscle have certainly equated to more physical power, and thus meant that those who possessed these characteristics had a greater chance of defending themselves and their offspring from predators. Through this mechanism of "becoming fit for purpose" certain qualities became advantageous in a population. Not surprisingly, then, those who had them had the upper hand in mate selection and, ultimately, in gene proliferation.

Darwin himself explained how the functional aspects of body language (sending the message) acquired the status of metaphorical. He argued that some gestures had a purposeful role (pinching one's nose to block an unpleasant smell, for example) which over time applied the meaning across the situation and became metaphors (suggesting a foul smell). Most of all, successful living in a group requires a system of communication. Body language most likely has its roots in pre-speech form of information sharing. Animals rely, for example, on olfactory information much more than we do; however, we still do share certain gestures and facial expressions with our closest genetic primate relatives. Hence nonverbal communication evolved as a representation system for states and qualities that benefited human survival.

But how does this notion translate into the present-day environment? Take an example of height. A primate's height used to signal high or low dominance among our ancestors, and not surprisingly, studies of successful business leaders consistently show they tend to be taller than average in the general population. Hair growth quality might have been an indicator of health, thus high-flying managers are more likely (than average) to have their own head hair. Intelligence, a gauge of one's ability to process information correctly and rapidly and use it effectively in novel settings, gave a powerful leverage not only to individuals but to the group as a whole. Predictably, contemporary leaders also tend to be highly intelligent.

Another evolutionary advantage of developing a complement to the speech system of communication is the reduction of cognitive load. Since our brain has only a limited capacity for storage of incoming information (it is restricted to *seven* pieces of information, plus or minus two), combined with the temporal pressures of memory (any information has to be transferred from the initial reservoir of short-term memory to the infinite long-term memory's storage during that time or it will be lost), it is very useful to receive some messages effortlessly, without any thinking involved. Figure 1.2 is a graphical illustration of this idea.

THREE MEDIA, THREE CUES

Some people in business prefer to communicate certain messages in writing while others prefer using face-to-face meetings. Research has

15

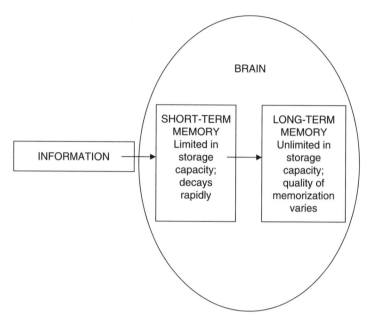

Figure 1.2 **The brain's short-term and long-term storage capacity**

shown that the choice of a communication medium can greatly affect the degree of clarity or ambiguity of the message being sent. Oral media (for example, telephone conversations and face-to-face meetings) are preferable to written media, such as notes and memos, when messages are ambiguous (requiring a great deal of assistance in interpreting them), but written media are preferable when messages are clear.

What leads someone to choose one mode or media of communication over another? Why not drop a note in a pigeonhole rather than phone the other person? Why race up three floors to find a person is not in when you could have used an e-mail?

One obvious answer to the question of choice of medium is economy and efficiency. Telephones are faster, letters and memos can be duplicated and so on. However, there are various important psychological advantages and disadvantages to the various media that are well understood but seldom discussed explicitly. Certainly, face-to-face or

TABLE 1.2 **Media for sending and receiving body language cues**

Medium	TV, Face-to-face	Radio	Print E-mail
Cues	Verbal, Vocal, Visual	Verbal, Vocal	Verbal

video-conferenced communication offers the best option for sending and receiving body language cues.

Verbal cues

We communicate daily using three types of medium. First, we write e-mails (and letters); we text and scribble notes; we compose reports, advertising scripts and so on. A lot of businesses require the ability to write well, to communicate clearly, succinctly and unambiguously on the page. The tools are words and numbers, diagrams and graphs.

The issue at work is how to write documents that communicate meaning most efficiently. We have many choices and options: to use pie-charts, graphs or tables when communicating data; whether, when and why to use color, capitals or italics. These issues are often much more pronounced with PowerPoint presentations. Critics and consultants in this area have numerous "rules" that prevent boredom and fatigue caused by information overload as well as helping people to process the information.

All this refers to verbal communication: communication by words alone in whatever font, color or size one may choose. The limitations of words alone can easily be seen in daily e-mails, where people add emoticons like :-) or :-< to indicate their emotional reaction to a statement. These are innovative, affect-laden, new and imaginative forms of punctuation.

Further, nearly all print media, even rather serious financial reports, use pictures to enhance or illustrate the script. Some favor cartoons, especially if they succinctly and wittily convey an important message. Many PowerPoint presentations attempt to "sex up" the whole process by using pictures and "special effects", particularly if the content is dull or very emotional.

Verbal communication is the most precise. It is therefore the experts' preferred communication medium: lawyers, accountants, engineers and scientists communicate primarily by this cool, efficient medium. Colleagues at work e-mail one another despite being two doors away. Children "txt" each other while in the same room or building.

Vocal cues

We also use the telephone a great deal: witness the travelling public and the number now using mobile phones. A phone call is quick, convenient and usually cheap. In addition to what people say, we get a range of vocal cues: their accents and vocabulary; their speed of speech, and hesitations, whether they lisp or stutter; how and when they laugh.

Actors have voice training, as do some journalist and politicians. There are "golden rules" about "pitch, pause and pace" in speeches. The gravitas, the sexiness, as well as the irony of the message can be conveyed by the voice. Huge amounts of money are spent by advertisers in "voice-overs": a recognizable person's voice brings a great deal to the communication.

Vocal cues are nonverbal cues. They indicate a person's place of upbringing, social class and education. They are clues to emotional state and to unconscious processes. The parapraxis or "slip-of-the-tongue" is a well-known Freudian observation, where people say the wrong word, often the opposite of what they mean. There are also "slips-of-the-pen", but those of the tongue are more common and often more embarrassing.

We listen to the radio, talk on the phone and buy tapes and disks of speech, poetry and so on. The growth of the audio book – which is recorded by an author or an actor – attests to its popularity. But consider how marketing people choose the actors to read books. Should they be male or female, distinctly northern or perhaps Eastern European?

People try to "hide behind" the spoken word. They take elocution lessons to change their accent and adapt speech styles involving "pitch raises", or "hip phrases" such as "kind of" or "like". They do so to ingratiate themselves with others, to join groups, to become accepted or acceptable. But they can "leak" their real background and emotions.

VOICE AND EMOTIONS

Vocal cues are full of emotions, and these emotional overtones can be detected easily. We can distinguish between a happy and a sad voice with no difficulty. However, is it possible to detect lying from the affective coloring of the voice?

That is what voice risk analysis devices claim to do. They are similar to polygraphs or lie detectors in their function and are used to try to detect whether people are telling the truth, especially over the telephone. These gadgets have been tried out by many businesses, from insurance companies to local councils, to detect false applications and dishonest claimants. The idea behind the technology is relatively straightforward: lying is stressful; thus, when a person lies, his or her vocal patterns change. Stress-induced voice alterations are, however, not always obvious and cannot be picked up by a human ear. The changes in voice tremors are subtle and insidious but can be spotted by sensitive "voice risk analysis" systems. The technology is said to account for individual differences in voice tones and pitches too. After all, some people are naturally shyer than others and might feel tense when making an honest insurance or benefit claim.

Yet it is not clear whether this technology works as a "liar catcher" or a "liar deterrent". The accuracy rate is far from infallible and the final decision on whether the caller is lying or not still has to be made by a human agent. On the other hand, similarly to lie detectors, voice risk analysis systems seem to work because people believe they do. When warned about being monitored, liars' detection apprehension increases. This, in turn, results in more stress and more visible voice quality changes, but it also simply discourages unconfident liars to make a fake claim.

Visual cues

For most people, the essence of all good communication is face-to-face. The more important the communication, the more likely it is that people will want to *see* the other person, and preferably not on a video link, which can seem stilted, artificial and unnatural. Interestingly, they cannot always articulate what they want to see, but believe they can communicate better face-to-face.

This book will discuss the many visual cues that occur in everyday behavior, from body posture and gesture to eye contact patterns. Visual cues include how people dress and how they move; how they sit and when they fidget; and how attractive they are.

When we see people face-to-face we also get other silent cues. We get olfactory cues – their scent – which can be powerful indicators of their health, and age and diet. If we shake hands we get details of the other person's body temperature and perhaps their anxiety level. We get information about how they present themselves to the world through their use of make-up, jewelry and even hair dye.

The richness of nonverbal, visual communication is the topic of this book. It should be pointed out that while one may get pure visual cues in a photograph and pure verbal cues on the printed page, often they co-occur. The telephone call includes verbal and vocal cues, while face-to-face communication has all three.

Verbal communication media

Consider the letter or its electronic equivalent, the e-mail. It has a number of obvious advantages. Unlike the telephone call or face-to-face meeting (unless this is audio- or video-taped), the letter or printed e-mail is a record of the communication. Hence it is the preferred medium of lawyers, bureaucrats and those concerned with the extraction of money or information. The letter, particularly if produced on a computer, may also be revised so that a precise tone, meaning or deliberate ambiguity may be communicated. Letters and e-mails are a more private means of communication than the telephone or face-to-face meeting, and in some cases they are cheaper than other methods. However, there are some doubts about the security of e-mails.

Curiously, however, two of the major drawbacks of the e-mail are also its major advantages. Letters take time, and feedback is postponed. We tend to impart bad news in writing when we feel inadequate to deal with the feedback we might receive. Angry, but unassertive, people of all ages frequently write letters and e-mails of complaint after receiving poor service, rather than deal with the matter immediately, face to face – often because they are afraid of the negative, aggressive or direct feedback they are likely to receive.

We also write when feedback is likely to embarrass us. People who have recently become bereaved, and sometimes the dying themselves, often explain how they received many letters, gifts and flowers but, strangely, people visited infrequently. As people usually respond in the same medium through which they were initially contacted, the caring friend can expect nothing more threatening than a grateful letter of acknowledgement.

Another advantage of the letter – but less so of the e-mail – is the opportunity it offers for impression management. First, there are the letter-heading and logo features, as well as the quality of the paper. Some people immediately rub the letter heading as a Braille reader might, just to check whether it is embossed. Business letter-headed notepaper is used to identify with the organization. Letters also allow one to state formally one's qualifications and job title.

Vocal communication media

The telephone offers numerous advantages over the letter. Feedback is immediate, if the person is available. It has a rather different legal status; that is, there is no record of the conversation. One can queue-jump, often quite effectively, unless the person with whom one wishes to speak has a filter mechanism such as an unhelpful personal assistant.

But the telephone has two other major advantages, certainly over the face-to-face meeting. The first is that you may speak to somebody while knowing practically nothing about him or her. What psychological or demographic variables can one recognize from a telephone voice? Sex? Probably, though we have no doubt all made embarrassing mistakes in this area. Age? Perhaps people under 10 or over 80 years might sound different, but it is very difficult to make accurate judgments. Education, race? Very unlikely. What about detecting a person's emotions, or whether he or she is lying? Again, unless at the extremes of anger, fear or depression, it is very difficult to detect a person's mood or indeed his or her implicit intentions when communicating over the telephone. We have all, no doubt, experienced surprise at seeing a favorite radio personality on television and finding that he or she is older or younger, balder or more hirsute, plainer or more attractive than one has imagined. Indeed, radio presenters' looks and shape may account precisely for why they are on radio as opposed to television in the first place.

Of course, not knowing much about the other person may be advantageous to either party. Just as you cannot know the age, looks or disabilities of the person to whom you are talking on the telephone, nor can he or she know such things about you. Hence the use of a "telephone voice" – an attempt to present an image through accent and tone of voice that is specious but desirable. The telephone offers some of the major advantages of face-to-face communication, such as speed of feedback, but crucially hides the tell-tale nonverbal cues that allow one to detect how honest, sincere, committed, truthful and so on is the person with whom you are talking.

The telephone offers one other major advantage, though there may be exceptions to the rule. Because one pays for a call in terms of a multiple of time and distance, the average time spent on the telephone is considerably shorter than the average spent face-to-face discussing exactly the same problem. Niceties and trivia are usually reduced and one gets to the point of the communication far more quickly. People may feel the need to provide refreshments when meeting face-to-face, or may be interrupted by a third party. However, business telephone calls are rarely too long, and furthermore one has a whole host of possible excuses (lies) as to why they need to be terminated (a call on the other line, knock at the door, and so on).

But most people prefer to communicate face-to-face, though, of course, in doing so they lose some advantages of the letter and the telephone as outlined above. They need more than verbal (written) and vocal (audio) cues to give and receive complex messages. Academic ethnologists, zoologists and psychologists have tended to rewrite the songwriter's words, "It's not what you say, it's the way that you say it", so emphasizing the role of nonverbal clues, such as eye-gaze patterns, body posture, movements, gestures and the like in communication. The crucial point is the medium you choose to "say it" through.

CONCLUSION

All animals communicate nonverbally continuously. Unlike animals, human beings have developed the power of speech and the ability to also express thoughts and intentions verbally. Yet a good deal of how we are understood, interpreted and evaluated happens via the "nonverbals" that accompany our speech.

Communication in the business world is extremely important. Communicating effectively and efficiently is highly valued, as is "being a good communicator", which usually means being charismatic and motivational. While body language is particularly important in some situations, it is also possible to over-emphasize the power of the medium by attributing to it more significance than it is capable of delivering.

2

THE SIGNAL SYSTEM

What are the major components of body language? What are the most important nonverbal behaviors we need to attend to? What do very specific behaviors tell us? Traditionally, researchers have "split up" the different types of bodily communication. Thus there are books, papers and experts on eye gaze as well as experts focusing on gestures alone. Some concentrate on cross-cultural differences in one or more types of body language, while others look for the body language indicators of specific emotions such as anxiety. As technology has progressed, so has research into such areas as olfaction (the sense of smell). No doubt soon there will be MRI or brain activity studies of body language.

CHANNELS OF COMMUNICATION

There are many ways of drawing up lists of the major body signals. In fact our everyday language shows how we note and understand different aspects of body language.

Body language is made up of various signals: the quick glance, the wry smile, the well-known gesture, body posture, the light touch, the badge on the lapel and the choice of perfume, for example. Each, alone and together, can provide a powerful and subtle form of communication to complement the spoken language.

There are innumerable English phrases that seem to relate to body language. Consider the following:

- *Touch*: "I touched her for a fiver". "I felt touched by his concern". "Her plight touched me".

- *Posture*: When people are comfortable they usually balance their weight on both feet. Hence we have "well-balanced", "take a firm stand", "know where you stand on this". When uncomfortable, many people shift their weight from one foot to the other and can be seen to be "shifty characters".
- *Eye contact*: "I see what you mean". "Seeing is believing". "I can't see any other solution".
- *Gesture*: "He gave me the cold shoulder". This indicates that a person rejected what was being said and metaphorically turned away in disgust.
- *Territory/distance*: "I feel close to him". "She is very standoffish". "Back off from me, buster!" "I prefer to keep her at arm's length".
- *Orientation*: "I dislike people who are always taking sides". "I feel diametrically opposed to everything he does".
- *Odor*: "I like the sweet smell of success". "He has a nose for where the money is". "Yet she still came up smelling of roses". "He is always sticking his nose in other people's business". "She always sticks her nose in the air". "I will ensure that I rub his nose in it".
- *Body state expression*: Feeling is often expressed in terms of body language. Thus we: "shoulder a burden", "face up to" other people, issues", try to "keep our chin up" or "grit our teeth" in the face of pain, have a "stiff upper lip", "bare our teeth" on occasion, "catch the eye" of another, and "shrug off" misfortune.
- *Dress* is also revealing of personal characteristics: one may be "dressed to kill", "dressed to the teeth", "'too big for one's britches" or "'wear one's heart on one's sleeve".

See what they say: eye gaze

The eyes are, indeed, the messengers of the soul. We "keep our eye in", "have an eye to the main chance", "keep our eyes open/peeled/skinned", "see eye-to-eye with others" but "turn a blind eye to certain events". Some people are hiding something – there is "more than meets the eye". Some individuals are the "apple of one's eye", and others a "sight for sore eyes". You may prefer "not to bat an eye" or to "pull the wool over others' eyes'". And you can be "up to your eyes" in trouble. We can accurately label emotions just from the changes in appearance of the eyes, which is why talking to people wearing dark glasses can be so problematic.

Where, when, and *how* we look are all part of the phenomenon of eye gaze, one of the most important and primitive ways of communication. Gaze plays a crucial role in conversation. Looking at another person is a way of getting feedback at particular points in the conversation. It is also used as a synchronizing signal. People tend to look up at the end of utterances: this gives them feedback and hands over the "conversational baton". People also look up more at the end of grammatical breaks, but look away when hesitating, talking non-fluently or thinking. There is often mutual eye contact during attempted interruptions, laughing and when answering short questions. Gaze functions to encourage and persuade in all human beings. Examples are shown in the box below.

- A looker may invite interaction by staring at another person who is on the other side of a room. The target's studied return of the gaze is generally interpreted as acceptance of the invitation, while averting the eyes is a rejection of the looker's request. We deal with embarrassment by looking away. It discourages conversation. We ignore and punish behavior simply by gaze aversion.
- There is more mutual eye contact between friends than others, and a looker's frank gaze is widely interpreted as positive regard. Lovers really do gaze more into each other's eyes.
- People who seek eye contact while speaking are regarded not only as exceptionally well-disposed by their targets, but also as more believable and earnest. Politicians "sweep" the room with their eye gaze. Salesmen know how to look at each member of their audience.
- If the usual short, intermittent gazes during conversation are replaced by gazes of longer duration, the target interprets this as meaning that the communication is less important than the personal relationship between the two people.
- The amount and type of eye gaze imparts a great deal of information. Pupil dilation, blink rates, direction of gaze, widening of the eyes all send very clear messages.

The causes and consequence of pupil dilation are particularly interesting because it is one of those communication behaviors that neither party (sender or receiver) are much aware of during the communication. Consider this: people are shown two identical photographs of a woman, with the only difference being that on one of them her pupil size is detectably and artificially enlarged to be double the normal, natural size. When asked to rate which one is more attractive, 60–80 percent of people shown the photographs will nominate the woman with falsely dilated pupils. However, if you ask them to point out how the photographs differ, very few identify the manipulation of pupil dilation. They point to skin, hair texture, lips or face shape, but rarely the pupils.

Pupils dilate for various reasons. In bright light they contract; in dim light, expand. But they also dilate with strong emotions such as sexual excitement or rage. The latter visibly manifests in cats or dogs that are about to fight. What is more, people respond to others who appear to be sexually attracted to them. Women used to put belladonna plant extract (which literally translates as "beautiful woman") in their eyes to cause pupil dilation (and, consequently, eye-sight problems, unfortunately). This could be a painful and dangerous process, but was considered worth the risk to attract men. Thus the man, unaware of why he was attracted to the woman, responded to the dilated pupils.

This is an example of the power of visible signals. Not one that is perhaps the most relevant or applicable in the workplace, however.

Consider the factors that determine the amount of eye gaze:

1. *Distance*. In elevators, we turn to face the door because we are forced to stand too close together, and reducing eye gaze helps to lessen the discomfort of having our body zones invaded. Note how conversation before, during and after the ride changes. As soon as the distance between people drops below 6 feet (1.8 meter), their eye contact decreases.
2. *Topic of conversation*. It is no accident that Catholic confessionals and psychiatric couches are so arranged as to attempt to reduce the amount of eye contact between priest and the individual in the confessional, and the therapist with the patient in the room. When people are talking about shameful and embarrassing things or looking inward, it is better that they sense but do not see others, and that those listening do not (cannot) stare at them. People often find that they can have "good conversations" walking or doing a cooperative activity, such as washing up, because they are close to, but not looking at, their companions. Intimate talk can be inhibited by eye contact.
3. *Conversation task*. Doctors look more at patients when talking about emotional rather than physical symptoms or conditions.

People look more at cooperators than competitors. Persuaders look more when trying to influence.

4. *Attention.* Hitch-hikers, charity-tin shakers and others all maximize eye contact to increase attention. People look at each other about 75 percent of the time when talking, but only 40 percent of the time when listening. One looks to get, and keep, the attention of others.

5. *Interpersonal relationships.* People look at those they like more than those they do not like. Their pupils dilate more when they are looking at someone they like. Gaze also signals dominance: more powerful people are looked at more (partly because they tend to look more and speak less). Threat is also indicated by gaze. Direct gaze signals threat, while cutting off or averting your gaze is likely to signal appeasement.

6. *Cooperation.* The extent to which people are willing to cooperate rather than compete is often communicated by gaze patterns. The amount and type of gaze is important. The common meaning of a high level of gaze is that the gazer is interested and attentive. However, combined with certain expressions it could as easily indicate threat.

7. *Personality.* Extroverts look more often, and for longer, at their interlocutors than introverts. The confident, the bright and the socially dominant look more while it is the opposite for the socially anxious. Females look more at those they are talking to compared to males.

8. *Physical appearance.* People look less at the disabled, and at less attractive individuals, and more at the able-bodied and those who are more attractive.

9. *Mental illness.* Many psychopathologies are associated with reduced and/or "odd" gaze patterns; in particular, autism and paranoia. Schizophrenics and depressed people tend to avert eye gaze.

10. *Ethnicity.* People from contact cultures such as those in the Near East look more than those from non-contact cultures such as those in Europe.

People also disguise eye contact by wearing dark glasses or shades. Blind people do so to indicate their blindness, but also because they cannot always "face" a person. Often, to avoid the embarrassment of not being able to "look a person in the eye" when appropriate, blind people wear tinted glasses. Security people also wear dark glasses so that possible suspects cannot see the direction in which they are looking.

Traffic police wear reflecting, mirrored glasses to reduce the possibility of an argument. Irate or nervous drivers can be put off a confrontation if they not only cannot see the eyes of the policeman but are also forced to see their own eyes. They experience objective self-awareness, seeing themselves as objects and not seeing those they are engaging in conversation.

Most of us know people who close their eyes while speaking. Such "eye blocks" may occur because a person is bored or feels superior. They deny both speaker and listener the opportunity to receive and give feedback. Shy, introverted people also tend to have a less open eye gaze.

The way rooms are furnished can maximize or minimize eye contact, as with the psychiatric couches and confessionals described above. But the position of chairs, desks and other office paraphernalia might also be a clue to a person's preferred mode of communication and their personality (given that they chose or arranged the furnishings themselves). It can also dictate how close you are to one another, how easy it is to look at each other in the eye and the angle of contact (orientation). It can be very uncomfortable sitting face-to-face at a very close distance, or particularly relaxing.

Some quirky individuals encourage others to choose where to sit from a number of options. The seats might differ in height, "stiffness" and distance. They believe it might symbolize the type of interaction and communication they prefer or intend to have.

Facial expression

The face is a highly expressive region. It is "readout" of emotions: immediate, spontaneous, honest and uncontrollable. Knowing this, however, we expend a lot of effort trying to control it. The eyes, mouth and eyebrows are all able to move independently, allowing for many different expressions. The nose can be flared or wrinkled in a sneer. Skin color, texture and moisture can give a great deal of information about an individual's mood and state of health. Simple line drawings of eyebrows, forehead and mouth in different expressions can send at least ten emotional messages. Happy facial expression is usually drawn with the eyes and smile lines pointing up; angry or sad face with the mouth line down, as in inverted U; and surprise is indicated with both mouth and eyes taking the shape of an O.

We can detect or infer with high accuracy specific emotions from the face, including surprise, fear, disgust, anger, happiness and sadness.

TABLE 2.1 **Judging personality from facial features**

Physical facial features	Personality judged as
Thin lips	Conscientious, highly moral, respectable
Thick lips (in females)	Sexy, amorous
High forehead	Intelligent, highbrow, bright
Protruding eyes	Excitable, explosive
Positive curving mouth	Cheerful, easy-going, funny, well-adjusted
Wrinkled face	Aggressive, determined, quick-tempered
Dark complexion/coarse skin	Hostile, boorish, sly
Wearing make-up	Sexy, frivolous
Wearing spectacles	Intelligent, dependable, industrious

We can detect "level of threat" from the face, as well as the health of another person.

Certainly, many facial expressions – such as startle responses or expressions of pain – appear innate, rather than learnt or culturally variable. But there are cultural rules about appropriate expressions in various social settings. Thus one is expected to look cheerful at weddings, miserable at funerals, and excited at sports matches.

People are known by their faces. People "put on" faces and many believe that, after a time, one's face says a lot about one's personality. Whether this is true or not, studies have shown that people make judgments based on facial features, as shown in Table 2.1.

As with eye gaze, the facial expressions of people at interviews, in committee or while working with customers send powerful messages about their inner states, particularly if one observes how the expressions change in response to what is being said.

One of the most interesting and important features of facial expressions is, first, their speed of change; and second, their congruity. The more genuine the expression, the more the pieces "fit together". The fake smile occurs with the mouth but not with the eyes. Further, the smile is very quick to both appear and disappear.

The face can reveal our physiological reaction very subtly. We blush and we sweat with embarrassment and stress. A quick "flash" of the eyebrows can signal surprise and disgust. The expressiveness and importance of the face to everyday communication is best illustrated when it is masked. The face-masked, burqa-wearing woman can seem threatening. It helps if the eyes are visible, but these too may be hidden behind a "grille". Equally, people learn to put on a "poker face" so as not to give away any information to what are they thinking. The face is designed for expression. We learn to read faces and what they say.

The salesperson, the negotiator, the motivation speaker all need to be skilled readers and senders of facial expressions.

The smile has also attracted a good deal of attention. Ventriloquists smile, as do sophisticated liars – both to put others off. The smiling expression helps the ventriloquist to deceive observers, while in the case of the "bare-faced" liar it makes others less alert to what is going on.

The science of smiling

Smiling may be natural or faked. The broad, genuine, expressive and spontaneous smile can be defined physiologically in terms of what muscles do to different parts of the face; lips, cheeks or eyes. There is also the wry, miserable smile, often lopsided, that indicates recognition of the vicissitudes of fate. The polite smile – often more like a grimace – is as much a sign of embarrassment as happiness.

The smiling or laughing face is often not very different from the howling or tearful face. Some people – women more than men – cry with joy; we talk about things as being "frightfully jolly". People sometimes laugh as a response to shock, or when embarrassed. Funeral wakes are often characterized by laughter. Genuine laughter increases breathing rate and depth, while lowering blood pressure and heart rate. Crying, as uniquely human as laughing, may accompany laughter and may be as much a sign of joy and relief as of shock or sadness.

The "science of smiling" was founded by Charles Darwin, whose centenary was celebrated in 2009. He noticed that smiling is universal, whereas many other nonverbal behaviors of body language (such as gestures or touch) differ between cultures and are therefore probably learnt. Babies born blind smile in the same way as sighted infants. Human babies begin smiling at around five weeks of age: babies learn that crying gets the attention of adults, but smiling keeps it.

Darwin also observed that smiling and laughter often occurred together and therefore had similar origins. Happiness, he thought, was similar to amusement. Smiling, it is argued, is the outward manifestation of happiness, and serves to begin to connect us to others. We are, as people say now, "prewired" to connect with others via this system. Interestingly, some researchers have shown that people who cannot smile, because of facial paralysis, say, have more difficulty in social relationships.

However, there maybe cultural differences in rules of smiling: when etiquette dictates whether it is appropriate to smile or not. For example, it has been demonstrated that in America, people smile more in the south than the north (cut by the Mason–Dixon line).

We know that, on average, women smile more than men. When they are two months old we can observe that baby girls smile more than baby boys. We know that powerful men smile less than less powerful women. Also that smiling is linked to testosterone: the higher the level of the hormone in men, the smaller and fewer are their smiles.

It has been suggested that the English smile less than many other groups because of their ideas about the virtues of the "stiff upper lip" and not appearing emotional. And they also keep their teeth hidden and pull their mouths sideways rather than up. One explanation for the common pursed smile of the English is that for a long time a small mouth was considered more attractive and desirable.

Smiling is what psychologists call "the expression of positive affect". The sequence of events goes like this:

1. Most external events (seeing a person, hearing a joke), but also internal events (such as a memory) arouses, through brain activation, an emotion.
2. This effects the facial nerves that control the production of emotional expressions *but also* other physical systems such as heart rate and skin conductance.
3. The actual expression is modified by other nerves that are activated by thought (cognitive) processes.
4. There is feedback from the face to the brain.

So smiling is not only a manifestation of happiness, but also increases happiness. In fact, impressive physical evidence has demonstrated not only that smiling is a consequence of feeling happy or contented, but also that putting on a smile can induce physiological change in body temperature, heart rate, skin resistance and so on. That is, adopting a smiling expression can lead to positive moods (and vice versa). It also has the added advantage that others tend to smile back.

Reciprocity and contagion

There is much evidence of body language mirroring. We automatically copy the facial expressions of others. We reciprocate and in social groups it can be contagious. People respond to those who smile, and evaluate them differently and more positively than those who do not. As the old saying goes: "Laugh, and the world laughs with you; cry and you cry alone".

This sets up a *virtuous* cycle for the smiler and a *vicious* cycle for the non-smiler. Thus in sales, hospitality and negotiation situations, the person who smiles first increases the possibility of the other person(s) smiling, which increases trust and liking and, therefore, also cooperation and helpfulness. Smiling helps to bond people together.

There is also physiological evidence that smiling has specific biological consequences. This is even truer of laughter and there is evidence of a feedback loop. Smiling has hormonal and physiological consequences which make people feel better and want to smile more. Smiling self medicates and heals.

Types of smile

All body language researchers have attempted to come up with a full category scheme for the different smiles one notices. Zoologists noted that chimpanzees have two smiles: a *submission face* (lips retracted, teeth exposed) and a *play face* (lower jaw dropped and corners of the mouth pulled back). The submission face is designed to appease.

Smiling in humans can indicate dominance. If you watch two people of different social rank, you will see that the dominant person smiles more in "friendly situations" but less in "unfriendly situations".

Psychologists have made many distinctions among human smiles, but at the most fundamental level the distinction has been between *genuine* versus *fake* smiles. Fake smiles are used for various purposes – often to pretend to show enjoyment, or sociability or agreement. These are easily noticeable because they involve the mouth and not the eyes. Technically we can define the physiological difference between a genuine and fake smile: two muscles are involved (*zygomatic major* and *orbicularis oculi*). Real smiles involve *both* of these muscles, but fake smiles involve the former but not the latter. Fake smiles involve the mouth more than the eyes: they are, in a sense only half the story.

Another distinction has been between *open- and closed-mouth* smiles. One writer (Judi James, 2008) has identified fourteen different smiles, which she calls the mirthless, the stretched social rictus, asymmetric, upturned, mouth-shrug, perfect, suppressed, tonsil-flasher, secret, uber-flirt, aggressive, lower-jaw jut, clencher, smug and know-all!

The world's expert, however, is Paul Ekman, who has studied all the facial muscles and psychological motives to understand the nature of smiles. He has a useful list:

1. The *felt* smile, which is long and intense and shows all signs of positive feeling associated with amusement, contentment, pleasure from stimulation.
2. The *fear* smile and *contempt* smile are misnomers because neither are related to positive emotions, though both can have a "smily mouth" and dimples.
3. The *dampened* smile is a real smile where people attempt to suppress or conceal the extent of their positive emotions.
4. The *miserable* smile is a "grin and bear it" smile indicating stoicism about negative emotions.
5. The *flirtatious* smile is partly embarrassed because the person gazes/faces away from the person of interest/contact.
6. The *Chaplin* smile is a contorted, supercilious smile that in effect smiles at smiling.

Ekman also notes deliberate, *but not* fake smiles that sign particular messages; for example:

1. The *qualifier* smile, which takes the edge off a harsh message and can "trap" the recipient into returning the smile.
2. The *compliance* smile is an acknowledgement that a bitter pill will be swallowed without protest.
3. The *coordinated* smile is a polite, cooperative smile showing agreement, understanding and acknowledgement.
4. The *listener response* smile which simply indicates that everything heard has been understood. It is an encouragement to the speaker to continue.

Politicians, movie stars and media people practice smiling. So do those in the hospitality business. There are things they learn *not to do:* open your mouth, unless laughing; producing a sudden flash smile; or having a choreographed smile that bears no relation to what you are saying. Saying cheese produces fake smiles. People well-known for smiling very little (Vladimir Putin, Charles Bronson, Margaret Thatcher) have a reputation for being tough and non-submissive, which is the impression they want to portray. Smiling effects a person's reputation, and those in the "reputation business" know that.

Detecting false smiles

There are many reasons why people smile. We know that when people are lying they tend to smile less than when telling the truth, because they do the opposite to what people expect of those who are telling a lie. Police studies have shown many times that people accused of serious crimes (such as smuggling) and less serious ones (such as speeding) tend to smile more and more genuinely when innocent than those who are later proved to be guilty. You can detect false or *counterfeit smiles* by looking for four things:

1. *Duration*: How long it lasts. False smiles last longer.
2. *Assembly*: They are put together (eyes, mouth) and taken apart more quickly than real smiles.
3. *Location*: False smiles are "voluntary" and involve mainly the lower part of the face, whereas real "involuntary" smiles also involve the upper part of the face around the eyes and eyebrows.
4. *Symmetry:* If the smile appears more on one side of the face (often the right side) it is more likely to be false.

DIANA, PRINCESS OF WALES

In a brilliant and highly detailed analysis of one, albeit famous, person, Peter Collett from the University of Oxford identified six quite different smiles:

- *Eye-puff smile*, to widen the eyes and make people feel more protective/nurturing of her.
- *Spencer smile*, which was authentic, heartfelt and genuine.
- *Pursed smile*, which occurred at times of shyness and embarrassment.
- *Dipped smile*, which involved lowering the head so the eyes look up showing childlikeness.
- *Head-cant smile*, which meant tilting the head to one side to show she was unthreatening.
- *Turn-away smile*, which gives two opposing messages (approach/avoidance); Darwin called this a hybrid expression and it is considered "irresistible".

Smiling at work

Those in certain businesses such as the service and entertainment industries, are encouraged to smile so that it becomes a natural part of their work activity. It is relatively easy to teach this, because it has such obvious quick and immediate rewards to those who smile: they feel better, others respond more positively, and they succeed in their task more quickly and more often. Thus they feel better about themselves and their task, and smile more naturally more often.

Gestures

Hands, heads and feet can be used to produce a very wide range of signals, signs and other movements. Hand movements accompany speech and can be used to point to people, objects, self; show spatial relationships (in/outside; up/down); show spatial movements (round-and-round); beat time by showing rhythm or tempo; show a particular movement (punching, kicking); draw a visual picture (spiral slide, odd-shaped room).

Traditionally, it is argued that most culturally recognized gestures have relatively specific meanings (see Table 2.2).

TABLE 2.2 **Gestures and their meaning**

Gesture	Meaning
Nod head	Agreement
Shake fist	Anger
Rub palms	Anticipation
Clap	Approval
Raise hand	Seeking attention
Yawn	Boredom
Rub hands	Cold
Beckon	Come
Extend hand	Invite to dance/join in
Point	Give direction
Thumb down	Disapproval
Shrug shoulders	Lack of interest
Pat on back	Encouragement or commiseration
Pretend to shoot oneself	Faux pas
Outline female body	Attractive female
Rub stomach	Hungry
Wave hand	Goodbye
Shake hands	Greetings

The Anglo-Saxon world is surprisingly gesture-poor, possibly because of the richness of the English language. The "teeth flick" (meaning anger), the "cheek screw" (meaning "good") or the "eyelid-pull" (meaning "I am alert") are unknown in Britain.

How frequently people gesture is a function of many things: whether others can see them (though many gesture a lot while speaking on the telephone); how excited, involved and enthusiastic they are; when the topic is complex; when the listener seems not to be paying attention; when the speaker wants to dominate the listener; when the topic is concrete and about manual activities (pitch a tent, tie a tie) rather than abstract; and those with weaker verbal skills.

It is possible to distinguish between many different types of gesture. Ekman and Friesen (1972) have distinguished between:

- *Emblems*: sign language, often rude, sometimes part of a task- or occupation-specific culture. They are a shorthand (pun intended!) substitute for words.
- *Illustrators*: movements that accompany and amplify speech. The size of the fish that got away and the place of the pain in the body are both illustrators.
- *Regulators*: gesture movements such as those of an orchestral conductor. They attempt to regulate conversation: to "shut someone up", bring others in, encourage people to continue.
- *Adaptors*: anxiety displacement movements that may reveal emotions.
- *Displays*: often ritual gestures of powerful emotions or symbolic quality, such as the clenched fist, the Nazi salute, the laying on of hands.

If a person taps his or her temple with a forefinger it can mean "crazy" or intelligent: opposite meanings from the identical gesture. This hand-to-brain contact could mean a "bad brain" (stupid fool) or a "good brain" (very bright, clever). The context and the culture determine the meaning of gestures. Yet many gestures extend well beyond specific or national boundaries.

Gestures can say something of the *emotional state of others*, particularly their level of excitement or anxiety. Self-touching gestures: the neck-scratch, collar-tug or fingers in mouth are often particularly telling of shame, doubt and presentational anxieties. Gestures also give information about personality. Extroverts tend to be more expansive, while people with depression have fewer, slower, more hesitant and non-emphatic gestures. Neurotic people touch their faces and hair often, scratching and pulling; they indulge in wringing their hands, interlocking their fingers, and opening and closing their fists.

There are many gestures which, in Anglo-Saxon culture, are easily interpreted. These include rubbing hands together (excited expectation, or simply being cold). Clenching hands (in front of the face, on a desk or in front of the crotch) may signal confidence or frustration; steepling hands (up or down) is usually a positive gesture of confidence; thumb displays (holding your jacket lapels, sticking your thumbs out of a pocket) are thought to show superiority, even pomposity, possibly even lay oneself open to ridicule.

Hand-to-face gestures are particularly intriguing and nicely characterized in the three wise monkey states known as "Hear no evil, see no evil, speak no evil". *The mouth guard*, possibly disguised as a fake cough or used to conceal a yawn, is often associated with lying – as is the nose touch. It has been suggested that if a speaker touches his or her mouth he or she may be lying, while if the listener does it, it suggests that he or she feels the speaker is lying!

The eye-rub (see no evil), *the ear-rub* (hear no evil), and the neck-scratch, collar-tug or fingers in mouth (no nail-biting) are often seen as signs of deceit or uncertainty – or simply anxiety. It may be that anxiety or anxiety about lying causes physical tension, which leads to the gesture, rather than it being the manifestation of an unconscious idea.

Touching the chin, cheek or jaw is usually associated with thinking (evaluating what is being said or making a decision) and occasionally with boredom. *Rubbing the back of the neck* is often interpreted as a sign of frustration ("pain in the neck"). *Folded arms* or using bags, flowers or books as a barrier is usually interpreted as defensiveness or nervousness. Equally, *leg or foot crossing* with ankle locks is usually interpreted as coldness or defensiveness. Precisely when these gestures are adopted or changed (particularly in terms of what is being said at the time) is a very important clue to their interpretation.

Pease (1984) has noted various other sorts of known gestures:

- *Straddling a chair* (sitting backwards) – using the back of the chair as a defence against aggression.

- *Fluff-picking* (picking imaginary fluff off clothes) – approval or deliberately withholding evidence.
- *Both hands behind the head* – controlled, dominant, confident.
- *Hands on hip/in belt* – sexual aggressiveness or sizing one another up.
- *Tie-straightening* – preening in males as a courtship gesture.

Equally, one can use various props such as cigars, pipes and spectacles to send gestures. How and where smoke is blown, how cigarettes are held, when spectacles are put in the mouth are all interpreted as meaning something, whether the "actor" meant it or not. Indeed, film actors deliberately use certain actions to convey the motives and mood of their character. Anything put in the mouth may be thought of as a gesture of reassurance or possible aggression.

Gestures are important at work. Leaders sometimes "choose" symbolic gestures such as Winston Churchill's V for Victory sign. They become recognized by the way they do things – point, adjust their glasses, fiddle with their cufflinks.

Posture

A person's posture may result from early psychological rather than physical experience. Adolescents may hunch or stoop to disguise breast development or excessive height. Long periods of depression may lead to the adoption of the depressive's characteristic sagging pose even after recovery has been made. Some argue that just as body posture is an index of emotional health (tensed muscles lead to bad posture), so you can change (relax) emotional states by changing posture. Indeed, the Alexander Technique is based on diagnosing and correcting posture. Yoga and Chinese t'ai chi aim to improve general well-being through exercising or manipulating the body.

The three main human postures are *standing, sitting* (which includes squatting and kneeling) and *lying*. Shown "stickmen" figures, people can easily, accurately and reliably identify states of mind or qualities such as suspicion, shyness, indifference, puzzlement and so on. Thus one can signal relaxation by asymmetrical arm and leg positions, a backwards and possibly sideways lean and hand relaxation. The arms, legs and trunk alone and together can give strong messages of states such as anxiety, sexual flirtatiousness and humility.

Some researchers have noticed how body movement communicates various desires in courtship or psychotherapy. Nonverbal cues of courtship readiness include preening the hair and adjusting the stockings. Cues from positioning include facing one another with the torso leaning inward so as to exclude others. Actions of appeal might involve flirtatious glances, crossing the legs or exposing the palm of the hand. Posture in a selection or appraisal interview can give a good indication of how tense or relaxed a person is. A conference speaker's posture can also give an insight into his or her level of confidence.

Women used to be taught "deportment". Ballet is the physical and often extremely beautiful expression of emotion. Catwalk models learn to move in a particular fashion.

Body posture conveys clues about the health and mood of individuals. At work we want our managers to be fit and positive. This message can be put across in how they sit and stand, and how they change their posture.

Many have observed the "postural echo" or the idea of matching. People seem unaware that they mimic or copy the posture (and gestures and speed) of those to whom they are talking. It happens all the more with people one likes. This phenomenon has also been called emotional contagion and occurs when two skilled people are communicating about strong emotion.

Bodily orientation

One of the few things business people can control fairly easily is the way in which they orient themselves to others. This is usually done by the way that furniture is arranged. Thus one can interview across a desk (face-to-face, diametrically opposite); over the corner of a desk (at 90° in a cosy corner), or side-by-side, facing outwards.

Orientation of the body (the pointing of torso, feet) has been thought of as indicating where people's thoughts are, or where they really want to go. People standing and talking can face each other at various angles (head-on, side-by-side), and they can, through orientation, include or exclude others. Opening to a triangular position, while conversing with two or more people simultaneously, indicates acceptance.

Body pointing as well as the less obvious but also less conscious feet-pointing often indicates the person to whom ideas are addressed, who is favored in a conversation and who is liked or disliked. Seated body orientation (as well as distance) is, equally, very indicative of the nature of a relationship. Chairs can be arranged to symbolize or control a relationship, or may be moved over time to redefine it.

Inevitably, sitting opposite a person often symbolizes opposition. It is no accident the British have a two-party oppositional system, given the architecture of the House of Commons. People leave restaurants more quickly when seated opposite one another, unless tables are particularly wide. Sitting side-by-side often symbolizes cooperation and support, but it can be uncomfortable if people are seated too close together or if they feel they are not getting enough eye contact.

Round tables are democratic and connote cooperation. There is a business organization called the Round Table, and King Arthur's knights sat at a legendary round table. Various United Nations tables are round(ish) – symbolically indicating the equality of all in the circle. Theatre "in the round" too has a quite different feel for both audience and actors. Round tables are becoming more popular in business, tending to replace the more common formal square, oblong or rectangular shapes. Square tables can be awkward – at least some people have to sit diametrically opposite one another. Square tables also have a more closed and exclusive feel than round tables, which appear easier to join.

Rectangular and oval tables are still found in boardrooms and cabinet meetings. The person who has the greatest power tends to sit in the middle, or more commonly at the head, while the rank of those attending is defined in terms of distance from that person.

Most work is undertaken sitting down and sitting still, but some managers have discovered the benefits of having meetings standing up. This index of emotional health usually ensures shorter meetings. Leaning on something is considered to be a disrespectful posture (like the person at the bar, the farmer at the gate) because it signals inattention and relaxation.

Angle and distance of chairs from one another is important, but so is height. Sometimes chairs, like thrones, are elevated to symbolize power and influence. Pease (1984) has noted that desk seating positions (at rectangular tables) can be in several different positions:

- *corner position*: indicating friendly, casual communication but with a partial barrier (this position is favored by GPs);
- *cooperative position*: people sit next to each other;
- *cooperative defensive position*: people seated opposite each other with the barrier between, but an understanding that half the space on the table/desk is one person's territory while the other half belongs to the other person; and

- *independent position*: diagonally opposite, at maximum distance, avoiding eye contact.

Room layout can dictate orientation, which may help or hinder the communication intended to take place in that setting. This is why conference rooms' layouts are so important. You can walk into a room and detect by its design what sort of communication tends to occurs there. Does it encourage participation and provide an opportunity for all those present to engage in the talk, or is it only convenient for the speaker and the members of the team seated in the front row?

Territory

The study of space is called *proxemics*, and the study of how humans communicate through their use of time is called *chronemics*. Strictly speaking, territory is not a bodily signal. But we do signal differently when in different territories, and often send clear defensive messages as to what delineates a territory. Like animals, people try to establish and maintain territories, albeit fleetingly. The "unmanned" towel on the beach, the coat on the chair and the suitcase on the seat all indicate that somebody has staked out that territory. We all know the different feel a meeting has if it is held in the boss's office; if the boss visits you in your office; or if you meet in an assigned meeting room. Most houses have public and private rooms – areas designated as being appropriate for outsiders and insiders. The same is true of public buildings – for example, hotels, which have "staff only" signs. Often there is a dramatic difference in the quality of décor between different territories: plush to drab, carpeted to bare floors.

Just as actors differentiate between front-of-house and backstage, so businesses differentiate between front-house and back-room. Indeed, we have the term "back-room staff". Dress, language, posture and physical contact are all quite different in these different zones. It is possible to make distinctions between different "psychological" zones. First, there is a very *private zone* in the office. It may be the employee's small but very personal workstation and locker. Then there is the shared *inner-group zone* of the working department or division. Here, people have marked out favorite chairs and so on that are known to, and respected by, all those in the group. Comfort with interpersonal distance is a function of several features: sex (men having narrower intimate zones than women); culture (Anglo-Saxons like more distance than Latins); and area population density (rural people stand further away from each other than do urban dwellers).

It has become common to distinguish between four zones: *intimate* (less than three feet), into which professionals are not allowed to intrude – apart from medical and quasi-medical people; *personal* (three–four feet), which one may have to share in aeroplanes, for example; *social* (four–twelve feet), for most strangers and colleagues at work; and *public (more than twelve feet)*, for all other interactions.

Meetings held in public spaces are quite different from those in private space. The use of space is also very culturally different. The Japanese see the shape and arrangement of space as having clear, tangible meaning, yet in public they cling close together in crowded groups. Americans carry a two-foot bubble of privacy around themselves. For privacy, some people – for example, Arabs – retreat into themselves; others retreat behind closed doors.

Territory is important in business, particularly when entering another's territory. How close should one approach the desk or chair of another is associated with that person's status. People who enter a room and remain near the door signal a lower status than those who walk right up to the executive's desk. The time between door-knocking/entering and hearing/answering is also status-related. The more quickly the visitor enters the room, the more status he or she has, while the longer the executive takes to answer, the more status he or she has. A senior manager can walk into a subordinate's office unannounced, yet the latter has to wait outside the office of the former to be allowed in. Subordinates leave the senior's office when the telephone rings, while the former does not always answer the telephone, to give the boss the full attention he or she deserves.

Physical areas have special significance because they are the territory of a particular person and are associated with high/low status people in particular social roles. The physical layout can determine how people use space in waiting rooms or common rooms – as designers of airports or hotels know very well. The "trick" is to give people a sense of being in private territory while ensuring the maximum number of people can use the facility.

The physical environment

The size, shape and furnishings of rooms effect how people communicate in them. The House of Commons in London appears to suggest a two-party system: us versus them; blue team versus red. Churchill memorably remarked that we shape our buildings and afterwards they shape us. Rooms leave cues to who lives and works there; how they interact, and how frequently. They tell of status, power, inclusion and exclusion.

The Chinese have passed on their interest and belief in feng shui. The main presumption of feng shui, which literary translates as wind-water, is the presence of life energy chi and its two states of *yin* and *yang*. Feng shui is the practice of balancing negative and positive charges of chi through the design and architecture of the physical environment. It is believed that success in all areas of life, including health, relationships and career can be achieved through the harmonization of living and working space around people. Objects are positioned in a certain manner to attract or reflect chi in the right proportions.

Though feng shui is uniquely Asian, Westerners seem to be intrigued by the tradition too, to the extent that there are international groups and associations claiming that feng shui should be regarded as a scientific discipline. However, despite its popularity, feng shui seems to be based on superstitious beliefs of lay people rather than on hard scientific evidence. Though similar in concept to bipolar magnetic fields, there is no proof of the existence of such a life force as chi. On the other hand, it might be that by arranging individual objects and structures in an organic or holistic manner, and by relating individual parts or objects in the structure back to the whole space a building occupies, a deeper level of comfort is achieved. Alternatively, popular feng shui might be nothing more than the placebo effect.

Environmental psychologists know that people evaluate and behave in rooms according to they way they appear. They can be stylish, light and airy, as well as comfortable or functional, or conformist. They also know about environmental modifiers that can change mood and behavior. These include sound (music), lighting and smell. Supermarkets are very aware of the power of sound and smell on behavior.

What of the structures and design of rooms and of the possibility of movable objects. How do people like to sit in restaurants? Which tables are more popular? What is the ideal shape? The answer to these questions is: four-person, round tables placed against a wall.

Note how people rearrange their space to introduce or remove perceived barriers. Equally, they personalize spaces with objets d'art or bric-a-brac. Consider how neighbours fight over territorial invasion.

The world of business is replete with many fine examples of how people choose and use spaces to control communication and show rank. Thus executives have their corner offices, with bigger windows, on the top floor. They have more space higher up; some are even en-suite. They may have "protective" outer rooms with guards (that is, personal assistants). They have maximum privacy and control. They have big desks but uncluttered offices. They are more likely to have a meeting table than files, filing cabinets or even computers. They are decision-makers, not knowledge workers – and it shows.

Architects know that the way they design prisons, old-people's homes, or student dormitories can profoundly influence interactions in them. Proximity and propinquity affect the amount of contact, which often grows into liking, but density and over-crowding have significantly negative consequences on social interaction.

The quality of conversations can be powerfully determined by *conversational distance*. We have already mentioned the so- called *social-consultative distance* which varies between 1.5 feet and ten feet and is most commonly used in everyday interactions. However, should you sit side-by-side, opposite or at right angles to someone? How far apart should you be? Is it always beneficial to have a barrier (that is, a desk or table) or not? It is clear that the seating alone is instructive: it can be changed to indicate leadership, dominance or cooperativeness (see Figure 2.1).

Look at Figure 2.1. Which arrangement would you prefer, and why? Which would be better for negotiation and which for information shar-ing? Which would be better for a business lunch or a romantic dinner?

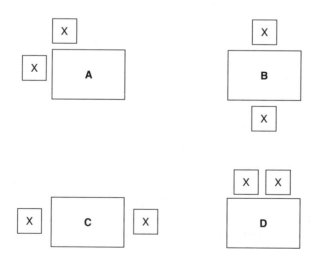

Figure 2.1 **Two chairs at an oblong table: four possible positions**

The moral of the story is simple. The physical environment reflects how we move and our distance and angle in relation to one another. It symbolizes, contains and encourages certain conversation topics and tasks. An astute awareness of these factors in business can have very significant consequences.

FEEL THE UNSPOKEN

Touch (or body contact)

Touch is probably one of the most powerful and primitive means of contact and communication. These days, we live in a non-contact culture – hence the power of touch. Children explore the world by touch, until the inhibitions of our society penalize it. Touch has a primitive significance of heightened intimacy. In the 1960s psychotherapists used so called "encounter groups" and "T-groups" to explore the therapeutic benefits of touch (among other things). Argyle (1975) noted that, in Western society, there are many types of body contact:

Patting head, back
Holding hand, arm, knee
Slapping face, hand, bottom
Guiding hand, arm
Punching face, chest
Embracing shoulder, body
Pinching cheek, bottom
Linking arms
Stroking hair, face, upper body, knee
Laying on hands
Shaking hands
Kicking bottom
Kissing mouth, cheek, breasts, hand, foot
Grooming hair, face
Licking face
Tickling anywhere.

People in Anglo-Saxon culture touch for various reasons: attempting to persuade or obtain a favor; when sympathizing; when giving orders and advice; when excited or happy. Most people can distinguish between the *professional* touch (of doctors, hairdressers) the *social* touch (of greeting or farewell); the *friendly* touch (of sports people when they celebrate, or among families); and the *sexual* touch (to bring about or increase arousal).

Body contact is dictated by relationship: whom, where, when and how much. Touching one's spouse, children, friends, relations and strangers is governed by very different rules. Touch can signal sexual arousal, nurturance or dependence, affiliation and aggression. It is often used as an interaction signal in greetings and farewells and in guiding others. Touch is used with great meaning at grand ceremonies, such as confirmations, ordinations and weddings. It often signals the passing on of a continuous chain of authority. It is used in prize-giving and initiation rites. You are more likely to touch when asking a favor or trying to persuade someone; and when giving information or an order rather than when receiving or responding to one.

Many gestures are easily recognizable, though often unacceptable at work: the shoulder, waist or full embrace (hug). People can detect and correctly classify such gestures as being functional/professional versus social/polite or friendly.

The 'meanings' of touch are many:

- *Positive emotions and affect*: from nurse, therapist, carer, symbolizing affection, support and reassurance.
- *Negative emotions*, such as anger and frustration: hitting, slapping and squeezing another person.
- *Specific and discrete emotions*: stroking and patting for sympathy.
- *Playfulness and humour*: tickling, "false" punches.
- *Influencing and persuading*: holding the upper arm while shaking hands.
- *Conversation control and interaction management*: tapping a person to remind of something.
- *Responsiveness*: touching to indicate agreement, empathy, involvement in the conversation.
- *Task related*: this is the functional, directional touch when engaged in cooperative tasks.
- *Symbolism*: usually of warmth, friendship and inclusion.

The handshake is one of the most over-interpreted of body signals. We are told that it is an integral part of personality and a symbol of a power struggle. Whose hand is "on top", how vice-like the grip and the weight-on-the-foot relative to the hand are all supposed to provide information. The hand has "palm power": one can have a submissive, recipient, open gesture – like a beggar – or a more aggressive, palm-down gesture.

The handshake can be described by the nature of the grip, the power of that grip, the number of "pumps" and who reaches out first. The dominant handshake is characterized by a palm down, firm but short shake.

Various typical handshakes have been described:

- *glove or politician*: both hands used by one party to cover the opponent's hand, trying to give the impression of honesty.
- *dead fish*: cold, clammy, limp.
- *knuckle grinder*: the macho handshake which squeezes the fingers only.
- *stiff-arm thrust*: no bending of the arm.
- *arm pull*: sometimes found in children.

Another interesting quandary in the "modern" handshake is what to do with the other (left) hand. One can leave it limp at one's side; or grab the other person's wrist, elbow, upper arm or shoulder to show various attitudes such as sincerity, honesty or a caring quality.

Some handshakes, of course, have no hidden meaning. Those with arthritis or whose hands are integral to their career, such as surgeons or musicians, may avoid handshakes or give weak shakes, not because of their lack of confidence or power but because of their fear of damaging their hands. Handshake gestures may have been learnt in childhood and have little to do with carefully thought out patterns of dominance and submission.

People also self-touch. This is often associated with cleaning, grooming and attending to appearance. Such touching is also associated with comforting or protective gestures because it appears more in situations of stress and anxiety. People can "leak" their fear, disgust or prejudices by self-touching.

For those of us living in a non-contact culture, the power of touch is all the more real. People can be disarmed by touch, a trick known to many. Touching is heavily pre- and proscribed. When, where, how and why we touch each other is dictated by a range of social rules never more so than at work. The handshake, the pat on the back and the few other contact behaviors are all carefully prescribed, and breaking the rules can have very serious consequences.

Withdrawal of touch is also a powerful means of influencing. A shaky, feeble handshake is readily ascribed to a weak or unconfident personality by many. Not responding to socially accepted touching, such as air kissing or hand giving, can be a serious breach of social rituals.

Odor

For too long, psychologists neglected the role of smell in communication. Odor is a powerful communication system among animals, and we humans are all personally aware of the olfactory consequences of such things as stress and sexual excitement on our own bodies. People know that some smells are able to summon powerful memories. There is now considerable interest in "pheromones", a term coined in 1959 from the Greek *pherein* "to carry" and *hormon* "to excite". The chemical secretions are used by all primates to mark territory, assert dominance, repel rivals and attract mates.

Adults have scent glands under their arms and around their genitals; body hair traps scents which are powerful markers. It is the way in which clothes capture, turn stale and "chemicalize" these body odors that make them unpleasant.

People in Western societies seem determined to eradicate and replace natural body odors. For many, the morning begins with the use of soap, toothpaste, mouthwash, scented shampoo, deodorant and cologne or perfume. Individuals have distinct, reliably detectable body odors (sweet, musky, lemony) that are a function of health and diet. Doctors have been urged to use their sense of smell in diagnosis. Animals are now being trained to do so as they have acute odor sensitivity.

Anthropologists have pointed out that odor communicates racial, cultural and family traits that help to identify us and relate to a range of acceptable and avoidant behaviors. Because smells are so clearly associative, environments are deliberately "sprayed". The smell of baking bread and freshly brewed coffee has been used to help sell houses. Some shops use the pine and spice smells of Christmas to try to induce greater sales in the festive season. Hospitals and dentists try to hide or mask smells associated with those places because of the extent to which they are associated with pain and anxiety.

To demonstrate the power of odor, one study required men on a selection skills course to evaluate the merits of a particular woman for a secretarial job. The only difference between her and various other interviewees (she was a trained actress) lay in the perfume she was wearing. Surprisingly, she was evaluated as more able and technically skilled when wearing a popular perfume. In this sense the scent gave her a "halo effect" – smells nice, is nice; smells good, is good.

It seems that the human odor-communication system is primitive, and operates for most of us beneath the level of awareness. Few people are able to send or detect complex messages or signals by the choice of chemicals to spray on themselves, and most are not in a position to alter voluntarily the central nervous system in order to induce particular scents. Most of us operate on the pleasant/unpleasant dimension and are utterly reliant on the erratic feedback of others to determine reaction.

Equally, the social problem of telling somebody about "bad breath" or "unpleasant odor" is fraught with embarrassment. All this leads to the conclusion that most of us have very little idea of the effect our natural and unnatural scent has on those we meet.

Smell at work

How do you design shops, arrange products and create ambiance to maximize sales?

Researchers have found that you need to get people in the right mood to maximize impulse buying. So how to (quickly, cheaply and efficiently) change mood? The answer is in things such as smells and music. Both have immediate associations. They have been described as emotional provocateurs, which appear to be both powerful and primitive, and they seem to work at an unconscious level.

Music is used to quicken the heart and the pace (for example, marching music) as well as to relax people. Few state occasions, or indeed any with rites-of-passage significance, take place without music to signify the mood and meaning of the occasion.

Scientists are now also beginning to play with smell or, if you prefer, aroma. It is now perfectly feasible to develop cheap, synthetic but impressively realistic scents of anything you fancy. Baking bread, warm chocolate, sea breezes, "new car smell", or new-mown grass – it is all possible!

Smells can make you hungry; or relaxed; or even cross. Some researchers have attempted to use smells to increase sales. They found the best smell to pump into a petrol-station mini market was the smell of "starched sheets", because garage forecourts are dirty, oily places and people have a clear concern with the cleanliness of the food (especially fresh pastries) on sale in the shop. The exceptionally clean association of starched sheets "does the business". People's concerns about cleanliness disappear and they buy more.

Smells have associations, some of which are shared. As noted earlier, buildings such as hospitals and rooms such as dentists' surgeries have distinct smells that can almost induce phobias. Christmas has its own smell, as does the seaside.

Individuals too have specific smell associations. Thus unique smells like Earl Grey tea, Pears soap, or particular perfumes can have unusual effects on individuals. And the same smell can have opposite effects on two different people. The smell of tea, for example, can bring both pain and pleasure: memories of boredom to some, and excitement to others.

Smell is also powerfully linked to individual autobiographical memories. Along with hospitals, railway stations have distinct smells that quickly evoke emotional associations. Neurological studies have shown that this is not surprising, given that the primary olfactory cortex of the brain is linked directly to the amygdala and the hippocampus – the basic structures for the experiencing of emotion and emotional memory forming. What is more, smell does not seem to be integrated with the rest of memory knots (visual, verbal, phonemic and so on representations of an object or idea); it is also the slowest among all the other stimuli to be processed.

We know that smell is generationally linked as a result of shared product experiences and lifestyle. Far fewer people bake bread or live in the country than used to formerly, hence the comforting feeling associated with the scents of warm bread, or cut hay or fresh horse manure, may work on people of only a particular age cohort.

Certainly buildings and different parts of them have characteristics smells as a function of who works in them, what they do and how they are furnished. Some smell of cleaning materials and others of food of various types. Aromatherapy may not, as yet, be an accepted therapy, but there is no doubt that people do change their behavior in response to smell. The whole perfume industry is based on this simple point.

Many organizations and the people in them pay a great deal of attention to smell. These include hotels and restaurants, and airlines and other transport systems. They want often to convey the message that things are clean and orderly, and they do this with scent. People may not be conscious of the smell but do respond to it very obviously.

People, of course, douse themselves in scent, from shampoo and toothpaste to perfume. Women know how men respond to certain perfumes. Various studies have shown that people who have a particularly desirable smell are judged, quite inappropriately, as being clever, more productive, as having higher morale and so on.

Music and smell work on mood. And moods do not last long, though they can profoundly influence both thinking (decision-making) and behavior (shopping, for example). The process can even be semi-subliminal: while people are initially aware of particular scents, they remain unaware of how their purchasing behavior has been changed by them.

Those studying attraction (the effects of body odor), decision-making and brain chemistry are curious as to precisely what physiological consequences occur once positive and negative moods are induced and familiar scents are detected. But they still do not know how people are able to distinguish between pepper and peppermint, or how wine tasters do their job. It was not thought of as a very serious area of enquiry until the commercial consequences were spelt out.

It is possible to imagine many positive and negative consequences of increasing our knowledge of the link between smell and mood, and mood and behavior. Some will object to a twenty-first-century version of a new "hidden persuader"; others will be pleased to find that someone has thought to ionize and aromatize their working, travelling and shopping environment.

BEYOND WORDS AND SOUNDS

Voice and speech pattern

It is a common notion that words convey the meaning of what is being said. However, vocal properties of speech can stress, highlight, or change completely, one and the same statement. Thus, voice and speech patterns, such as pauses, accents, emphases, intonations, variations in pitch, tempo, rhythm and tonality work in a similar fashion to punctuation. A classic school exercise illustrates this idea: '*A woman without her man is nothing.*' Once you have decided which words to punctuate, the intonation will follow accordingly. What is more, depending on how you choose to stress each of the words and where you pause in the sentence, the overall meaning of the statement alters dramatically. Compare the following: "Call me fool, if you will" with "Call me, fool, if you will" or "Panda eats, shoots and leaves" with "Panda eats shoots and leaves".

Vocal and speech patterns communicate various things:

- emotional states (anger, joy, sadness);
- dimensions of personality (extraversion/introversion, masculinity/ femininity);
- group affiliation, such as social class or regional background;
- assertiveness, dominance, credibility.

Dominance, for example, is characterized by faster speech, fewer pauses, louder voice and more pitch variations. Sadness can be detected through lower tone and volume of speech. Extraverted individuals usually speak faster and use more pitch variations.

Research into voice and speech patterns is the study of how things are said, not (so much) what is said. It is the study of prosody. Consider the six sentences below. Place emphasis on the words in italics and you will see how the meaning of the sentence changes:

- *The* director gave cash to his PA.
- The *director* gave cash to his PA.
- The director *gave* cash to his PA.
- The director gave *cash* to his PA.
- The director gave cash *to his* PA.
- The director gave cash to his *PA*.

Voice researchers, coaches and actors can identify, and when appropriate reproduce, very specific and recognizable types of voices. Voices can be thin or flat or nasal. They can be breathy or tense or throaty. They can be shrill or sexy; strained or tired. They convey meaning and impression, often different for males compared to females. Consider the "voice-over" in advertisements. A throaty (husky) voice in a male is often used to indicate wisdom and sophistication, while in a female a similar voice might seem boorish, lazy and less intelligent. Think of how voice trainers work with actors and politicians.

Some voices are quite simply more pleasing than others. They are in part a function of our age, social class and emotional state. We can and do change various acoustic features (pitch, tone, tempo, rhythm) to adjust to whom we are speaking and the topic of the conversation.

Those in the business of persuasion tend to speak faster and louder with more pitch variation; they are often very fluent, non-hesitant and speak with fewer pauses.

We use vocal cues to do conversational turn-taking. A conversation is a two-way process with (ideally) a speaker and one (or more) listeners. The question is, how do we "coordinate" speech automatically and effortlessly so that all those interested get a turn to speak. We *yield* to another person to give them a turn. We also vocally *request* a turn, often by "starter-starts" such as trying to begin another sentence "And I... But... But..." or back-channel murmurs like "Yeah", "Uh-huh" spoken fast meaning "Get on with it; I want a go".

Some people (note politicians being interviewed) engage in *turn denying* and *turn manipulating*. To do this they increase their speed and volume of speech when others are trying to interview them; they decrease their pauses and eliminate all silent breaks or hesitations.

Many therapists and researchers are particularly interested in hesitations, pauses and slips of the tongue as well as when and why people "go silent". There are grammatical pauses (the end of the sentence; before a conjunction; before an adverbial clause) as well as non-grammatical pauses. There are "um, er" pauses and empty pauses. There are pauses for effect and pauses for uncertainty.

Equally, there is the power of silence. Skilful inquisitorial interviewers all know the power of silence, particularly when refusing to accept "their turn" in the conversation. They might ask a direct question, "Did you have sex with that woman?" The other person responds, "No, I did not", but the interviewer then chooses to remain silent, thus putting pressure on the interviewee to speak further. The silence here indicates an unwillingness to accept the answer.

There are places of silence (courtrooms, hospitals, churches), which encourage rumination and reflection. Skilful orators, chairmen and actors know how to use (albeit very short) silences (more than pauses) to accentuate, to punctuate and to convey powerful emotions of sadness, love, or even disgust.

Silence can reward thoughtfulness and contemplation as well as ignorance. It can indicate that one is evaluating a statement or coming to a conclusion. Silence occurs in revelations when something is hidden or becoming known. Perhaps because we live in such a noisy, communication-filled world, silence is all the more powerful as a communication style.

Finally, there is the fascination with parapraxis or slips of the tongue, made famous by Sigmund Freud. This occurs when people use the wrong word, often the opposite of what they meant to say. Analysts claim that the incorrect word reflects what people really believe and want. A famous pun captures the definition of Freudian slips precisely, "A Freudian slip is when you intend to say one thing, but instead you say your mother." Evidently, they are mainly of a sexual or suggestive nature. Spoonerism is another example of slip-of-the-tongue mistakes. Spoonerisms are, however, distinguishable from other speech errors by their pattern of substitution: it usually involves a changeover of the first or last letters or syllables in an expression, such as "You have hissed my mystery lessons" instead of "You have missed my history lessons".

Although psychoanalysts claim such mistakes are evidence of repressed desires and sexual urges, cognitive psychologists have noticed the rules according to which such mistakes happen. V. Fromkin generated a list of principles governing slips of the tongue:

- *stick* in the *mud* > *smuck* in the *tid* (consonant segments exchange)
- *a*d h*o*c > *o*dd *h*ack (vowel segments exchange)
- una*ni*mity > unamity (syllable deleted)
- easi*ly* enough > easy enough*ly* (suffix moved)
- *tend* to *turn* out > *turn to* tend out (words exchange)
- *my sister* went to *the Grand Canyon* > *the Grand Canyon* went to *my sister* (whole phrase exchange)

To cognitive psychologists, these errors show how language is organized and structured in our memory, not the power of untamed sexual urges.

CONCLUSION

We communicate by verbal, vocal and visual cues. The way we look before we open our mouths already conveys messages about us. The way we sit, stand and move tells others about our mood, our health and our motives. Our gestures, eye contact patterns and posture can contradict or underline our verbal message. How close or far away we prefer to stand, and at what angle, is important. The quality of our voice, our clothes and jewelry are noted by others. Together, these cues, processed quickly and often without awareness, create impressions that can have an impact on all we do, and these impressions sometimes are all we have to secure a deal. That is why body language at work is important.

Body language can be unpacked or understood through various channels, cues or mechanisms: from touch to odor, gaze to gesture. However, while they tend to be researched and discussed separately, they co-occur. Thus, anxiety or anger are communicated by all channels simultaneously. Both researchers in the area and popular writers on the topic have come to the conclusion that it is safest and wisest to interpret body language signs together; that is, to look for patterns of nonverbal behavior, to spot them appearing one after another or simultaneously, or, put simply, to analyze clusters of signals rather than single, individual cues.

However, when there is a multitude of signs and signals, there are usually too many to pick up instantly. That is why it is so fascinating to watch (true) experts' commentary on film clips. They usually draw your attention to very particular, seemingly insignificant cues that, in context and with interpretation, seem to mean so much. Naturally, those involved tend to be politicians, celebrities or royalty: in other words, people who tickle public curiosity. The analyses are usually even more interesting when the people concerned are trying to hide or disguise their emotions or intentions (and TV producers make sure to include such extracts to boost the ratings). What these examinations do show, however, is that, with skill and knowledge, body language reading can reveal a great deal, but that it is easiest when the reader is not taking part in the actual interaction. Not only does it give the advantage of being able to concentrate on minute details not noticeable to the naked eye in real time, but also provides them with an opportunity to look a the same clips again and again. Perspective and distance have always been of benefit for those in the know and with know-how.

3

EVERYDAY SIGNS AND SIGNALS

As well as the thoroughly investigated cues and channels discussed in the previous chapter, there are many other nonverbal cues we use to communicate from day to day in our working lives. In this chapter we shall consider briefly three of these: physical appearance, dress, and color. Each has clear analogies in the animal world. For many animals there is a clear correlation between their physical features and strength or reproductive success; nearly all animals – for example, peacocks – send signals using special feathers and markings; and most have a purposeful coloring.

THE INFLUENCE OF NONVERBAL SIGNS IN IMPRESSION FORMATION

How long does it take to form an impression? Body language research points to the obvious answer: not long at all. In fact, it take just few seconds for us to make up our mind about another person. More importantly, it shows that this inkling is appearance-based, which has clear implications for business and work settings. It is therefore not surprising that people spend a huge chunk of their time, and place much importance on, grooming, polishing and improving their looks.

What sort of information can we detect from the outward image? Potentially, we can infer both qualities and states mind of people. As pointed out earlier in the book, we detect emotional states from facial expressions; for example, joy and sadness, anger and frustration, disgust and surprise. More than that, we deduce *characteristics* of people too, such as their competence, intelligence, dominance and status, simply by looking at them for a very brief length of time.

56

The area of psychological research that studies impression formation uses a paradigm called *thin slices of behavior*. Participants are presented with a peek, a tiny slice of information for five seconds or less which shows a person either static (photographed) or active (video-taped). They are then asked to rate the person shown against a number of traits and qualities. The findings have been astonishing. Students' teacher evaluations prior to the start of classes correlated highly with the ratings given to the same teacher at the end of the course.

We have an amazing ability to pinpoint other people accurately on a range of different personality and qualities scales without any deliberation or conscious thought on our part. These unconscious impressions also tend to be more correct than if people are given time to consider their choices.

PHYSICAL APPEARANCE

It makes evolutionary sense to judge the book by its cover. Physical appearance is used extensively in the animal kingdom as a crude divider. It separates males from females, young from old, and one subtype of species from another. It is the same with humans: facial and body symmetry is indicative of good genetic health, while asymmetry is a sure sign of some mutation and imbalance. Beautifully proportioned buttocks signify mating potential in women, while a firm, muscular build is evidence of sexual maturity in men. Overall, we use appearance to discriminate between good and bad, new and old, ripe and raw.

Started by the ancient Greek philosophers and passed on to the modern-day media, the debate about the role of physical appearance in our life is ongoing. Francis Galton first tried to measure various physical features and relate them systematically to personality traits and behaviors. Oscar Wilde's book, *The Picture of Dorian Gray* is based on the idea that appearance betrays inner character. Nowadays, more than ever before, there is much pressure on fitting the bill and looking right.

It seems that we have implicit ideas about how looks are linked to inner traits and characteristics. Recent research in the currently reviving area of physiognomy shows that physical and facial appearance is consistently related to judgments of credibility, trustworthiness, aggression and dominance. It could be that the development of both bodily features and personality traits are influenced by the same stimuli – for example, exposure to sex hormones. Digit ratio, for example, or the relationship between index and ring finger lengths, is claimed to be connected to such psychological traits as dominance and assertiveness. Men generally regarded as more dominant apparently also have longer ring fingers. Women who tend to be less domineering have slightly longer index fingers. Thus the connection between these, at first glance unlikely physical and psychological features, is explained through the influence of the same hormone, – testosterone – during foetal development. Testosterone, a male hormone, simultaneously affects both a foetus's skeleton structure and its personality characteristics, thus resulting in both "manly" and "womanly" finger ratios, and dominant or submissive personalities.

BODILY ATTRACTIVENESS

Evolutionary psychologists have studied the facial and bodily correlates of attractiveness that are related to youth and health (and fecundity). It is possible to describe characteristics of the body and face that are consistently rated attractive by others:

- BMI: Body Mass Index or shape, which is weight/(height × height). An attractive shape has 21–26 BMI points.
- WHR: Waist-to-Hip Ratio in females. A desirable score is 0.7 to 0.8.
- CTH: Chest-to-Hip ratio in men (less than 0.95).
- LTR: Leg-to-Torso Ratio (higher ratio or longer legs is preferred in women, smaller ratio or shorter legs in men).

As well as such "crude" body indexes, there are things like symmetry, height and skin texture. There are a whole range of characteristics that signal health and attractiveness. Consider hair: this indicates age (bald, grey) and race as well as fitness. Many cultures require body hair to be removed, especially by women.

People attempt to improve their attractiveness by various methods. These include possibly dangerous and certainly expensive plastic surgery, but also cosmetics and nearly always clothes. Clothes are used to enhance and disguise, to flatter and to distract: to change the state of both wearer and observer.

Below is a table listing bodily and facial features on which evolutionary psychological research has concentrated. Looking at the sheer number of variables that were investigated experimentally, it is possible to conclude several things. First, it shows that there are many details that constitute a "perfect" shape or look. Second, how important symmetry is to the concept of physical attractiveness. From face to figure, from fingers to toes, symmetrical body parts are consistently rated as being more attractive. It is also clear that certain forms and magnitude of bodily features are associated with beauty more than others. Thus some of the most frequently studied variables are shape and size.

Body component	Variables of research interest
Face	Symmetry, masculinity
Eyes	Shape, color
Nose	Shape, size
Lips	Voluminosity, color
Mouth	Oral hygiene
Figure	Symmetry, proportion, WHR ratio
Shoulders	Shape, breadth
Buttocks	Shape, size, firmness
Stomach	Size, shape, tone
Arms/Legs	Symmetry, length, proportionality to body
Hands/Feet	Symmetry, size, skin
Static measures	Height, weight
Dynamic measures	Manner of walk, personal space, body language

Source: Adapted from Swami and Furnham, 2008.

People seem to always have been fascinated by beauty and the beautiful. However, is it true that in these politically-correct, litigiously-obsessed, image-conscious times, that physical appearance cues, as much as ability and experience, affect our judgment? Is it the survival of the handsomest? Surely no one now dares to differentiate between job candidates on the basis of how they look, except, of course, in the theatre, movies and fashion, where it is all-important.

Though many would argue that beauty is in the eye of the beholder, academic studies in the area reveal a somewhat different picture. In fact, research on physical looks makes a rather depressing reading. Various well-conducted criminological studies have shown that physical features frequently sway judgments of innocence and guilt. The scared, small-eyed, heavily-built, shaven-haired defendant has far less of a chance of being judged correctly innocent than the large-blue-eyed, neotonized cherub. Attractiveness influences both juries and judges: bail levels, fines and jail sentences are often partly a reflection of the defendant's looks.

There are a host of studies on physical looks that show how certain features trigger reactions. Shown pictures of the same person wearing spectacles or not, attached to a CV, people rate those wearing glasses as being more intelligent. The effect has much less impact during interviews, where voice, vocabulary and answers to questions can overpower the simple prop of spectacles. But looks count, often subtly and very imprecisely.

Attractiveness is usually defined as "the degree to which one's facial image elicits a positive response". The results from many experimental studies support the "What is beautiful is good" phenomenon. As noted in the previous chapter, this is also called the *halo effect* and means that physical attractiveness is associated with many other (quite unrelated) characteristics and traits. Thus those who are considered attractive are thought of as being more intelligent, more socially skilled, more moral, more adaptable, and more agreeable than those who are deemed to be less attractive.

LOOKING THE PART

Consider the job of the casting director of a play or film. It is as interesting as it is challenging. It is, of course, a selection job. Out of the many, many hopeful applicants for the role, those must be chosen who in some way best encapsulate looks, voices, mannerisms and personae of the characters. Villains have to look like villains; and heroes like real heroes. Seductive lovers and vulnerable princesses all have to have the "right body".

The whole package needs to fit. The voice might be right, but the stature wrong. The look may be frightful and menacing but the physiology too puny to magnify the effect. Most directors want to be a little original, a little quirky. Hence the curious mixture of heroes on American detective shows, from bald, lollipop lickers to short, square, binocularly-challenged individuals.

Obituaries of film stars show how they tended to play similar roles. No doubt because they *looked the part*. Often people who knew these characters intimately reported that in effect they were quite unlike their celluloid characters. "Bad guys", characterized by gruff, monosyllabic one-liners, were often amusing raconteurs in private life; while matinée idols off-screen could be selfish, loutish and vulgar.

This is all very well in the "arty" world of drama and theatre, but what happens in business? To what extent are those who select managers influenced by their ideas of what a manager should look like?

Photographs are often used to accompany CVs, and selectors used to call for them. They do not dare to do so now, lest they be thought of as being influenced by the person's (facial) appearance, indicating race and age as well as physical attractiveness. But height, body shape, skin texture, hair length and quality do make a difference, for both men and women. Indeed, there are "consultants" who sell their skill at helping you to maximize your assets and minimize your limitations. The great rise of cosmetic surgery may be seen by some as a good business investment. They know that in the selection process, in presentations, and probably at assessments, it really does help to look the part.

The job application process has, for most people, dropped the habit of asking for a "recent" photograph. In the past, this was mainly for the purpose of identification. Impostors have been known to take tests for other people. And photographs can help to jog the memories of interviewers, who might see as many as a dozen candidates in a row.

The use of photographs is now impermissible because of a new discrimination: *lookism*. This is a close cousin of heightism and weight-ism, which could be called *shapism*. The lookist/shapists argue that people do better at work (are selected, promoted, rewarded) on their looks more than on their performance, which is unfair. Survival of the prettiest! The beautiful shall inherit the earth.

Unfortunately, there is abundant research evidence available to prove that this is true. Overweight people (as seen from photographs) are less likely to be selected for interview and, if they make it to that stage, are less likely to get the job. Very short people, particularly men, don't fare too well. The bald and bearded, those with thick lenses, or poor skin, or uneven teeth, are all handicapped. "What is beautiful is good." Attractive people spend less time in mental hospitals; they receive smaller/lower fines and prison sentences; and are more likely to be elected leaders of their fellows.

In one study conducted in the mid-1980s, a group of researchers sent a CV with photo attached to a group of public health administrators. In a letter, the supposed enquirer requested information and guidance on how to "get into" a public health career. The results showed that identical letters but with pictures of overweight (as opposed to normal weight) writers received both fewer responses and less encouragement to start a career in the area. Even when the applicants were judged to be equal overall in (mainly facial) attractiveness, there was evidence of bias against the overweight.

Studies on the perception of overweight job applicants all seem to show that they are thought to be "careless", "greedy" and "lazy". One study showed that overweight sales people were rated as less trustworthy, less punctual and less polite than their normal-weight colleagues. *Fat-ism exists*. Fat people are less likely to be selected for specific jobs.

One study used video-taped interviews and another used actors made up in theatrical costumes and good make-up to appear to be either average or overweight, with the same person asking identical questions in identical interviews. There remained bias against the overweight. So it's harder to get a job if you are overweight. And there is worse news: some studies have shown that there is a negative correlation between weight and pay – heavy people are paid less.

Heightism, lookism and weightism are soon to be on the agenda of the "discrimination at work" enthusiasts. They are certainly right to point out that attractiveness does affect every aspect of our lives, and our success at work. But the real issue is how best to deal with that fact.

There are three problems with the issue of the psychology of attractiveness, the issue of lookism and issues of discrimination. The first is the problem of subjectivity. There is often considerable agreement about the very beautiful and very ugly, but much less consensus about those in between. There are websites, support groups and fan clubs of people with very particular characteristics. Some individuals find plump voluptuousness attractive. Beauty, indeed attractiveness, like contact lenses, might be almost entirely in the eye of the beholder. This makes legislation on discrimination or even laying down guidelines very problematic.

But the second issue is much hotter. It has been suggested that looks are related to job performance: attractive people out-perform their less attractive colleagues. There are various mechanisms suggested to account for this. At the simplest, social learning theory level, attractive people are more self-confident as a result of the way they have been treated in the past. They have been privileged, favored and rewarded. Evolutionary psychologists have proposed the unthinkable and suggested there are good reasons to believe attractiveness is linked with intelligence, which is itself a good predictor of job success.

More obviously, the public respond well to more attractive people. Better-looking people are more persuasive. They sell more, get more tips, are liked more by others. Unfair, perhaps, but then life is unfair.

Third, some activities require a certain shape. People might need a certain strength, agility, ability to stretch and so on. They might need 20/20 vision. Have all these issues have been considered in disability legislation?

There might be downsides to being good-looking with an ideal shape. People with good looks can be arrogant, narcissistic, spoilt: think supermodels or teenage actresses. They can be lazy, relying on their looks rather than other skills, perseverance or simply hard work. They may also be very low on empathy and insight because they have not had to learn these skills.

There are two powerful reactions to the above observations. The first is the shrill cry of unfair discrimination from the *conspiracy theorists*, who see prejudice everywhere. There are no doubt associations of the short, the fat, and many other groups that believe they are discriminated against. Their argument is that physical characteristics play no part in how well they do the job, and that they are therefore victims. Some would even call for height quotas and the like, ensuring that by law as many top executives are below the average height as above it.

Battling for the other side are the *covariance theorists*, who point out that height and weight are in fact linked to social class, which in turn is linked to education, which is linked to skill, knowledge and attitudes. Thus the reason why top people tend to be slimmer and taller than average is that these are covariates of education, which is indeed a good predictor of success at work.

There can be strong or weak variants of either the conspiracy or covariance theories. Thus one could try sociobiology as a strong version of covariance theorists. It might go something like this: mate selection is partly a function of physical attractiveness. Women like fit, bright, wealthy males; males like pretty, fecund women. The more you "fit the bill" the bigger the choice of spouses you have, and vice versa. Thus certain physical types do better. Alpha males with trophy wives are top of the chain. True for the mountain gorillas of Burundi; but true also for the management team in Banbury.

How to reduce the attractiveness bias

Politicians and lawyers immediately plump for legislation, making the former smug and the latter rich. An alternative answer comes from the classical musical industry, where "blind" auditions were introduced in selection players for symphony orchestras. Judges could only hear, but not see, the musicians playing and selected the applicants to be in or out based on their abilities, not their outward appearance. The same principle has already been applied to business. Candidates are frequently asked to take IQ and personality tests *before* they are invited to a selection interview.

However, interviewers can easily be biased too. Charming, outgoing, lively, attractive people leave better impressions than their introverted, shy, less attractive but equally competent counterparts. Hence the structured selection interview. The traditional, rambling, unstructured interview relies on instinct and intuition and feeds prejudice, particularly judgments made based on body language, which may or may not be relevant to the job. They are desperately unreliable and invalid. The structured interview is different. It ensures that all candidates are asked identical questions in the same order. In addition, the questions are limited to *salient features* of the candidate's ability, knowledge and skills. Further, when evaluating the candidate after the interview, a consistent logical and mathematical scoring system is used. The interviewers are also trained in what to look for, thus the structured interview certainly moderates the bias against those who are less attractive.

So there are two morals here: one for the interviewer and one for the interviewee. With litigation mania and ever more lawsuits around fairness in selection, it pays to introduce structured interviews. In short, this means focusing on job-related factors, and evaluating actuarially rather than intuitively. For the interviewee: attending Weight Watchers, wearing make-up and high-heeled shoes, whatever works for you, can make a difference.

Perhaps beauty is not in the eye of the beholder after all. But it pays to know that books are judged by their covers. In this sense, we communicate by our appearance, which we can do something about. We can dye our hair and have plastic surgery. We can have laser surgery on our eyes, wear contact lenses or spectacles of many different styles. We communicate our age, values, wealth and status by how we present ourselves to the world. We "make a statement" with our looks alone.

LIPSTICK INDEX AND FOUNDATION FACTOR

It has been known for some time now that sales of make-up increase during bad times. Shares of leading lipsticks brands jumped up immediately after 9/11, and the recession current at the time of writing has proved to be particularly successful for sales of liquid foundation.

These facts do not come across as particularly surprising. Many speculate that make-up helps women "to put on a brave face" during times of instability. Others are more practical minded and point out to the general trend of downsizing in a recession: it makes economic sense to buy an inexpensive lipstick to spice up an already-worn outfit than to spend money on a new dress.

Either way, make-up's primary function is to reduce or draw attention to facial features. Lipstick helps women to "paint on a smile"; and it accentuates and corrects the shape of the lips. Foundation's main purpose is to create a flawless complexion, to smooth out skin imperfections, to make the face glow, wholesome and fresh. Overall, it is all to do with beauty, which, in turn, is associated with youth and fecundity, and these qualities are desirable whatever the current state of economic affairs.

DRESS

The whole fashion business is designed to enable people to send signals about wealth, taste and values, as well as to make in- and out-group statements (that is, who is in the tribe, who are "their people"). Clothes make a strong visual statement about how you see yourself. They are the value system of the individual made visible. Notice the way that jewelry, watches, spectacles and so on are marketed, often emphasizing the communication functions of each item. Various consultants make a good living advising business people about which colors they should choose or avoid, as well as about types of material and clothes that will make them look taller, slimmer, more serious or part of a particular group.

Badges, rings or cufflinks can indicate allegiance to groups or to organizations – often educational – that one has been associated with in the past. Ties, for men, can signal hobbies (golf-club designs), humour (male chauvinist pigs), as well as club membership. One of the American investment banks, for example, pioneered "pink shirt Fridays" for their employees, to build the team spirit, encourage loyalty and promote pride in group belonging. Spectacles can be used to emphasize facial features or to give an impression of studiousness, frivolity or practicality. The material used for clothing and accessories – crocodile-skin products, ivory or fur, for example – can indicate ecological values, or lack of them. Fashion consciousness – the keen sense of what is currently in (and out) – is another signal that may be sent by clothes. "Power dressing" seeks to imbue the wearer with significance. People tend to accentuate and hide certain features in order to attract or distract. The signalling system of clothes is not perfect. Noise in the system originating from subgroups, and cultural differences in meaning, inevitably leads to some messages becoming lost or mixed up.

We have all had the embarrassment of arriving at a party either over- or under-dressed. It is embarrassing because we signal our expectations about formality, measured by the guests, food, wine and so on. Being under-dressed can insult the hosts; while being over-dressed insults your intelligence. Both mean you read the invitation wrongly; you made a social gaffe.

Sexuality, power and wealth may be signalled by subtle dress-code cues, but only those "in the know" can pick these up. Ultimately, dress signals personality and values more than other specific messages. One can also make "fashion statements", but only the fashion-conscious will be able to read them. There is also the rather sad spectacle of the "fashion victim" who invests, in every sense, far too much in the signalling system. One can be taught the language of dress but it is too crude a communication system to be particularly useful.

Some people are more "clothing aware" than others. It has been suggested that clothing choice and awareness relate to:

- *manipulation*: people can wear outfits aimed at deception for their own ends;
- *social class*: better-educated people from a higher social class are sometimes more clothes-sensitive, though some "at the top" flout clothes sense while some "at the bottom" are extremely clothes-sensitive;
- *self-concept*: clothes are a second skin and reveal confidence;
- *social values*: clothes can indicate conservatism or radicalism, and where one stands on the practical/impractical (sensible/creative) dimension;
- *mental health*: disturbed people often wear bizarre clothing, or pay little heed to their appearance.

Clothing has an effect on both wearer and observer. People may use clothes to try to induce a state of well-being in others. It has been demonstrated that you are more likely to give information to someone if you like the way he or she is dressed. The fact that clothes affect the wearer is embodied in the simple phrase, "When I look good, I feel good."

Uniformed organizations – hotels, airlines or nursing services, for example – have to consider how their uniforms suggest not only cleanliness and efficiency but also status and rank. Clients prefer to see their professionals dressed in a certain way to indicate the latters' education and know-how, and to signal an appropriate relationship between "them" and "us".

But clothing choice at work may be severely limited by dress codes – even by "dress-down" days, on which people are required to wear "casual" clothes. Dress "off duty" may be more revealing, because it is less constrained. The idea is that your clothes not only reflect your attitude but also influence it. People are supposedly more comfortable in more relaxed clothing. Dressing down, in theory, lowers stress, blurs false barriers between "Chiefs and Indians" and promotes general well-being. This may or may not be true, and requires verification and specification: when, for whom, where, and why.

What are the rules for, and effects of, dress? Some organizations rejoice in having a smart uniform. Airlines probably come top of the uniform league outside the military. Not only are the uniforms smart and fashionable, but staff have to follow rigorous rules about such aspects as how they wear their hair; how much jewelry they are allowed; even rules about fingernail length and color.

Various organizations, such as rail companies, that gave up uniforms, have reintroduced them. For the customer, uniforms have many advantages. First, staff are easily identifiable. It's often embarrassing, in a bookshop, for example, perhaps asking several people (customers) for assistance before you find the person you need (actual staff). Second, you can (usually) distinguish the person in charge; that is, uniforms give a signal of rank. Third, uniformed staff can reinforce the brand. They can wear the logo and literally make the brand come alive.

Some uniforms are as much functional as fashionable. Others are meant to improve hygiene or safety. On the other hand, some organizations either have dated, tacky uniforms that few could wear with pride, or allow staff to add idiosyncratic touches. Fast-food outlets often have semi-uniformed staff.

Read a child's storybook and you will see that everyone on the high street seems to have an outfit. The baker with his tall hat; the butcher

TABLE 3.1 **Interpretations of various modes of dress**

Outfit	Interpretation
Suit, tie, shirt	Formal, standard business attire
Short skirt/low cut blouse or top	Usually too revealing, frivolous; not suitable for work
Jeans and t-shirt	Casual, informal
Track suit	Unless worn during physical exercises, shows lack of any dress sense
Latest designer piece	Communicates unconventionality, individuality and purchasing ability
Dress	If well tailored and of darker colors, it makes a good work outfit. Judged as feminine, especially when juxtaposed with trouser suits

with his apron; the tailor with his tape measure. Thus it is not surprising that many people have come to expect their professionals to be dressed in a particular way. Indeed, there are strong associations evoked by various types of clothes (see Table 3.1). A few years ago the *British Journal of Psychiatry* published a paper showing six pictures of male and female doctors. They went from the formal collar and tie, white coat and stethoscope slung around the shoulder to the completely dressed-down doctor in "smart casual" wear. What did people prefer? They liked the professional medical look with the white coat the best.

Some people are lucky to have attire choice at work: the lecturers may choose to wear smart suits or casual outfits. There is also choice within the uniform. Sometimes there are uniforms for special occasions. People expect and like to see a university's Vice Chancellor in full finery for a graduation, or undertakers in old-fashioned formal attire for a funeral.

Dress in all organizations follows a spoken, or rather an unspoken code. Dress code is part of the corporate culture and something newcomers pick up soon after joining an organization. Certain things are *de rigueur* and some are *taboo*. It has been said that you had to be very rich, very senior (or very stupid) to wear a brown suit or brown shoes in the City.

They used to say "If you want to get ahead, get a hat". Perhaps that applies to all apparel: dress for success. Dress alone is not enough to become successful but it can certainly send an instant message of status, professionalism and allegiance. It is a communication system, as all fashion-conscious people know.

68

COLOR

People color their hair, they have preferred colors in their wardrobe. Some people seem only to wear black, others choose highly saturated colors. Skin color for centuries has been a carrier of many stereotypical messages. Color conveys meaning.

The same is true for business. Virgin has a bright, saturated red; Barclays a distinctive turquoise; Lufthansa a goldish-yellow, and BP a range of greenish yellows. Aer Lingus's green has changed over the years, as did Air Canada's red.

In our culture there are color codes. Red is the color for danger: it means stop, prohibited, on fire. Yellow and black used together mean warning of danger. Black lettering on a yellow background is the optimum for legibility. Green means safety, exit, rescue services. Blue is for helpful signage.

There are idioms and adages which refer to color. We talk about being "off color", "coming out with flying colors", "sailing under false colors". There is also "feeling blue" and being "green with envy".

Yet a lot of nonsense is spoken about color. This is the evidence-free, naïvely enthusiastic world of color therapy and color consultants. There is an army of chromophiles offering psychological diagnoses and interventions and claiming that it is possible to change or enhance image by the use of color: you can become more intellectual if you wear blue-greys or blue-greens or muted blues; appear more secure if you combine earth tones or deep shades of colors with "bright accents" of gold, ivory or white.

Color can be used for several purposes. It can enhance various perceptual effects like distance, temperature and excitement. Red, yellow, violet and brown "bring things closer" while blue and green help make things look further away. Orange and yellow imply warmth; blue and green are cool colors. And green (mental hospital green in particular) is meant to be "restful"; while red is stimulating and violet aggressive. You may be able to make a (deceptively small) room look bigger through colored paint or light. Or you may make a cold room look and "feel" cosy.

Color is known to also affect mood. In general, colors at the long wavelength end of the spectrum such as red and orange can induce feelings of high arousal, while short wavelength colors such as blue and green induce feelings of calm. A number of studies have made comparisons of the arousal properties of various pairs of colors. Thus, violet has been shown to produce greater arousal than green; red produces more arousal than blue. Red lighting produces greater arousal than either blue or green. The above demonstrations used measures of physiological arousal. At a more subjective level, it has also been found that people feel more excited and stimulated by red, orange and yellow than by green and blue. Blue tends to associate more with feelings of being calm, peaceful and serene. Green has no strong association at a psychological level with such descriptions of how one feels.

Further, color can influence how well people learn new things or perform on educational tasks. Color coding, for example, has helped people distinguish between broad categories of things and actions (e.g. hot/cold, on/off). Coding has helped people develop maps of their environment or mental guides to help them find their way around complex buildings. Color can help to attract or direct attention to different aspects and features of complex materials such as maps and diagrams, and can thus serve as an aid to learning and performance. The different arousal properties of colors can also be useful. Warm colors, because they are arousing, facilitate activity and may help certain tasks. The wrong colors under the wrong circumstances can, however, be a hindrance to learning. It has been found that some people prefer cooler colors when working on complicated mental tasks, while warmer colors are often preferred when doing boring, repetitive things.

Sometimes color also affects behavior but usually only under certain circumstances. Work with the mentally ill has indicated that different colored lighting can produce different reactions and patterns of behavior among patients. Specific examples of this were that magenta had a quieting effect in one study, while its replacement with white light after one month caused patients to get much more excited. Blue had a prolonged quieting, soothing effect which was noticed by staff and patients alike. Yellow used with depressed patients had a slight stimulating effect, and red produced even more stimulation.

The color of ink has been found to affect handwriting: handwriting with green ink is nearer to normal than when done with red ink. The performance of factory workers has also been found to vary with lighting color. One study, which examined men working at factory machines, measured output under the effect of different colored lights. White was best, while colored lighting produced signs of nervous excitement. There was no evidence of a stimulating effect of red or a soothing effect of blue.

Thus color can, indeed, be used effectively to change stimulation levels and memory, improve signage, communicate urgency and safety and, of course, improve the aesthetic beauty of the environment.

However, color affects behavior only tangentially, spasmodically and in the short-term, through affective and cognitive mechanisms. That is, moods and memories are most obviously affected by color. There are, nevertheless, clear and consistent findings on color associations and preferences.

Females show a greater preference for red, violet and yellow and a greater dislike of green than males. They also prefer highly saturated, brighter colors than do males. Still, we don't know if this is true in other cultures and other historical periods, or indeed why this sex difference occurs. There is evidence that color preference is cultur- ally learnt, as different colors have very different associations across different cultures. This inevitably limits the generalization of these findings.

Extraverts tend to prefer arousing, warm colors (such as red), while introverts prefer cool, calming colors (for example, green). Extraverts choose and prefer bright, pure colors, whereas introverts prefer more subtle shades. Sensation-seekers prefer red, while sensation-avoiders prefer blue.

Young children seem to associate different colors with different emo- tions: love, anger, and pain with red and black; happiness, strength and "life" with blue; and honesty with white. As they get older, children shift away from a preference for warmer colors (especially yellow) to cooler colors (in particular, blue).

Dark-eyed people tend to prefer colors at the red end of the spectrum, and light-eyed people at the blue end. This is probably because of the presence of a pigment, melanin, in dark-eyed people, which acts as a light shield.

Colors have symbolic associations, but these vary across cultures. In the West, colors often have these meanings:

- Red – charity, divine love
- Green – faith, gladness, hope and joy
- Black – wisdom, constancy, as well as evil, falsehood, error
- White – purity, truth

- Blue – hope, faith, modesty and fidelity
- Yellow – jealousy and change.

Design and marketing people take color seriously. Color has symbolic value. Color creates impressions. Color can be memorable. However, there is no evidence to suggest that color works in more subtle ways on the human psyche; your perceived gravitas will not be affected by the particular hues in your tie.

CONCLUSION

This chapter looks at how we present ourselves, and in particular at how we make statements with our clothes and our attempts to look more attractive. The cosmetic and fashion industries are dedicated exclusively to serving modern humans' powerful needs to present themselves in a particular way (though many would argue that businesses exploits these motives or creates them artificially).

We change our clothing and our appearance regularly to send messages. Some people are more skilled at this than others. It is not simply a question of style or fashion sense. Many differences in this ability stem from cultural upbringing (some are more conscious of their appearance than others) as well as individual inclinations to follow the "horde" or "fit the bill". The entertainment industry has "wardrobe" department dedicated to making sure that people look right for their roles. Politicians and high-flying executives are sometimes given advice on what and what not to wear: from color of tie to jewelry.

Nevertheless, everybody acknowledges the communicative power of physical attractiveness. It seems to transcend both geographical and temporal borders. Ancient Greek and Roman statues of perfectly-shaped male and female bodies will always inspire awe and admiration. Though many non-Western cultures have had different standards of beauty, these art works are still appreciated worldwide, and not the least for the attractiveness of the models. Hence the attempts of people to look more attractive to their colleagues at work.

4

COMMUNICATING ATTITUDES, EMOTIONS AND PERSONALITY

SHOWING EMOTIONS

Body language sends messages – messages about emotions, attitudes and personality. Therapists have argued that it can shed new light on the dynamics of inter-family relationships: that, at times, it is a signal from the unconscious. This is because, to a large extent, we express our emotions most clearly through our body language. We do this partly because we cannot help it; we can "do no other", because strong states such as guilt, shame, embarrassment, anger, boredom and sexual excitement have strong physiological reactions. We "leak" our emotions because our central nervous system reactions can cause blushing, sweating, pupil dilations, changes in breathing and so on.

We also express our emotions nonverbally because we do not always have the vocabulary to express them verbally. Occasionally people do not have enough insight into their emotions or feel the need to report them – even if they wanted to do so. Indeed, it has been reported that on occasion people notice their physiological reactions and nonverbal communication and infer their emotional states from these. Thus, if I notice I am sweating, I conclude that I am anxious.

A famous "shaky bridge" experiment showed how easily we mis-attribute emotions. An attractive female researcher stopped young men on either a wobbly wooden bridge or a solid stable one and asked them to answer a set of questions. She gave them her number to discuss the details of the study further if they wished to do so. Not surprisingly, more men from the "shaky bridge" condition called up the girl. Walking on an unstable surface can be a

> tense experience even for the bravest among us. In response to the potential danger, hormones rush through the body preparing it for the "fight or flight" response. However, sexual attraction produces similar kinds of bodily reactions: palms of the hands sweat, pupils dilate, and heartbeat intensifies. Therefore men in the experiment misattributed their excitement to being attracted to the researcher, not to their fear of walking over the bridge.

Various body signals are related to the messages we send. Facial expressions, eye movements, gestures, posture and tone of voice all deliberately (or unconsciously) give clear impressions about how we feel. As part of growing up in our culture we learn how to decode emotions in other people. There are tests that allow researchers to investigate the accuracy and reliability with which people interpret a combination of signals such as anger, contempt, disgust, fear, joy or surprise.

EMOTIONAL LABOR

Are some jobs, such as selling or working in the burgeoning hospitality industry, unique? Some jobs have a pretty intangible product, called service, and some are heavily reliant on state-of-the-art technology. What does it take to succeed in the service industries?

Staff in people industries (customer service, hospitality) do have common features. They are selected to be jolly, optimistic, attentive and empathic. They have to be considerate "people-people". Further, they need to have consistently high presentation standards.

In the early 1980s, in a study of airline steward staff, a researcher, Arlie Russell Hochschild, wrote a book called *The Managed Heart: Commercialization of Human Feeling*. In this book she argued for a new concept: *emotional labor*. She pointed out that many jobs require physical and mental labor, but some, uniquely, require emotional labor.

The idea is simple: service staff are required to express emotions they do not necessarily feel. They are required to smile, to be positive, to appear relaxed whatever they are actually feeling. Hochschild called this *surface acting*. However, in some jobs people are almost required to feel the emotions they are expected to display. This is called *"deep acting"*. The idea is that (canny) customers can spot the false display of emotion, so service staff in these circumstances have to learn the "inside-out smile".

So such service staff have to learn to become *method* actors. They must really experience emotions to be able to portray them convincingly. Karl Marx said that workers were alienated from the products of their labor. Equally, Hochschild believed that service workers, whose emotions are "managed and controlled" by their employers, become alienated from their real feelings. The sorts of emotions shown are patience, friendliness, curiosity, while suppressing boredom, frustration and anger.

Thus service staff have not to be inauthentic but (sort of) *learn authenticity*. Hochschild believed this costs too much, in that it causes psychological damage in the long term. Yet there remains controversy, not so much about the concept but rather if it is essentially damaging in the way it estranges workers from their true feelings.

One way to control and aid expression of emotion is through the use of *scripts*. Service staff are encouraged to act – to learn their lines; to portray a character. This teaches them the appropriate emotions, which may, in time, become how they truly feel.

There is nothing new in scripts. Sociologists in fact argue that they are a good thing, because they can both help workers to distance themselves from their "performance" and reduce the likelihood of a mishap. Young staff seem to like scripts. They help in interactions with difficult and demanding customers, and control volatile exchanges. As they become more confident, quite often staff personalize the (suggested) script with their own idiosyncrasies. Staff believe scripts help and protect them. Further, everybody knows that it is just surface acting.

Similarly, uniforms can act like stage clothes. They can inform and protect. They help to identify who is who. Is a uniform a barrier? Does it mark people as servile and powerless? Much depends on how smart it is, what is it that people are serving, and who are the customers.

Service staff have to "fake" being eternally polite, cheerful and courteous. They have to cope with people being rude, dismissive or over-familiar. Some have to deal with uninvited sexual innuendo.

All service staff have a "backstage" – in the galley, the kitchen, even the cloakroom. Here they can be themselves, let off steam, react in the way that they would naturally. Behind the scenes they can mock difficult customers. They can get their own back and enjoy the camaraderie of the oppressed. Rest breaks are times to become the real self; to take off the make-up; to recover a sense of self-worth.

Training reduces the negative effects of emotional labor. What is more, some people are clearly more suited in terms of their emotional "make-up" for service jobs. Emotional labor requirements also differ from culture to culture. However, are service jobs becoming increasingly de-skilled? Evidently not, if social and emotional skills are taken into consideration.

Acting is as much nonverbal as verbal. The office, certainly the shop, the restaurant and the hotel all represent a stage that requires a certain amount of acting.

ABILITY, ACCURACY AND SKILL

Are some people simply better nonverbal communicators than others? How, when and why have they acquired the implicit and explicit knowledge and skill to be expert communicators?

Tests have been devised to measure this, but one thing seems clear: self-appraisal is not a good predictor of actual skill. All too often, those with surprisingly little insight and skill believe they are very good nonverbal communicators, while those with considerable knowledge underestimate their ability. Nearly everybody believes they are a good listener, which is demonstrably false. And others genuinely believe they can nearly always detect when people are lying to them, which is, undoubtedly, not the case. Self-awareness of nonverbal sensitivity and flexibility is therefore not a very good measure of it.

However, we do know that:

1. *Gender*: overall, females are better decoders than men. They read emotions better and are better lie detectors, though it does seem that men may be better at detecting (and, perhaps, responding to) anger.
2. *Age*: people get better as they get older, but this skill peaks around the mid-twenties.
3. *Intelligence*: there is a very small positive relationship between intelligence and nonverbal communication. Studies on children have, however, shown that bright children are better at nonverbal communication, which may also help their achievements in school because it improves their relationships with teachers and peers.
4. *Personality*: data from tests shows that people who are extroverts rather than introverts; stable as opposed to anxious; agreeable more than disagreeable; open rather than closed to experience; instrumental rather than fatalistic; and democratic compared to autocratic, do a better job of sending and receiving nonverbal communication.

5. *Race*: results are mixed, but it seems that people quite naturally are better at decoding the messages of those of the same race.
6. *Mental patients*: most psychotic patients have a particular difficulty with nonverbal communication, as do those on the autism/Asperger syndrome spectrum. Indeed, for the latter group, it is their inability to read body language signals that most clearly defines their condition. However there are some mental disorders, such as antisocial or narcissistic personality disorders, that make sufferers particularly good at nonverbal communication. There is also some evidence that neurotic people maybe very perceptive at decoding the emotional signals of others, but surprisingly unable to control their own.

Those who decode well do not necessarily send well, though the two are closely related. Being proficient at sending nonverbal messages is a function of many things: experience and practice; knowledge and skill; motivation and confidence. The issue lies mainly in self-awareness and emotional control.

One characteristic that seem to summarize this skill has been called *self-monitoring*. Snyder (1974) came up with the concept of self-monitoring, a personality trait that is very much to do with awareness and flexibility. Self-monitoring is the tendency to notice (visual, vocal, verbal) cues for socially appropriate behavior and to modify one's own behavior accordingly (see Table 4.1). Individuals can be classified into two groups with regard to their level of self-monitoring. Those who score highly on the trait of self-monitoring are characterized by sensitivity to social clues indicating socially appropriate behavior, and using those cues to modify self-presentation. Low self-monitors are thought to be relatively insensitive to social cues, and tend to maintain a consistent self-presentation across different situations. High self-monitors emphasize the public self and, like actors, seem to be asking "What role should I be playing in this situation?" Low self-monitors are more interested in their personal value systems and private realties. The central question asked by the low self-monitors is "How can I look like the person I truly am?"

Clearly, high self-monitors are good at reading nonverbal cues and adjusting their behavior accordingly. Socially, they are highly flexible and adaptable.

Snyder (1987) distinguished between the hard and soft sell in advertising – the former being about quality (for example, intrinsic merit, functional value) and the latter about image. He argued and

TABLE 4.1 **Self-monitoring**

High self-monitors	Low self-monitors
Prefer (and choose) careers in theatre, PR, law, politics, diplomacy	Consider themselves sincere and compassionate, thus choose careers in social services or "helping" professions
Happier in, more confident about and more successful at selling	Work best when in groups of people like themselves
Respond to "task-orientated" rather than "relationship-orientated" leadership	Respond to "relationship-orientated" rather than "task-orientated" leadership
When choosing a career path, are influenced by other candidates' appearance, demeanour and mannerisms	When choosing a career path, are most interested in linking the job to their inner disposition

demonstrated that high self-monitors rated image-orientated advertisements and products as being more appealing and effective, and would be willing to pay more for the product. By contrast, low self-monitors reacted more favorably to product-quality orientated advertisements. He also showed that the same principle applied when encouraging a person not to consume a product. Thus high self-monitors may be put off smoking because of the consequences of bad breath and smelly clothes, while low self-monitors may be more concerned with health consequences (for example, coughing, sore throat).

High self-monitoring consumers are those who purchase the sleek, flashy, sporty-looking car despite its possibly poor performance and handling characteristics, the ones who use the toothpaste that make their teeth look the whitest (even if it threatens the enamel of their teeth), and the ones who drink the "super premium" beer – that special imported beer that says something about its drinker's status (even if it tastes no better than the less expensive domestic brands). These image-conscious high self-monitors clearly choose *form over function.*

By contrast, low-self-monitoring consumers purchase the nutritious breakfast cereal (even if it isn't the one endorsed by the Olympic gold medal winner), the ones who use the mouthwash that is purported to kill the most bacteria (even if it does leave their breath with that faint medicinal odour), and the ones who choose the energy-efficient refrigerator (even though it's not available in the most designer-styled finish). They choose *function at the expense of form.*

Snyder (1987) published his short measure of the self-monitoring trait, which you are welcome to try for yourself. There are 18 statements, which you might judge as being true or false of you. Put a T if you agree with the statement or an F if you disagree with it. Then check your score against the explanation provided below. Test yourself!

1. I find it hard to imitate the behavior of other people.
2. At parties and social gatherings, I do not attempt to do or say things that others will like.
3. I can only argue for ideas which I already believe in.
4. I can make impromptu speeches even on topics about which I have almost no information.
5. I guess I put on a show to impress or entertain others.
6. I would probably make a good actor.
7. In a group of people I am rarely the centre of attention.
8. In different situations and with different people, I often act like a very different person.
9. I am not particularly good at making other people like me.
10. I'm not always the person I appear to be.
11. I would not change my opinions (or the way I do things) in order to please someone or win their favor.
12. I have considered being an entertainer.
13. I have never been good at games like charades or improvisational acting.
14. I have trouble changing my behavior to suit different people and different situations.
15. At a party I let others keep the jokes and stories going.
16. I feel a bit awkward in a company and do not show up quite as well as I should.
17. I can look anyone in the eye and tell a lie with a straight face (if for a the right end).
18. I may deceive people by being friendly when I really dislike them.

There are 9 statements which are true of high self-monitors and 9 statements which are true of low self-monitors. Thus, if you indicated T for Q 4–6, 8, 10, 12, 17–18 and F for Q 1–3, 7, 9, 11, 13–16, you are a very high-monitoring individual. You are likely to be extremely socially aware and sensitive to nuanced body language.

On contrary, if you marked T for Q 1–3, 7, 9, 11, 13–16 and F for Q 4–6, 8, 10, 12, 17–18, you are a true low self-monitor. You do not pay much attention to either your own or others nonverbal behaviors in social interactions.

A medium score would comprise from a mixture of agreeing and disagreeing with both high and low self-monitor items. An average score would represent a person who is adept at reading some social clues and exhibit a degree of control over their own nonverbal behavior, but does not take too much notice of body language in their social life.

There is a skill in being a sender and a skill in being a receiver of nonverbal communication. Those who are interested in, and skilled at, people-watching need to know certain facts to understand how and why people behave as they do towards one another:

- Who the people are and what is their relationship – their position, status, relationship, social class, education.
- The physical and social setting for the behavior – the social rules and expectations governing that setting.
- The real and hidden purpose of the interaction – why the people are meeting.
- The frequency, duration and etiquette associated with the communication.

Communication occurs in a particular setting for a particular purpose, though the latter may not always be clear to the communicators. Skilled observers notice small things that, together with verbal content, enrich the understanding of what is really going on. That is why NVC pundits are asked to watch politicians so closely; and why politicians take advice from other experts on how best to deliver their message. This is of particular interest when famous people are under duress or have been accused of lying.

COMMUNICATING ATTITUDES

We also communicate interpersonal attitudes through body language. There are clear signals for friendliness and hostility. Watching two people talk, even without hearing the content of their speech, it is possible to understand who is – or at least feels – dominant, and who is, or feels, submissive. For example, liking, and affiliation, is sent as a message by:

- A higher incidence of body contact such as touching or stroking;
- Closer proximity in standing or sitting;
- An orientation to each other that is often side-by-side;
- More mutual gazes or smiling;
- A posture with more leaning forward, more open arms and legs; and
- A softer, quieter tone of voice.

Equally, human hostility signals look remarkably like those of animals – with harsher voices, more frowning, more teeth-showing and a tense posture.

There is evidence off all sorts of sex differences, but these are also related to particular personality types and particular cultures. Thus, compared to men, it seems that women adopt a more open-arm, open-leg posture to males they like and to those of higher status. Males, compared to females, show more evidence of vigilance in relation to physical threat – more direct orientation, more eye gaze and a much less relaxed posture. In general, people with psychotic disorders are very poor readers of body language, while neurotic people are particularly good, being highly sensitive to signals of rejection. Overall, women seem more sensitive than men, particularly where the latter are in technical professions. Most often we disclose our emotions by using displacement activities – behaviors designed to cope with anxiety, aggression or boredom. People waiting for an interview may go through excessive preening/grooming (brushing clothes, checking jewelry), and eating, drinking or smoking without needing to, as well as demonstrating recognizable behaviors such as foot-tapping, fiddling with objects and pretending to read (flicking through magazines or newspapers without really taking anything in).

Crowding at concerts or cinemas, in elevators and on trains or buses results in unavoidable intrusion into other people's intimate zones, and reactions to this invasion are interesting to observe. There is a list of unwritten rules that people in Western cultures follow rigidly when faced with a crowded situation such as a packed lift or public transport. These rules include the following:

- You are not permitted to speak to anyone, including a person you know.

- You must avoid eye contact with others at all times.
- You are to maintain a "poker face" – no emotion must be displayed.
- If you have a book or newspaper, you must appear to be deeply engrossed in it.
- In elevators, you are compelled to watch the floor numbers above your head.

We often hear words like "miserable", "unhappy" and "despondent" used to describe people who travel to work in the rush hour on public transport. These labels are used because of the blank, expressionless look on the faces of travellers, but they are misjudgments on the part of the observer. What the observer sees, in fact, is a group of people adhering to the rules that apply to the unavoidable invasion of their intimate zones in the crowded public space.

Source: Pease (1990), p. 22.

Some nonverbal signs in everyday conversation are shown in Table 4.2.

Our ability to attribute other people's states and attitudes relies on reading the body language. A surprised person looks so because their initial body expression has changed to a "new look". The effect quickly passes and the nonverbal behavior typical to the person resumes.

Attitudes (like/dislike; approve/disapprove) are judgments we make about things, objects, people and so on. These are not stable, but rely

TABLE 4.2 **Nonverbal signs in everyday conversation**

Seeking information	Verbal	Higher duration of utterance, faster reaction-time latency, more speech interruption
	Visual	More frequent gazes in the direction of the other speaker
	Proxemic	Shorter spatial distance in standing or seating arrangements
Permission to speak	Gesture	More frequent head nods and chin thrusts, more expansive hand and feet movements, larger postural shifts
	Visual	Larger pupil size, increased eye-blinking
Surprised response	Verbal	Reduced verbalizations
	Facial	Raised brows, eyelids opened wider, dropped jaw, open mouth
	Visual	Increased pupil size, change in eye contact, raised hands

on immediately available information, most of which is provided via the nonverbal system of communication. That is why judgments or attitudes can be, and constantly are, altered.

INTUITION

To describe somebody as perceptive, intuitive and insightful may refer to his or her being particularly nonverbally literate. Some professionals have to be good at reading bodily cues so that they can understand their clients better. Psychologists and GPs, waiters and comedians, after-dinner speakers and lawyers gain a great deal if they are able to understand the motives, reactions and emotional states of their "clients".

A central question remains as to whether both the giving and receiving of messages via nonverbal behavior is innate or culturally learned and transmitted. Certainly, we know, for example, through studying facial expressions of blind people or the touch behavior of those from different continents, that nonverbal behavior has biologically adaptive origins but also cultural modifications. Smiling, shaking the head for "no" and the shoulder-shrug are pretty well, but not totally, universal. But others are learnt. And they are learnt as a part of growing up. Witness the child, the adolescent and the adult telling a lie. As adults, most of us have learnt to be less obvious and more sophisticated in our nonverbal behavior when we lie. This makes us, and indeed everybody else, more difficult to read. Yet it remains difficult to sustain for long either the faking or repression of emotions that have been manifested nonverbally.

Yet we all know that much nonverbal behavior is governed by rules. Indeed, an old saying that one person's freedom ends where the other person's freedom begins illustrate this idea quite clearly. Disconcerting behavior such as shouting, quarrelling, or exaggerated manner of speech or gesture has always been frowned upon, or indeed prohibited, since it disregards the rule of common courtesy. Thus, Debrett the most authoritative etiquette guide notes that even in most public of experiences members of civilized societies are asked to show respect towards other people's privacy.

Some nonverbal behavior is nothing more than rule-following. But what one can tell intuitively from seeing "good manners" nonverbally is that people know the rules and are prepared to conform to them. Not following the rules could mean either ignorance of, or antagonism towards, social etiquette.

It has been suggested that women are more intuitive than men, that they are better readers of nonverbal signals, and as a consequence, are more skillful senders of body cues. This may well be true. It may be a function of biological differences – the need for women in childcare to be very sensitive to the signals of their pre-verbal children. Or it may be because the structure of society means that women are often less powerful than men. Inevitably, subordinates are more attentive to the moods, needs and whims of their superiors than vice versa. This interpretation *may* help to account for women's increased sensitivity to nonverbal cues – often referred to as intuition.

EMOTIONAL INTELLIGENCE AND READING THE SIGNALS

Since the mid-1990s, the idea that EQ or Emotional Intelligence Quotient is more important in business than IQ or Intelligence Quotient has been taking hold. EQ is defined as inter- and intrapersonal intelligence. It has been argued that it consists of three categories of adaptive abilities, all of which are related to sending and reading nonverbal signals. They are the expression of emotion; the regulation of emotion in oneself and others; and the utilization of emotion in solving problems. Different writers on the topic have emphasized slightly different things, but all stress the importance of the perception, appraisal and expression of emotion; and understanding, analyzing and emphasizing emotional knowledge. You cannot be emotionally intelligent without being highly literate in body language.

In short, EQ is about *emotional literacy*, and emotional literacy is about reading the cues of nonverbal communication. However, it should be pointed out that it includes the ability to send, receive *and* regulate cues. Many neurotic people are very sensitive to the moods and feelings of others. Often they can partly disguise their own feelings, but not usually for long, as they find it difficult to regulate their own moods. The high-EQ person is more resilient and psychologically robust that most people classed as neurotic. He or she knows how to find and sustain positive emotions and tends to be optimistic, with a strong ego.

But high-EQ people know when to speak or indeed to listen to others about personal problems, when to share emotions with others, how to present a good impression of themselves, and how to complement and charm others. In the chapter "Managing with Heart" in his book *Emotional Intelligence*, Goleman (1996) argued that teamwork, open lines of communication, cooperation, listening and speaking one's mind are characteristics of emotional intelligence (EI), and are essential at work.

In business, empathy and compassion are in, and the manipulative, jungle-fighter boss is out. Leadership and being a good manager is about being attuned to the feelings of the people managers have to deal with (up, sideways and down). There are many applications of EI, including being able to see grievances as helpful critiques, which is using feedback effectively; creating an atmosphere in which diversity is valued rather than a source of friction; and networking effectively.

But would you prefer the CEO of your company to have a high EQ or a high IQ? Do you want a cold but clever boss, who understands the business, keeps his or her eye firmly on the bottom line, reads the market signals, but is little clumsy, shy and gauche? Or would you prefer the perceptive, empathic, socially adept boss, equally able to charm customers, employees and the media? Naturally it is desirable to have both, but what are the consequences of being all head with no heart, or vice versa?

The former, high-IQ person, may be respected but not particular liked, whereas the latter is often greatly loved but not respected for his or her business acumen. It is not common to find a boss with both high IQ and high EQ. Perhaps the best solution is to have a good mix of IQ and EQ on the board – but could they get on with each other? One does suspect that the bright board members might despise the warm, sensitive ones, who in turn might be offended by what they would perceive as intellectual arrogance.

But the good news is that whereas IQ cannot be learnt, EQ can. You can learn various intellectual tricks, but it really is not likely that you will be able to raise your (adult) IQ much. On the other hand, it is relatively easy to acquire EQ skills through "social skills", "interpersonal skills", "assertiveness", "counselling" and "communication skills" courses. Much of this training is about being observant about one's own nonverbal behavior and that of others. It is about sensitivity and flexibility in reading a wide range of emotions, both verbally and nonverbally.

YOUR PERSONALITY IS SHOWING

Can one understand another person's personality from his or her body language? Nearly all personality theorists agree that two of the absolute fundamental dimensions of human personality are *extroversion* and *neuroticism.* These are the basis for the famous Galen system: phleg-matic (low E, low N); choleric (high E, high N); sanguine (high E, low N); melancholic (low E, high N). Both extroversion and neuroti-cism can be reasonably accurately inferred from a close reading of body language. Extroverts tend to be active, sociable, impulsive, expressive, irresponsible risk-takers not prone to reflection, while neuroticism is characterized by low self-esteem, unhappiness, anxiety, obsessiveness, guilt and hypochondria.

Extroversion

We all know extroverts are loud, outgoing and talkative. But few understand the "mechanism" behind the trait. In short, extroverts are "stimulus-hungry", under-aroused, in need of excitement.

Typical extroverts are sociable, have many friends, need to have peo-ple to talk to. They crave excitement, take chances, often stick their necks out, act on the spur of the moment, and are generally impul-sive individuals. They are fond of practical jokes, always have a ready answer, and generally like changes. They tend to be carefree, easy-going, optimistic and like to "laugh and be merry". They prefer to keep moving and doing things, tend to be aggressive and lose their temper quickly.

Typical introverts are quiet and retiring, introspective, fond of books rather than people. They are reserved and distant except to intimate friends. They tend to plan ahead, "look before they leap" and dis-trust the impulse of the moment. They like a well-ordered mode of life and keep their feelings under close control. They seldom behave in an aggressive manner, and do not lose their temper easily. They are reli-able, somewhat pessimistic, and place great value on ethical standards.

Extroverts trade-off accuracy for speed in their search for excite-ment. They are more likely to have accidents, more likely to break the law, more likely to take drugs and to smoke. The exhibitionis-tic thrill-seeking of the extroverts is as biologically hard-wired as the peace-seeking of the introverts, who are quite content with a book, a chess game or a stroll in the countryside. Physiologically over-aroused, the introvert is as stressed by more stimulation as the extrovert is pleased by it.

Hence the extrovert sees the introvert as being boring, inadequate and secretive, while the introvert sees the extrovert as attention-seeking, shallow and noisy. The two extremes choose different envi-ronments in which to do differently preferred jobs with colleagues of

TABLE 4.3 **Possible speech variations according to personality traits**

Speech and language	Introvert	Extrovert
Form	High	Low
Code	Elaborated	Restricted
Grammar	More nouns, adjectives, prepositions	More verbs, adverbs, pronouns
Vocabulary	Correct	Loose
Accent	Received pronunciation	Local
Speed	Slow	Fast
Paralanguage	Few dysfluencies	Many dysfluencies

their own type. *Ambiverts*, to use the correct term for those in the middle of the spectrum, tend to get on fairly well with both types as long as they are not too extreme.

Extreme extroverts are fairly easy to detect nonverbally. They move and talk faster than normal, tend to fidget more and are more prone to boredom. Extroverts look and touch more than introverts, prefer more dramatic clothes, gesticulate more dramatically and show a wider range of facial expressions. But it is the area of language that introversion–extroversion can be clearly detected. Extroverts will talk faster than introverts, have fewer unfilled pauses in their speech and be quicker to respond in everyday speech.

It is suggested that extroverts differ from introverts on a number of speech and language dimensions: *form*, which refers to the degree of formality in the language used; *grammar*, which refers to the types of words a person chooses to use; *vocabulary* or lexicon, which refers to how many words are used, and how correct and how unusual they are; *accent*, which refers to regional and class-related ways of pronouncing words and phrases; *speed*, which refers quite obviously to the speed at which people talk; and *paralanguage*, which refers to dysfluencies such as "ums", "ers" and so on. What is being suggested in Table 4.3 is that, compared to extroverts, introverts generally use more formal speech with more careful grammatical constructions, perhaps a bigger vocabulary, and so on.

Neuroticism

Emotionally unstable people – those with negative effectivity – are not difficult to spot. For example, they seem to have more headaches than stable people. It may be that they simply notice headaches more than stable people, or call attention to them more often. But the traits associated with neurosis are well known: being anxious, moody, lonely, pessimistic. Such people tend to have more phobias and are more prone to depression. They look stressed, nervous and worried a lot of the time.

It is not difficult to spot clues to neurosis in a person, though it may be confusing if one person's emotional instability is primarily a function of anxiety, but in someone else one of depression. Consider the following:

- The anxious person and the depressed person seem to adopt expressions of surprise, fear and gloom that stay with them. Actors know how to present the model of a depressed person facially – the scowl, the lack of expression.
- Depressed people tend to avoid eye contact, whereas anxious people have a gaze pattern that darts about, ever on the lookout for a potential threat. Overall, those who are emotionally stable establish more mutual eye gazes for longer periods than do those who are emotionally unstable. Depressed people show a few, hesitant, nonemphatic gestures, while those who are anxious are more prone to self-touching, along with aimless fidgeting.
- The posture of the depressed person is easy to recognize. He or she looks limp, lacking in energy – even ashamed.

It is in the area of body contact that one can see emotional instability most clearly. Neurotic people are often fearful of all contact. The obsessionality and hypochondria associated with neurosis make people fearful of catching disease by touching. Neurotics with low self-esteem worry about how "touch-worthy" they are. The guilt factor in neurosis can associate touching with sexual advances and hence it is unlikely to occur.

Certainly, by observing people over time in a range of situations, one can get a pretty good idea of their personalities from their nonverbal behavior.

CULTURE AND BODILY COMMUNICATION

The world has shrunk. Wherever you are right now reading this book, chances are there is already a McDonald's restaurant or a Starbucks coffee shop within walking distance or, if not, there will be one open very soon. Equally, the recent economic downturn has made international connections all too visible, with stock markets crashing one after another in a domino effect.

Despite the similarities they share, however, cultures are inherently diverse. Different historical events, geographical conditions and available resources have shaped the cultural psyche and produced the most peculiar of traditions. These traditions have been adopted into the culture and resulted in some behaviors typical of the mind set. For example, German people are famous for their punctuality, and the Spanish and Latin Americans for their lack of it. The English have a reputation of being reserved, cold and unemotional, while Americans are often spoken of as being bold, open and expressive.

Cultural differences and similarities are the hot topics on the agenda. How do you interact with your international business partners? How do you bring together a multicultural team of experts, and how do you ensure their work is successful? How do you pitch a business idea to, or make a deal with, a client from an "alien" culture? What are the pitfalls and traps that cultural unawareness might instigate? Communication in business is of the utmost importance. Take finance as an example. A vital building block of the economic and monetary system is a psychological concept of trust. Credit, from the Latin, *credo*, literally means "I trust you". Without trust between lender and borrower, no transaction is possible. How, then, do you build trust, or more importantly, how do you communicate your trustworthiness to your international business partners?

Body language definitely has a role to play here. Given that we form opinions and make judgments in a split second that are usually not only accurate but also pervasive and hard to change, your gestures and body posture can say more about you than your not very fluent local language. However, when it comes to international etiquette, and in particular where language barriers exists, people rely on nonverbal clues much more readily. Culture is by definition a set of shared rules, practices and symbols accepted as a norm in a particular environment. Culture dictates behavior as well as motivations, goals and actions, so it is not surprising that culture also plays a huge role in the display and expression of nonverbal signs.

Is body language universal?

Since Charles Darwin's work in the nineteenth century, it has been acknowledged that some forms of bodily communication, such as smiling and crying facial gestures, are innate and universal. They are recognized and displayed around the globe. Paul Ekman (2003), the eminent researcher of the psychology and physiology of emotions, studied facial expressions exhibited by people from different cultures. He came to the conclusion that facial expressions of basic emotions are physiologically based, evolved behaviors that do not differ much across cultures. Nevertheless, he also agreed that there are "display rules" as to *when*, *where* and *with whom* these expressions can be shown. These display rules are internalized by children during their social-ization into the culture. They are constantly reminded, encouraged, rewarded and punished in the home and at school for particular kinds of bodily communication. As the Dutch cross-cultural researcher Geert Hofstede (2005) put it, these rules become the "software of the mind".

Ekman lists six basic pan-cultural expressions corresponding to primary emotions:

- Fear
- Surprise
- Anger
- Disgust
- Distress
- Happiness.

However, facial expressions can easily be misread, misinterpreted or misattributed, because feelings, or cognitive awareness of emotions, can be experienced differently by different people. What is scary to one person, is only nerve-tickling to another. We interpret things with the help of pre-existent knowledge that is (i) culturally determined; (ii) sub-jective; and (iii) relies on imperfect memory. Hence it is paramount to know the cultural nuances and to read the signals correctly.

In business situations these rules are especially important. Stocking-up on etiquette books, researching the internet or participating in cultural awareness training courses is necessary homework that can bring success in your business dealings in a foreign country.

Body language versus foreign language

Despite popular claims that 70 percent of all information is processed by means of nonverbal unconscious channels, the ability to speak and interact in the language of your business partner is much more impressive. Though this book is about *nonverbal* communication, verbal or linguistic abilities cannot be discounted. Language is not only the product of culture but also its best transmitter. By learning another language, you become exposed to new categories of thinking and reasoning. Some languages also seem better for certain functions. Hence stories about George III – who purportedly spoke to his horse in German, his cook in French and his lover in Italian.

It seems that when language is shared, cultural communication runs more smoothly. The reverse is also true: lack of linguistic abilities can impair your business interactions. Harzing and Feely (2008) reviewed the topic of language barriers and their implications for international business. Better linguistic abilities are widely used in organizations as a source of power and means of advancement, especially in multinational companies. Language is also an influential in-group/out-group marker: are you one of us or one of them? It immediately establishes affiliation, thus creating or breaking boundaries in organizations. It can either reinforce existing links and maintain alliances, or impair relationships and impede the work.

So, when language skills are simply not there, we have to rely on gestures and their interpretations much more. Sometimes it is not words, but rather the manner in which they are spoken and what accompanies them that is of more significance. When stakes are high and emotions intense, especially in business negotiations, body language is the source of information to be taken into account.

Still, there is a way to make up for your lack of foreign-language knowledge: by hiring simultaneous translators. These are the intermediaries, the uniting bridge between the players in the game. And they are ever in demand, partly as a function of the remorseless growth of the European community and world trade in general. So we need people to translate Czech into Dutch, Finnish into Portuguese, and Polish into Greek, for example.

Translators of the written word are often scholars, but translators of speech need to be actors as well. They have various tasks. Sometimes they shadow their (literally) "great leader". So, in the old days it was not uncommon to see the American and Russian translators just behind their bosses, subtly, "sotto voce" and almost ventriloquently informing their man what the other had said. Interestingly, the leaders did not look at their co-linguist informants. They smiled, nodded and nonverbally looked at their opposite number directly.

Translators get the gist of what is being said, but sometimes they cannot copy *how* it is said. Can they get mocking irony, and if so, how is it translated? Americans cannot understand British irony, under-statement or humour. How would a translator convey these? Watch a dubbed favorite movie with a known star. The dubbing actor may do timings well but quality of voice is crucial. The chuckle, the sardonic laugh, characteristic patterns get changed and it makes a difference.

It is no wonder, therefore, that presidents look at each other while translators whisper in their ears. What is being said is important, but no less than how and when it is said. And for most it is less worrying that things are lost in translation than what they do not want, understand or intend is transmitted.

Cultural values and motivations

In the updated version of their classic book, Hofstede and Hofstede (2005) proposed five main dimensions that are very useful navigation tools around cultural differences: individualism–collectivism; high- and low-power distance; femininity and masculinity; strong and weak uncertainty avoidance; and long- or short-term orientation. These dimensions can be used to gain a snapshot view into values and drives of a particular society. Once you know where the country stands on these dimensions, you can deal with the members of the culture more successfully, anticipate their expectations, appreciate their values, and adjust your verbal and nonverbal behavior in a timely and appropriate manner.

Individualism–collectivism

This refers to the extent to which the society places importance on individual values and benefits or those of the extended group (see Table 4.4).

Working practices of individualist countries:

- Speaking one's mind and freedom of expression is highly valued.
- Healthy debate is encouraged between all members of the group regardless of position or status.
- Communication is "low context": what is meant needs to be verbalized, not left to conjecture.
- Silence in a conversation is looked upon as "socially inadequate".
- Conflict of interest is generally not appropriate and should be stated before any work is begun.

TABLE 4.4 **Countries' score on the Individualism dimension by region of the world**

	High Individualism	Middle score	Low Individualism
Asia & Oceania	Australia, New Zealand	Japan, India	Thailand, China, Singapore, Korea, Vietnam, Pakistan, Indonesia, Taiwan, Malaysia
Europe	UK, Ireland, Belgium, France, the Netherlands, Germany, Switzerland, Sweden, Norway, Finland, Spain	India, Morocco	Portugal, Greece
Eastern Europe	Hungary, Poland, Czech Republic, Estonia	Russia	Romania, Slovenia, Serbia, Croatia
Middle East & Africa	Israel	Morocco	West & East Africa, Arab countries
North & South America	USA, Canada	Brazil, Argentina	Guatemala, Ecuador, Panama, Venezuela, Columbia, Costa Rica

- Workplace relationships are based on the idea of "business transaction".

Working practices of low individualism (collectivist) countries:

- A 'one for all and all for one' attitude.
- Doing business in collectivist countries usually involves building personal ties and relationships and earning trust.
- Direct confrontation should be avoided; social harmony is much more desirable.
- Allegiance to the family and its interests is valued more than self-interest.
- Consequently, practices of nepotism and favoritism, though often outlawed, still exist and influence decision-making to a certain degree.
- Communication is said to be high-context: the meaning behind the communication is derived from the social context and situation.
- Silence in social situations is acceptable.

The individualism–collectivism dimension has a straightforward application to, for example, international management practices. An

TABLE 4.5 **Countries' score on Power Distance dimension by region of the world**

	High Power Distance	Middle score	Low Power Distance
Asia & Oceania	Malaysia, China, the Philippines, Bangladesh, Indonesia, India, Singapore, Vietnam	Thailand	New Zealand, Australia, Japan
Europe	France, Switzerland (French), Poland	Portugal, Belgium (Flemish)	Italy, Netherlands, Spain, Germany, UK, Finland, Norway, Sweden, Ireland, Denmark, Austria, Switzerland (German)
Eastern Europe	Slovakia, Russia, Romania, Serbia, Croatia, Slovenia, Bulgaria		Czech Republic, Hungary, Estonia,
Middle East & Africa	Arab countries, Morocco, West Africa	East Africa	Israel
North & South America	Guatemala, Panama, Mexico, Venezuela, Ecuador, Brazil, Colombia, Salvador	Peru, Chile, Uruguay	Costa Rica, Argentina, Canada, USA

interesting piece of research showed that people from a *collectivist* background performed best when a given task was defined in terms of a group goal and each member worked anonymously, while a similarly defined task resulted in decreased output by employees from *individualist* countries. These people performed best when working individually and their merit was similarly recognized. These conditions were, on the other hand, counterproductive for employees from collectivist countries. It is clear that people are motivated differently, and should be assessed and rewarded accordingly. Thus, Hofstede and Hofstede (2005) point out that management in collectivist countries is "management of groups", while governance in individualistic societies is "management of individuals".

Power distance index

This concerns such work features as decision-making style, status, power symbolism and hierarchy (see Table 4.5).

Working practices of high-power-distance countries:

- Structured, vertical hierarchies.
- Autocratic decision-making style.

- Superior–subordinate relationships are highly unequal, both in terms of pay and of status.
- Greater and closer supervision is expected.
- Possessions aim to reflect rank visually.

Working practices of low-power-distance countries:

- Flat hierarchies.
- Consultative decision-making style.
- The gap between salaries of top and lower workers is small.
- Discretionary autonomy in work tasks, less supervision.
- Expensive material possessions by top-level employees are discouraged.

A country's position on this dimension is especially useful when one needs to choose an appropriate level of contact in foreign organizations. It can also be helpful to determine what kind of support and authority is expected from the management in different countries. One can see power distance in the way people of different rank address each other. Power is usually manifested nonverbally. Dress often is a very clear indicator of rank.

Masculinity–Femininity

Here we are concerned with the degree of distinction or overlap between masculine and feminine gender roles (see Table 4.6). Masculinity is defined by such qualities as being tough, forceful and concerned about material possessions, while feminine values are associated with being humble, caring and concerned about quality of life.

Working practices of masculine countries:

- Concern for work.
- Merit-based rewards.
- Conflict is resolved through competition/fighting.
- Assertiveness, ambition and healthy aggression are highly desirable traits.
- "Live to work" attitude.

Working practices of feminine countries:

- Concern for people.
- Needs-based rewards.

TABLE 4.6 **Countries' score on Masculinity dimension by region of the world**

	Masculine	**Middle score**	**Feminine**
Asia & Oceania	Japan, China, Philippines, Australia, New Zealand, India, Bangladesh	Malaysia, Pakistan, Singapore	Taiwan, Vietnam, Korea, Thailand
Europe	Austria, Switzerland, Italy, Ireland, Germany, UK, Greece	Luxembourg	France, Spain, Portugal, Finland, Denmark, Netherlands, Norway, Sweden
Eastern Europe	Slovakia, Hungary, Poland, Czech Republic		Serbia, Romania, Bulgaria, Croatia, Russia, Slovenia
Middle East & Africa	Arab countries, Morocco	Israel	West Africa, East Africa
North & South America	Venezuela, Mexico, Colombia, Ecuador, USA, Argentina	Canada, Brazil	Panama, Peru, Salvador, Uruguay, Guatemala, Chile, Costa Rica

- Compromise is sought when in conflict.
- Differences are tolerated and respected.
- "Work to live" attitude.

This dimension is useful for pinning down a country with regard to its preferred negotiation style, conflict resolution and expected gender work behavior. Assertiveness and force are displayed in masculine countries; showing respect and reservation in feminine ones. Inevitable male–female interactions at work are different in masculine and feminine cultures. They are more "stereotyped" in the former, with males being dominant and females submissive.

Uncertainty avoidance

This dimension reflects the degree of tolerance of ambiguous situations and need for direction (see Table 4.7).

Working practices of strong Uncertainty Avoidance countries:

- Longer-term employment.
- More anxiety and need for expressiveness.
- Traditional, ritualistic behaviors supported by formal structures.
- Expertise is valued.

TABLE 4.7 **Countries' score on Uncertainty Avoidance dimension by region of the world**

	Strong Uncertainty Avoidance	**Middle score**	**Weak Uncertainty Avoidance**
Asia & Oceania	Japan, South Korea	Taiwan	Thailand, Bangladesh, Indonesia, Philippines, India, Malaysia, China, Vietnam, Singapore, Australia, New Zealand
Europe	Greece, Portugal, France, Spain, Italy	Austria, Germany, Switzerland (German)	Finland, Netherlands, Norway, UK, Ireland, Sweden, Denmark
Eastern Europe	Poland, Serbia, Russia, Romania, Slovenia, Bulgaria, Hungary, Croatia, Czech Republic		Estonia, Slovakia
Middle East & Africa	Israel	Arab Countries, Morocco, Iran	West Africa, East Africa
North & South America	Guatemala, Uruguay, Salvador, Peru, Argentina, Chile, Costa Rica, Panama, Mexico, Colombia, Brazil	Ecuador	Canada, USA

Working practices of weak Uncertainty Avoidance countries:

- Shorter-term employment.
- Less anxiety and need for expressiveness.
- Intrinsic rule following.
- Common sense and general knowledge is valued.

Knowing a country's position on this dimension is valuable for learning how rigid or flexible are its working practices (schedules, plans, deadlines), rule-following behavior, and differences in attitudes to time. People follow rules and laws. You can see this in the street: to what extent people obey or violate traffic laws. The same is true inside organizations, which are often beset by numerous health and safety rules. Low tolerance national and corporate cultures have more rules and follow them more closely.

TABLE 4.8 **Countries' score on Long-term Orientation dimension by region of the world**

	Long-term Orientation	Middle score	Short-term Orientation
Asia & Oceania	China, Taiwan, Japan, Vietnam, Korea, India, Thailand, Singapore, Bangladesh		Pakistan, Philippines, Australia, New Zealand
Europe	Denmark, Netherlands, Norway, Ireland, Finland, Switzerland	France, Belgium, Sweden	Austria, Germany, Portugal, Spain
Eastern Europe	Hungary	Slovakia, Poland	Czech Republic
Middle East & Africa			Zimbabwe, Nigeria
North & South America	Brazil		Canada, USA

Long-term orientation

Refers to the degree to which a particular culture is future-orientated and values diligence, prudence and persistence; or present- or past-orientated with regard to traditions and social requirements (see Table 4.8).

Working practices of Long-term Orientated countries:

- Results are slow.
- Patience is a virtue.
- Saving is encouraged.
- Personal networks are important assets at work.

Working practices of Short-term Orientated countries:

- Results are quick, or better, immediate.
- Impatience is a virtue.
- Spending is encouraged.
- Meritocracy.

Be prepared for quick turn-around and fast decision-making in short-term orientated cultures; short(er)-term profit goals are regarded as a valuable pursuit. In contrast, time is sequential in long-term orientated countries. The emphasis is on tradition, conservation and continuation. Time is viewed as a treasure, not a pressure.

The five facets described above reflect the basics of all variations across the globe. Of course, it should also be stated that countries' scores on these dimensions reflect a general inclination towards either end of the scale. Thus it would also be true to claim that some members of collectivist societies, for example, tend to be highly individualistic, or that some citizens of strong uncertainty avoidance countries are more inclined to risk-taking. However, these are deviations from the norm and consequently represent a minority.

These dimensions serve as practical guides to general differences between countries. They paint a broad-brush picture of countries' behaviors and motivations as applied to the world of work and business. It is best to take into account all five scales to gain a clear understanding of how to do business in a particular culture. Armed with this knowledge, it is relatively easy to adjust your body language to the expectations of the country you are visiting.

Cultural differences in nonverbal communication

Countries differ in their attitudes towards time, greetings, emphasis on polite etiquette, and tradition. They vary in the degree to which they show emotion through facial expressions. Some cultures (for example, Saudi Arabia) traditionally place higher emphasis on what is *not* being said, and those with such cultural traditions pay more attention to nonverbal clues such as pauses, gestures and so on. Others (the USA, the UK, Germany) are bold and straightforward in their communication, and appreciate their business partners being direct and honest. Nonverbal aspect of communication in such countries is regarded secondary to the spoken message.

Greetings

There are few areas where your body language can make or break a relationship. It all starts with an introduction, and, as easy as it sounds, traps await you at this initial stage. You need to know how people are addressed in a particular culture – what is an appropriate title; should one use a first name or surname, or both; and in case of so many foreign-sounding names, which one is which?

Consider body language differences in greetings as well: in parts of Europe it is appropriate to bow with a slight click of the heels; in Japan, the deep respectful bow is required; the gallant hand-kiss is used in France; the bear-hug is popular in Russia; Thai and Indian people use a peaceful "hands-together in prayer" gesture; and Anglo-Saxons use a hand-shake. Interestingly, greeting behavior may also vary between the regions of a country. In the south-east of France, for example, three kisses on the cheeks is the norm, while in northern France, four kisses are more appropriate. Number of kisses can also reflect status or affiliation. Indeed, the form of greeting can also be an indicator of rank, familiarity, or type of meeting.

Expressing agreement

There are generally two kinds of gestures that convey agreement. One involves different movements of the head; and the other, of the hands. Desmond Morris (2002) provides a description of five different types of head gestures which can say "I agree" or "I disagree" with you:

1. *Head nod*: gradual upward and downward movement placing more emphasis on the downward stroke. It is believed to be a universal sign for agreement, which has been recorded in most cultures and tribal societies. What is more, even children born deaf and blind still exhibit it. Morris explains the ubiquity of this gesture by pointing out the submissive connotation of this gesture as in bowing.
2. *Head shake*: from left to right in equal proportions. This gesture is said to correspond to the way infants refuse breast or food when they are full, hence always means no in most cultures.
3. *Head twist*– an incomplete head shake, with the head turning brusquely to one side and returning to the upright position. Carries a disagreement or negative meaning.
4. *Head sway*: while in most cultures this gesture means uncertainty or lack of agreement on the issue, in Bulgaria it happens to mean "Yes". Morris speculates that this peculiarity arouse out of verbal expressions for agreement in Bulgarian language, such as "I will give you my ear", which later literally became a sign of affirmation.
5. *Head toss*: or an "inverted head nod" means "No" in Greece and former Ancient Greek provinces (still!), especially when done together with eye and eyebrow raising.

Hand gestures expressing affirmation are said to be the substitutes for using the head. One of the most universal signs of agreement is a hand-shake which corresponds to head nod. A "No" can also be expressed through shaking your finger or the whole palm of your hand from side to side. Parents, for example, often show that to children in disapproval of their behavior. A palm wag also allows a person to distance and block themselves from the suggestion being made. A person can also close his or her eyes in disagreement, literally saying that they are not taking anything in. The Japanese are famous for never expressing their disagreement directly. For them, this ruins the harmony of a relationship. They give elusive "Maybe" answers instead of a direct "No".

Embarrassment

Embarrassment is also one if the universally felt emotions concerned with the feeling of doing something socially inappropriate, breaching the rules of etiquette. It is felt and displayed across the world in a similar manner: by blushing, suddenly dropping the smile, lowering the eyes and head.

On the other hand, it has been revealed that some societies control their facial expressions more than others. As such, Russians, followed closely by South Koreans and Japanese, come out on top in the battle of facial-muscle control, while Americans take the bottom place in the hierarchy.

The concept of "face" appears to be particularly important in business dealings with certain countries, such as China, Japan and countries of the Middle East. Members of these traditional, collectivist societies try to avoid showing their weaknesses at all costs. Losing face by making a mistake, for example, means losing respect and hard-earned status. However, it is also true to say that no one in any sort of position of power would like to be challenged directly in front of subordinates. Thus, while face-saving might be a special concept in some cultural encounters, it is just as relevant in most Western business dealings.

Time

Time is viewed differently across the world. For some it is flexible, fluctuating and cyclical; while others see it as rigid, constant and linear. Attitudes to time are of particular interest in business. One of the biggest pressures and advantages in any negotiations is time.

In the West, we are always short of time. Deadlines have to be met, delays are regarded as a sign of either lack of interest or ability, both of which are good enough reasons to turn the business down. However, Southern European countries, such as Spain, Italy and Portugal, and

their former colonies in Africa and South America, have kept a different sense of time. It is stretchable, non-pressurizing and adjustable to
the needs of individuals. Given this, decision-making takes longer.
For the Japanese, among others, matters of importance require no
rush, and they take their time making up their minds. The more valuable the deal, the more time the Japanese are likely to take to reach a
conclusion.

Obviously, these differences are a natural source of conflict. It is hard
to appreciate a system of time so different from the one a person is used
to, let alone to abide by its rules. Books on cultural communication
offer many examples of how misunderstanding the attitude to time in
another culture has resulted in lost business opportunities, contracts
and investments. Time differences also result in the degree of multi-
tasking that is possible, and how much concentration and attention is
given to individual activities.

Overall, some countries can be characterized as *time-bound* (Germany,
UK, Switzerland and Scandinavia, for example), whereas others are *time-
blind* (such as Spain, Portugal, Greece). Time-bound societies emphasize schedules, deadlines, time-wasting, time-keeping, a fast pace of
life. Time-blind societies are more relaxed and casual about time. Hence
what is considered to be late in one society is not necessarily so in
another. As societies become more time-bound, they have a more competitive attitude to time, and so "fast" is better. Hence fast-living, fast-
eating, fast-tempo, manic-type work behavior emphasizing "catching
up" and not being "left behind". Time-bound societies see time as linear, and societies that are time-blind, see it as cyclical. Time-bound
societies centre work around clocks, schedules, delivery dates, agendas,
deadlines. Confusion between the two attitudes can make for serious
misunderstandings at work.

Collett (1994) points out various other time-related distinctions that
relate to the world of work. The first is the time-blind culture's ability to distinguish between "sacred" and "profane" time. The former is
for eating, family and sleeping, while profane time is used for everything else. Hence, in Spain, meetings can easily be interrupted: the
time is not dedicated solely to the meeting. There is also the distinction between *monochronic* and *polychronic* time. Time-bound societies
are monochronic – people do one thing at a time, while time-blind
societies are polychronic, happily ignoring appointments, schedules,
deadlines and tolerating interruptions. There is also the issue of *time-
orientation*: past, present and future. Thus the British are thought to be
interested more in the distant and recent past, and therefore do not

invest much in the future, whereas the Germans have a longer view of the future, investing in basic research, education and training.

The understating and use of time is crucial in business. Not only does it lead to how, when, where and why work is done, but also people with conflicting ideas and theories may have very different conceptions and expectations, which can lead to misunderstanding and animosity.

Why do these differences exist?

There are many reasons why bodily communication differs from one culture to another. It may be in part a result of language usage: the number and subtlety of words for a feeling or an action must affect the necessity or preference for nonverbal behavior in expressing that feeling or action. The social etiquette of people sets out precise rules regarding nonverbal behavior. Books of manners set out very clearly how people are to behave. Nonverbal communication is also seen in the structure of society and in its subcultures. The lower-status groups have prescribed and proscribed ways of dealing with those from higher groups. Even differences in technology between one society and another can influence nonverbal behavior. The use of the telephone, for example, may increase sensitivity to tones of voice.

Interpersonal distance, eye gaze and bodily contact are culture-dependent, as are taboos on exposing parts of the body, including the palm of the hand, the sole of the foot and so on. Two strong, isolated cultures, such as those of the Japanese and the Arabs, may have very different, indeed opposite, languages of nonverbal communication.

CONCLUSION: WHAT DOES IT ALL MEAN FOR BUSINESS?

The fact that body communication is in part culture-specific means that cross-cultural communication is fraught with potential problems. Argyle (1993) has noted that Westerners often find interacting with the Japanese difficult because they are bewildered by the Japanese people's blank facial expressions and unexpected bursts of laughter. Northern Europeans find that Southern Europeans (and North Africans) stand too close to each other and touch too much. In one celebrated study, an observer watched how many times couples touched each other in restaurants: in Puerto Rico, it was 180 times per hour; in Paris, 110 times per hour; but in London couples did not touch each other at all.

Cross-cultural body communication at work is particularly fraught with problems – hence the many books on protocol, customs and business etiquette for particular regions. The lesson is often that one country's good manners are another's grand faux pas. Eating and drinking, greeting and the giving of gifts are all very culture-bound and require a knowledge of correct behavior. Gestures too do not travel: thumb joined to forefinger in a circle denotes OK in the USA, zero in France, money in Japan, and is an obscene gesture in middle Europe. The depth and frequency of bowing carries meanings in Japan, but nowhere else. Certainly, the "do's" and taboos of body communication in international business can lead to misunderstanding.

It is routine practice now for employees to be sent on cultural training courses before they are despatched on business trips to remote parts of the world. A few reasons for their popularity are listed below. They help to:

- Appreciate the local mindset.
- Understand local business practices.
- Learn the "don'ts" and taboos.
- Be aware of the differences between the visitor and the host country.

Fons Trompenaars, a famous researcher in the field of international management, noted that in order to succeed in international business, cultural differences need to be recognized, gain respect and achieve reconciliation. While learning the verbal language of another culture is a huge advantage for communication in that culture, it is equally important to "speak" the body language and be aware of the cross-cultural variations in body language to become a convincing and competent communicator in business.

5

LYING AND DECEPTION: REVEALING AND CONCEALING INFORMATION

More than anything else, business people hope to detect the real, infallible truth and catch liars by carefully analyzing the body language of others. In sales and negotiations, in business beauty parades and in interviews, people conceal and reveal, bluff and bluster, fabricate and exaggerate. We use all sorts of euphemisms for lying: dissimulation, impression management, distortion. Most people believe that the body always betrays the mind, that the torso leaks the whole truth, and that the trained and perceptive observer can "spot the 'porkie pie' (a lie) a mile off". If only that were true!

Cheating, sabotage, stealing and whistle-blowing at work, almost by definition involve deception of one sort or another. This chapter will look at the difficult, but important, business of the nonverbal detection of deception. How easy and reliable is it to spot if people are lying? Are some people simply better liars and liar-spotters than others? And what of the conscience-free, psychopathic liars – can they ever be detected? What are the best things to look for – the sure signs of lying?

Lying is, and will always be, a hot topic. It is at the centre of ethical and moral codes. It is essentially a false communication that benefits the communicator. It is usually deliberate and may or may not be successful. To be accused of *being a liar*, as opposed to occasionally *telling a lie* is serious business. There is a bewildering array of words and concepts that deal with those who don't quite tell the full truth – the whole truth and nothing but the truth. Fibs, fabrications, falsehoods and fudgings. Politicians "spin" the facts to the public. Organizations use public relations gurus to "sex up" products, messages and services. Individuals, as part of daily intercourse and to save embarrassment and hurt, say things directly or indirectly (possibly through euphemism) to each other. Notice the way that negative as opposed to positive feedback is dealt with at work.

One reason why the public is as well (or badly) informed about psychological issues is the number of popular articles on the topic. Some are based on interviews with authors, others on a sort of popularized précis of a book review.

Popular literature is full of advice on how to lie. Consider the following list of suggestions which can be often found in lifestyle magazines:

1. Keep calm. Avoid fidgeting, do not gesture or manipulate objects unless necessary.
2. Think ahead and prepare a plausible alibi. Do not over-rehearse or memorise your speech. Avoid using unconventional words that are out of your ordinary vocabulary.
3. Appear tired and disinterested. Give the impression that you do not see the point in answering absurd questions.
4. Seem preoccupied with some other activity.
5. Dodge challenging questions. Say "I do not know" instead of "I do not remember".
6. Appear irritable and bad-tempered: you are clearly insulted by the false accusations.
7. Try not to touch your face. If you do it by accident, cover up face with a fake yawn.
8. Do not cross your arms or legs. Keep the palms of your hands open
9. Maintain good, steady eye contact.
10. Try to believe what you are saying is actually true.

As we shall see, some of the above is simplistic, wrong and misleading. Indeed, these articles reinforce ignorance and explain why people are such poor lie-detectors themselves.

Verbal clues

- *Response latency* – the time elapsing between the end of a question and the beginning of the response. Liars take longer. They hesitate more than they do when not lying.
- *Linguistic distancing* – not saying "I", "he" or "she", but talking in the abstract even when recalling incidents in which he or she was involved.

- *Slow but uneven speech* – the individual tries to think while speaking but gets caught out. He or she might suddenly speak fast, implying something is less significant. It is the change in pace in response to a particular question that gives a clue that something is not right.
- *Over-eagerness to fill silences* – to keep talking when it is unnecessary. Liars overcompensate and seem to show classic signs of insubordination – as if caught out. Uncomfortable with what are often quite short pauses.
- *Too many "pitch raises"* – that is, instead of the pitch dropping at the end of a reply, it rises, as in a question. It may sound like "Do you believe me now?"

Nonverbal cues

- *Squirming/shifting* around too much in the chair.
- *Having too much – rather than too little – eye contact*, as liars tend to overcompensate. They know that liars avoid a mutual gaze so they "prove they are not lying" by a lot of looking ... but "a tad too much".
- *Micro-expressions* or flickers of expressions – of surprise, hurt, anger. These are difficult to see, though, unless the frames of a video are frozen.
- *An increase in comfort gestures* – touching his or her own face and upper body.
- *An increase in stuttering, slurring* and, of course, "Freudian slips". Generally an increase in speech errors.
- *A loss of resonance in the voice* – it becomes flatter, less deep, more monotonous.

For many observers, the problem is in distinguishing between lying and anxiety. The well-trained and arrogant liar may thus look innocent, while the truthful but nervous witness may look like a liar. The fast, nervous tics of the latter may be seen as classic signs of insubordination – as if they have been caught.

We know that people prefer, and are better at, concealment rather than falsification. It is easier to forget than to distort the truth. Falsification means "making up" things that are not true. It is self-evidently much easier to say things did not happen at all rather than to invent a "new story". It is also true that people do have more problems lying about emotions – particularly powerful emotions such as terror, rage, fear and despair. Recounting a story of events fifty years ago, some people cannot suppress their emotions, which manifest in their tears and trembling voice. The more ego-involving the activity, the more likely it is that people in all walks of life will have difficulty in disguising the truth.

Regular and sophisticated liars have found the best mask, or cover, for their lie is the smile. Smiling has numerous advantages: it is an easy and natural expression to make voluntarily; it is polite; but, most importantly, it conceals opposite emotions (dread, fear, anxiety).

Liars tend to be most careful, thoughtful and involved in their choice and use of words. They can rehearse, practice and become word perfect. They are also very conscious of their facial expressions during the lying episodes. But it is the voice and body that perhaps give most away, and therefore the cues to watch to catch both the naïve and the sophisticated. People are betrayed by their words if they are careless, if they make a (Freudian) slip of the tongue, or an emotional tirade when the words pour, rather than slip, out. We also know that there are various vocal indexes of deceit relating to lying pauses, hesitations and tone and pitch of voice.

Finally, there are a number of important, subtle body indexes of deceit, including gestures, emblems, illustrations and manipulations. Emblems are well-known gestures with precise meanings: illustrations are movements that accentuate speech: manipulations are movements like grooming, massaging, rubbing, holding, pinching, picking, scratching. The autonomic nervous system changes with emotional arousal. Certain body changes occur – sweating, blushing, pupil dilation, breathing pattern, frequency of swallowing, all of which are difficult to inhibit. These changes are the basis of the lie detector/polygraph, as we saw in a previous chapter.

DIFFERENT TYPES OF LIE

There are different types of lie. *First*, there is the white, social, "harmless", flattering, expedient lie: this is supposed to result from a desire to improve social intercourse by protecting another person's feelings. It is thought of as common and even beneficial – and is unlikely to cause the teller embarrassment. For many, white lies do not count as lies and are even considered a sign of social skill.

Second, there is the professional, entertaining, necessary, salesman's lie: expedient lying that distorts or omits facts in the cause of business.

108

For some, this is good business practice – but that really depends on whether one is the buyer or the seller. Certainly a case can be made for not telling patients or subordinates the seriousness of a situation, if this would only make things worse. However, a salesperson not mentioning the very unhappy provenance of a particular product – for example, a car that has been in a major crash – may be considered a serious lie of omission.

But it is the *third* type of lie that is naturally of most concern to those in business – the illegal, pathological trickster's lie, the lie of omission, in which vital truths are omitted; and the lie of commission, in which facts are distorted. It is difficult to ascertain the numbers of these types of lie that occur in business. Suffice to say that the consequences of these can be great.

One of the latest and most painful issues in business has been the issue of redundancy. Whether voluntary or forced, it is never painless to deliver the news of job loss. It is stressful for both the messenger and the recipient: one is "in the know", and the other either in ignorant bliss or anxious anticipation of the coming storm.

An urban legend goes that, at the peak of the latest financial crisis, an auto manufacturer announced redundancies in a shocking manner. The employees were *tricked* into leaving the main building and then informed that the company had to cut the manpower. After that, the workers were encouraged to try to go back in to the warehouse: those whose swipe cards worked kept their jobs, while those who could not gain entry had to go. Their rationale for staging such a performance was to eliminate any possible (and very likely) protests. Obviously, this story has to be taken with a grain of salt. No company, however large or influential, would have been able to get away with such a redundancy practice, even when times were bad. However, this example illustrates how tense and dramatic laying-off can be, and how far some would go to avoid presenting it personally.

Nevertheless, it does not have to be so bad. There are "good" ways of letting go of people or delivering any bad news, and it is possible to do it with due respect and dignity:

- Be tactful and considerate; separate the person from the problem.
- Be very clear and straightforward about the decision; vagueness only intensifies the situation and gives false hopes to the recipient. Give reasons, not justifications.

- Do not attempt to negotiate or "sugar the pill". Say it and shut up.
- Expect a shock response: anger, tears, disbelief. Normalize and validate the emotional response.
- Don't rush it. Give time for the information to sink in.
- Do it at the beginning of the week, not the end.
- Have someone else available immediately for advice – legal, financial or career guidance.
- Try to create a counselling atmosphere: a quiet room where emotions are allowed to escape without fear of embarrassment.

Many professionals – doctors, the police, lawyers, teachers – have to deliver bad news. It's neither easy nor pleasant telling people they are dying, a relative has died, they are going to prison, or they have failed an exam. It requires skill, tact and timing. Still, some do "duck out" of their responsibilities and, in effect, lie.

But this chapter is not about this type of lying. It is about deliberate dissent, dissembling, dissimulation. Telling "bare-faced" lies not to prevent hurt in others, but to prevent the teller from personally being caught. It is about self-serving untruths aimed at cover-up behavior. It is about denying things that happened (or were planned). It is frequently morally, legally and ethically indefensible. Liars can choose not to lie. It is a deliberate act which may be done by a good or bad person, with or without adequate justification.

Because to accuse another of being a liar is a serious social accusation, there are a range of synonyms and distinctions that are made either to refer to the motive of the person telling a lie or the way in which they lie.

The term "deception" does not have to involve lying. Camouflage, be it on animals or on soldiers' tents, is an attempt to deceive. Make-up and plastic surgery are also attempts at deception. False hair, false teeth, false padding are used not only by actors, criminals and spies, but by all sorts of ordinary people in an attempt to disguise their real appearance. Many of these attempts at deception are considered to be socially acceptable, sometimes even necessary. There are essentially only two ways of lying: to conceal or to falsify. As noted earlier, concealment is easier than falsification.

At interviews, giving speeches and in viva-voce examinations, people strive to "hold their nerves": to appear more confident than they feel. They may do this with the help of drugs, the use of particular thought-patterns, or other tricks that may or may not be successful. All this is considered to be normal, healthy – even desirable.

But there is, of course, another less acceptable, but no doubt equally common form of deception: telling lies. There are as a result all sorts of synonyms that attempt to normalize the act and make it more acceptable. But a lie is quite simply a falsehood; an untruth.

> A broken promise, a failure to recall and a misinterpretation of an ambiguous statement are not really lies. Note what Ekman (2001) writes:
>
>> I have come to believe that examining how and when people lie and tell the truth can help in understanding many human relationships. There are few that do not involve deceit or at least the possibility of it. Parents lie to their children about sex to spare them knowledge they think their children are not ready for, just as their children, when they become adolescents, will conceal sexual adventures because the parents won't understand. Lies occur between friends (even your best won't tell you), teacher and student, doctor and patient, husband and wife, witness and jury, lawyer and client, salesperson and customer.
>>
>> Lying is such a central characteristic of life that better understanding of it is relevant to almost all human affairs. Advice columnist Ann Landers has a point when she advises her readers that truth can be used as a bludgeon, cruelly inflicting pain. Lies can be cruel too, but all lies aren't. Some lies, many fewer than liars will claim, are altruistic. Some social relationships are enjoyed because of the myths they preserve. But no liar should presume too easily that a victim desires to be misled. And no lie catcher should too easily presume the right to expose every lie. Some lies are harmless, even humane. Unmasking certain lies may humiliate the victim or a third party. (p. 23)

Psychologists distinguish between several categories when looking at lying in interviews. One is between attribution – a tendency to attribute only desirable characteristics to oneself, and denial – the tendency to deny undesirable characteristics. In effect, both may occur together, though people do seem to prefer one over the other. Another distinction is made between self-deception – when people believe their own positive self-reports or lies, and impression management – when respondents consciously dissimulate to create the "right" impression.

There are a number of distinctions that can be made in this area:

- *Errors of omission versus commission.* Omission refers to leaving out facts (usually undesirable ones). Thus a job applicant may choose not to mention his/her age, education, jail sentences or bankruptcy. People believe that failing to declare something is quite different (and more acceptable) than telling a deliberate lie. That, of course, depends on the situation and the ethical code of the judge. In contrast, errors of commission are quite simply telling lies. These may involve exaggeration or fabrication and are done consciously with a specific purpose in mind.
- *Self-deception versus impression management.* Some people cannot, as opposed to will not, tell the truth. Self-deception involves conscious deception that a person does not believe is a lie. It is people believing in their own positive reports: some genuinely believe they are intelligent, insightful, humorous and so on, when all the evidence suggests that they are not. Alternatively, a person may falsify an exam grade they felt they deserved or hoped for rather than the one they received, to make a better impression. They may also – as they would say "in all honesty"– report feelings, intentions and behaviors that are patently at odds with those of others. And they feel this to be a quite an acceptable act: certainly not a lie. In this sense they are not lying, but neither are they telling the truth.

Self-deceiving is different from "giving a good impression", and may involve serious lies of omission and commission. Self-deceivers are in a sense deluded, but they do not have to have a mental illness to be in this position. Impression management is about what is now called "spin". Reports may be "sexed up" to make them more appealing.

WHY DO PEOPLE LIE?

Ekman (2001) believes there are essentially nine main reasons for lying. They are:

1. *Punishment avoidance.* Whether for an accidental misdemeanour or a genuine offence, everyone tries to avoid being caught.

This is the most frequently cited reason among both children and adults.

2. *Reward ripping.* If the "forbidden fruit" is too irresistible and can only be obtained through a lie, most people would engage in misbehavior. This is the second most frequently quoted rationale for lying.

3. *Protection of others from punishment.* The altruistic nature of human beings makes it the third most popular motive for lying.

4. *Protection from physical threats.* Ekman notes this is different from punishment avoidance. A girl lying about having a boyfriend who is picking her up from a nightclub to avoid unwanted attention from other males would be an example of such a lie.

5. *Approval of others.*

6. *Excuses that grant us leave in uncomfortable social situations.* Examples are numerous: pretending to have very important business to attend to, or an imaginary phone call to make or answer. Some are canny enough to supply an excuse from the very start of the meeting that lets them escape without the need for another explanation.

7. *Embarrassment avoidance.* Supplying a socially acceptable excuse for your behavior instead of revealing a real, perhaps humiliating, one.

8. *Confidentiality preservation.* However, because no warning is given about such an intention, this would count as a lie.

9. *Control and influence over others* by deciding which information should or should not be revealed to them.

According to Vrij (2000) people lie to make a positive impression on others; to protect themselves from embarrassment/disapproval; to obtain advantage; to avoid punishment; to benefit others; and to facilitate social relationships.

Clearly, some people lie better than others. Actors and politicians are skilled at this activity. Machiavellian manipulators are good too, as are adaptable and social people. Various factors, other than the liar's personality, increase their effectiveness and the probability of not being caught. But the chances of catching liars rise if the individuals are known to the lie-catcher; if they are familiar with the topic; if the liar is young, introverted or self-conscious; and if the liar is from the same ethic background as the lie-detector.

CATCHING LIARS: WHY THEY FAIL

Psychopaths rarely get caught lying in everyday life. Politicians, doctors and salespeople have to learn to disguise emotions and present their case in a particular way. But other people are unable to keep a "straight face" and so may get caught out telling the most innocent of lies.

According to Ekman (2001), there are essentially five reasons (listed below) why liars get caught out. They leak cues to their deceit in their body, voice or words.

Lack of preparation (bad lines)

A good lie requires preparation, rehearsal and memorization. A good liar should be able to anticipate when it is appropriate or necessary to lie; when to be inventive; that they must remain internally consistent; and that the story must fit the known/revealed facts. The right words must be used, but the liar must not take time thinking about what to say. Lies take rehearsal and being word-perfect. Curiously, where people are over-rehearsed, over-consistent and overwhelmingly convincing, they too may be caught out through their over-preparation. Con-men, for example, are used to telling the same series of well-prepared lies over and over again. They, however, often look too confident, their story appears too coherent. They do not display enough anxiety that one would associate with the occasion. Thus, while a lack of preparation is surely going to get you caught out by an inquisitive questioner, an over-rehearsed alibi coupled with unemotional confidence is also very likely to arouse further suspicion.

Lying about feelings (emotional escapes)

Lies that involve emotions are more difficult to carry off than lies about actions, facts, intentions, plans or thoughts. When a person is made angry, frightened or sad, physiological changes occur automatically (in the central nervous system), without choice or selection. Strong emotions triggered by particular memories are hard to conceal or control. Sadness, anger and so on return in the re-telling, but if they are not present this may indicate lying. Trying to look angry when one is not or calm when frightened is not easy. Portraying the feeling of being upset or angry takes considerable acting skill. Perhaps even harder is the concealment of strong emotions or sustaining a lie about a powerful emotional experience such as an accident or a crime.

Feelings about lying (old-fashioned guilt)

If a person feels guilty, silly or vulnerable about their deception (tax evasion, embezzlement, plagiarism) appropriate emotions are triggered which may be difficult to conceal. The more people realize or believe they are telling a serious lie, the more likely they are to show guilt. Such deception-guilt arises more from the action of lying than from the lie itself. It increases when the lie is selfish, when the deceit is unauthorized, when the liar is ill-practiced, and when the liar and his or her target are similar in terms of personality and social values. Guilt leads to shame, which is manifested in eye contact, body posture and so on.

Fear of being caught

Also called *detection apprehension*, this concerns being fearful about being caught and punished for the deception in the first place. This fear is a function of a belief in the aptitude and skill of the lie detector. Some people are believed to be particularly good at detection: police officers, psychologists and psychiatrists, customs officers. They have a reputation for being suspicious and difficult to fool, thus are likely to increase fear in the liar, which may show up in a variety of emotional expressions.

Some people seem to be natural liars, but others are easily detected when telling any lies. Natural liars (excluding psychopaths) tend to be individualistic and competitive. Another factor of importance is how high the stakes are (what is involved for the liar): the more at stake, the greater the detection apprehension. There are two punishments for every lie: that for telling the lie and that for the lie failing. The latter is about losing trust and being labeled a liar.

According to Ekman (2001) apprehensiveness about being detected in telling a lie is the greatest under eight very specific circumstances:

- the target has a reputation for being tough to fool;
- the target starts out being suspicious;
- the liar has had little practice and no record of success;
- the liar is specially vulnerable to the fear of being caught;
- the stakes are high;

- both rewards and punishments are at stake; or if it is only one or the other, punishment is at stake;
- the punishment for being caught lying is great, or the punishment for what the lie is about is so great that there is no incentive to confess;
- the target is no way benefits from the lie. (p. 641)

Deception guilt

This refers to feelings about lying, not feelings about guilt. At extremes, this guilt can induce shame and affects feelings of self-worth which can very quickly manifest themselves physically. People with a strict, moral upbringing naturally tend to be the most guilt-prone. The psychopath, of course, does not suffer from this problem.

There are a number of highly specific conditions which seem either to exacerbate or to reduce deception guilt depending on the individual in question. It has to be pointed out that lying is an extremely idiosyncratic behavior. While some patterns of behavior are common to most lying situations, they are not necessarily exhibited by all liars. Moreover, these behavioral patterns might not have anything to do with lying but be caused by completely different and unrelated sets of factors. Again, Ekman (2001) has specified eight of these most common deception guilt conditions:

- The target is unwilling;
- The deceit is totally selfish, and the target derives no benefit from being misled and loses as much as or more than the liar gains;
- The deceit is unauthorized, and the situation is one in which honesty is authorized;
- The liar has not been practising the deceit for a long time;
- The liar and the target share social values;
- The liar is personally acquainted with the target:
- The target can't easily be faulted as mean or gullible;
- There is reason for the target to expect to be misled; just the opposite, the liar has acted to win confidence in his trustworthiness. (pp. 75–6)

Duping delight

Some liars get caught paradoxically because of the observable and puzzling post-lie relief, pride, even smugness. Again, if these feelings are not concealed – and this can be difficult – it can lead to the liar getting caught. People can tempt fate, enjoy "misleading others" and

116

play games, only to be caught by duping delight. This problem occurs particularly, according to Ekman (2001) under three circumstances:

- The target poses a challenge, having a reputation for being difficult to fool;
- The lie is a challenge, because of either what must be concealed or the nature of what must be fabricated;
- Others are watching or know about the lie and appreciate the liar's skilful performance. (p. 79)

Yet people remain bad at detecting lies, for many reasons. Vrij (2000) lists seven. *First*, people do not actually want to know the truth. *Second*, there are no typical deceptive behaviors applicable to all people. *Third*, the difference between liars and truth-tellers are very small. *Fourth*, the rules of conversation prevent lie detectors from carefully analyzing an accused liar properly. *Fifth*, observers' judgment is often affected by their personal biases, misbeliefs and systematic errors. *Sixth*, nervous behavior does not mean lying behavior, though many believe that to be true. And, *finally*, most observers fail to take individual differences into account.

Helpfully Vrij (2000) provides the guidelines shown in the box below to uncovering deception via nonverbal behaviors.

---

1. It is only possible to detect a lie via nonverbal clues if the liar experiences some emotion such as fear or guilt, or if the lie is too complicated or complex to concoct.
2. Note disparities between the verbal and nonverbal behaviors. Consider possible explanations for their occurrence, but remember that lying is not the only possible one.
3. If you know a person well, pay attention to any changes that do not match their normal behavior. Consider reasons for such differences. Again, bear in mind that lying is not the only explanation for these deviations.
4. Lying should only be concluded if all other explanations have been successfully rejected.
5. The person in question should be allowed to talk. It will help you to look for those verbal–nonverbal mismatches, thus confirming or disconfirming hypotheses. It also makes it harder for the suspect to monitor their behavior as when talking they have to attend both to what they are saying and to how they

---

saying it, thus giving the game away. However, Vrij warns that the very act of questioning might produce changes in behavior.

6. Most frequently cited nonverbal cues of deception, such as gaze aversion or restlessness, have not been confirmed as very dependable deception markers. Vrij suggests using them as a guide to lying, but reminds us to take into account individual differences. Some people will show more of the "classic" cues when lying, while others may not exhibit any of them at all.

THE CLUES TO DECEIT

People communicate using verbal, vocal and visual cues. The words they choose, their voice quality and numerous body cues all provide information about their emotional and cognitive state, and whether they may be lying. The lie-catcher needs to notice and interpret these manifold and subtle cues. Expert, professional lie-catchers differ from the (often misguided) amateur by the cues they look for, the trust they have in these, and the way they are interpreted.

Liars leak deceit. Most try hard to cover up their deceit, but it is difficult to control words, voice, face, feet and hands all at the same time. The voice and the face carry important cues. Vrij (2000, p. 33) has identified seventeen nonverbal behaviors that may be directly related to lying:

Overview and descriptions of the nonverbal behaviors:

Vocal characteristics

1. *Speech hesitations*: use of the words 'ah', 'um', 'er', and so on.
2. *Speech errors*: word and/or sentence repetition, sentence change, sentence incompletions, slips of the tongue, and so on.
3. *Pitch of voice*: changes in pitch of voice, such as a rise or fall in pitch.
4. *Speech rate*: number of spoken words in a certain period of time.
5. *Latency period*: period of silence between question and answer.
6. *Frequency of pauses*: frequency of silent periods during speech.
7. *Pause durations*: length of silent periods during speech.

Facial characteristics

8. *Gaze*: looking at the face of the conversation partner.
9. *Smile*: smiling and laughing.
10. *Blinking*: blinking of the eyes.

Movements

11. *Self-manipulations*: scratching the head, wrists, and so on.
12. *Illustrators*: functional hand and arm movements designed to modify and/or supplement what is being said verbally.
13. *Hand and finger movements*: non-functional movements of hands or fingers without moving the arms.
14. *Leg and foot movements*: movements of the feet and legs.
15. *Head movements*: head nods and head shakes.
16. *Trunk movements*: movements of the trunk (usually accompanied by head movements).
17. *Shifting position*: movements made to change the sitting position (usually accompanied by trunk and foot/leg movements).

Vrij (2000, p. 104) also gives seven specific verbal indicators that often relate to lying (see Table 5.1).

Experts in the area, such as Ekman (2001), have stressed facial clues to deceit and how facial expressions can serve a lie, but also provide manifold, and very subtle, cues to the truth. He argues that the face can show which emotion is being felt: anger, fear, sadness, disgust, distress, happiness, contentment, excitement, surprise and contempt can all be conveyed by distinctive expressions. The face can also show whether two emotions are blended together – often two emotions are felt and the face registers elements of each. The face also shows the strength of the felt emotion – each emotion can vary in intensity, from annoyance to rage, apprehension to terror and so on (p. 125).

People, through growing up, learn facial display rules. But to the skilled observer there are a range of micro-expressions which yield the emotions behind them. There are a number of technical terms that help to describe expressions. For example, a "squelched" expression is where one (possibly natural) expression is masked or covered by another. Experts look for asymmetrical facial expressions which show up on only one side of the face, the exact location of these expressions, the timing of the expression (with both words and other expressions).

TABLE 5.1 **Seven specific verbal indicators that often relate to lying**

Verbal characteristic	Description
1. Negative statements	Statements indicating aversion towards an object, person or opinion, such as denials and disparaging statements, and statements indicating a negative mood
2. Plausible answers	Statements which make sense and which sound credible and reasonable
3. Irrelevant information	Information which is irrelevant to the context, and which has not been asked for
4. Overgeneralized statement	The use of words such as "always", "never", "nobody", "everybody" and so on
5. Self-references	The use of words referring to the speaker him- or herself, such as "I", "me" or "mine"
6. Direct answers	To-the-point and straightforward statements (for example, "I like John" is more direct than "I like John's company")
7. Response length	Length of the answer or number of spoken words

To experts such as Ekman, the face really is the mirror of the soul. He believes one can distinguish between eighteen different types of smile – from the contemptuous, dampened and miserable to the flirtatious, embarrassed and compliant. He also documents some of the characteristics that often accompany particular lies. False smiles are often inappropriate (when they occur, how long they last); they are often asymmetrical, they are not accompanied by the involvement of the many muscles around the eye, and they only cover the actions of the lower face and lower eyelid.

Ekman (2001) concluded:

> The face may contain many different clues to deceit: micros, squelched expressions, leakage in the reliable facial muscles, blinking, pupil dilation, tearing, blushing and blanching, asymmetry, mistakes in timing, mistakes in location, and false smiles. Some of these clues provide leakage, betraying concealed information; others provide deception clues indicating that something is being concealed but not what; and others mark an expression to be false.
>
> These facial signs of deceit … vary in the precision of the information they convey. Some clues to deceit reveal exactly which emotion is actually felt, even though the liar tries to conceal

that feeling. Other clues to deceit reveal only whether the emotion concealed is positive or negative and don't reveal exactly which negative emotion or which positive emotion the liar feels. Still other clues are even more undifferentiated, betraying only that the liar feels some emotion but not revealing whether the concealed feeling is positive or negative. That may be enough. Knowing that some emotion is felt sometimes can suggest that a person is lying, if the situation is one in which except for lying the person would not be likely to feel any emotion at all. Other times a lie won't be betrayed without more precise information about which concealed emotion is felt. It depends upon the lie, the line taken by the person suspected of lying, the situation, and the alternative explanations available, apart from lying, to account for why an emotion might be felt but concealed. (p. 161).

Experts, pundits and researchers – they are not necessarily the same – are often called on by the media to help analyze whether a (famous) person is telling the truth. The recent public inquiry into the war in Iraq has seen many high-profile politicians being scrutinised on record. Usually, all the experts have to rely on are brief video-clips.

There are some facts that are clearly true about lying:

1. You can observe stress signals produced by the autonomic nervous system: dry mouth; sweaty palms; shallow, uneven breathing; "tickly" nose and throat; blushing or blanching. These are observable when someone is under stress whether he or she is lying or not. It is very easy to confuse the two. Most people in interviews are, initially at any rate, anxious. Psychopaths are brilliant liars because they don't suffer guilt and thus do not become anxious when lying.
2. People are less conscious of their feet or legs: the further you are from the face the nearer you get to the truth. Sudden changes in foot-tapping, pointing feet to the exit ("I want to get out of here"), and simultaneous tight arm and foot-crossing have all been taken to indicate lying. Yet active extroverts fidget more, as do young children. Foot movements may be as reliable an index of boredom as they are of lying. The frequent crossing of legs may simply indicate an uncomfortable chair. It is critically

121

important to look at the synchronicity between what is being said and changes in nonverbal behavior during the conversation.

3. Posture is more sincere than gesture: it can be seen to be more unnatural and more forced when people lie. Because people seem less aware of their total posture, they may secretly signal various desires (to leave, for example) or that they are holding back the truth. However, the shape and comfort of furniture naturally have something to do with it.

4. Give-away, expansive gestures decline: because they feel they may be caught out, liars tend to sit on their hands, fold their arms, clasp their hands together. The lack of spontaneity may be an index of lying or fear – the fear of being caught. And some people are simply not as gesturally expressive as others.

5. Shifty gazes: when children are lying they look down or away. They look guilty but do not look you in the eye. Many an innocent person has been accused of lying because they avoid eye contact. But people avoid eye contact for many different reasons – perhaps they feel uncertain about their opinions, they are trying to remember facts, or they feel social embarrassment. Indeed, it is impolite in some cultures to look someone in the eye. And as we shall see, some liars are caught because, knowing this "rule", they stare too much. In this sense they "protested" too much and hence got caught.

Considerable and impressive research has been carried out on lying. The research may involve video-taping people when they are known to be lying as well as when they are known to be telling the truth. From an analysis of their "normal" non-lying interpersonal style, one can see the difference when they are lying. And one can vary the type of lie involved to see whether this makes any difference. One can perform these studies on men versus women, professionals versus tradespeople; those labelled neurotic versus the stable and so on, to look at individual difference patterns.

However, there is no hard and fast practice regarding catching liars. At interview it is good to relax people (to get them off their guard) and then to talk as much as possible. The more that is said, the greater the number of opportunities to be caught.

Collett (2003) used the concept of "tell" to specify signals or actions that "tell you" what somebody is thinking, even if that person does not know it themselves:

- *Detection Tells*. Whereas most people believe they are good at detecting lies, the opposite appears to be the case. They seem to fail at this all-important skill for five reasons. *First*, people prefer blissful ignorance, not wanting to admit that the other person is lying. *Next*, people set their detection threshold very high, but highly suspicious people might set it very low. *Third*, people who rely on intuition and "gut feelings" do not do as well as those who look for clues to deception. *Fourth*, people forget that all behaviors have multiple causes and that there are few single, simple indicators of lying. *Finally*, people look in the wrong places and for the wrong cues – fidgeting as opposed to smiling, for example. Collett then considered classic lying tells:
- *Eye tells*. People know about gaze patterns and control them, but continuous rapid blinking and unusually intent staring may be signs of lying.
- *Body tells*. Despite popular belief, hand movements and fidgeting are under conscious control and therefore unreliable indexes of lying. However, other neglected things such as leg and foot movements and self-touching are better indicators. Further, just as many liars appear to freeze rather than become increasingly animated when lying.
- *Nose tells*. Touching the nose really represents covering the mouth. The "Pinocchio syndrome" may simply be a result of anxiety and it remains unclear whether vasoconstriction (blood draining from the face/nose) or vasodilatation (blood increasing in the face/nose) occurs when people lie.
- *Masking tells*. These are masks (often smiles) that people use to cover or mask their negative feelings about lying. The straight or crypto-relaxed face masks seem to work best.
- *Smiling tells*. Smiles are used extensively by experienced liars because they both make others feel positive and also tend to make others less suspicious about the liar. But there are many types of smile – blended, miserable, counterfeit. Clues to the counterfeit smile lie in the duration (they last longer), assembly (they are put together and dismantled more quickly), location (confined to the lower part of the face) and symmetry (they are less symmetrical).
- *Micro tells*: These are very fast, short-lived, micro-momentous expressions that are difficult to see live but can be seen on a second-by-second videotape playback. They may relate to tension release or anger, or a whole range of emotions associated with lying.

- *Talking tells.* Despite the fact that most people believe nonverbal cues are better than verbal cues to lying, in fact the reverse appears to be true. Collett (2003) lists eleven of these:
  1. Circumlocution: beating around the bush with long-winded digression.
  2. Outlining: broad-brush, detail-free account. Liars rarely expand when asked, while truth-tellers do.
  3. Smoke-screens: confusing, non-sensible statements.
  4. Negatives: liars are more likely to use negative statements.
  5. Word-choice: fewer self references (I, me) and more generalizations (everybody, always).
  6. Disclaimers: excessive use of "I know this sounds strange", "Let me assure you" and "You won't believe this, but...".
  7. Formality: becoming more tense and formal, liars say things like "do not" instead of "don't".
  8. Tense: liars use the past tense more to distance themselves from the events they are describing.
  9. Speed: liars slow down because of the strain on their various capacities.
  10. Pause: liars pause more, with more traditional dysfluencies, like "um" and "er".
  11. Pitch: this rises with emotion.

Collett (2003) provides the would-be lie-catcher with some good advice – see the box below.

Although there is no guaranteed method of detecting lies, there are certain things that you can do to increase your chances of spotting a liar:

- To detect a lie successfully you need to set your criteria so that they're neither too high nor too low. That way you'll avoid coming to the conclusion that nobody ever tells a lie, or that everybody lies all the time.
- Where possible, the actions that someone performs while they are supposedly lying should be compared with how they behave when they are telling the truth.
- To be a good lie detector you should also concentrate on behavior that falls outside conscious control or that people are likely to ignore.

- Given the opportunity, focus your attention on what people say and how they say it, rather than on what they do.
- It's important to work out whether the lie is likely to be spontaneous or rehearsed, and whether it's a high-stakes or a low-stakes lie. When the stakes are low or the lie has been rehearsed, the task of detecting the lie is much more difficult.
- To spot a lie you should always focus on a broad range of behavioral and speech clues. If you think you can spot a liar on the basis of a single clue, you're deceiving yourself. (Collett, 2003, pp. 239–40)

Despite numerous popular books and articles available that seem to imply you can "read people like a book" and it is relatively easy to catch liars, experts in the field say the precise opposite. One's ability to detect lies is multifaceted and problematic. In short, it depends on the nature of the lie, the personality and experience of both the liar and the person trying to detect the lie, and the context/situation in which the lie is told.

Ekman (2001) sums up ways of unmasking a liar (see the box below).

Success in distinguishing when a person is lying and when a person is telling the truth is highest when:

- The lie is being told for the first time;
- The person has not told this type of lie before;
- The stakes are high – most importantly the threat of severe punishment;
- The interviewer is truly open-minded, and does not jump to conclusions quickly;
- The interviewer knows how to encourage the interviewee to tell his or her story (the more words spoken the better the chance of distinguishing lies from truthfulness);
- The interviewer and interviewee come from the same cultural background and speak the same language;
- The interviewer regards the clues as hot spots, marking where it is important to get more information, rather than as proof of lying;
- The interviewer is aware of the difficulties of identifying the truthful, innocent person who is under suspicion of having committed an offence. (Ekman, 2001, p. 8)

From other research, Furnham (2000) pointed out that there are both verbal and nonverbal cues to deceit and that, contrary to popular belief, verbal (those related to the actual message) and vocal (those related to the quality of voice) cues may be as accurate and sensitive an index as body language. Indeed, it is precisely because liars believe there is more potential to catch them through their body than their voice that they concentrate too much on their body language and not what they are saying or how they are saying it.

How do professional lie-catchers (such as the police, customs officers) go about catching liars? Vrij (2000, p. 80) lists the cues police detectives typically pay attention to when trying to catch liars:

- Appearance, such as being untidily dressed
- Publicly self-conscious
- Socially anxious
- Display increased hand movements
- Are less cooperative
- Smile less.

There are some simple but important points to bear in mind when trying to catch liars:

- *Establish base-rate behavior.* What is the person like when they are normal, relaxed and telling the truth? Give people time to relax and see what they are like when it is unlikely that they are lying. Some people fidget more than others. Neurotic people are more anxious than more stable individuals most of the time. There are numerous idiosyncratic but stable nonverbal behavioral differences between individuals. It is too easy to mistake particular signs, such as sweating or avoiding eye gaze, as a betrayal of anxiety and a function of lying when it is perfectly normal everyday behavior for that person.
- *Look for sudden changes* in verbal, vocal or visual behavior such as movements. It is when behavior noticeably alters that it is most meaningful.
- *Note any mismatch* between what is being said and how it is being said, as well as any differences in anxiety level as certain topics are raised. When the eyes, the voice and the words spoken are not in emotional synchrony, it may well be a very good sign of lying. A forced smile or laugh to accompany the carefully prepared verbal line can be a powerful indicator that "something interesting is going on".

- *Formulate a hypothesis* as to the cause: what is the person lying about; what is the sensitive issue? Not everything is a lie. Why should they be lying about some issues and not others?
- *Test the theory* by bringing up a particular topic (in the area of the lies) and see if the nonverbal pattern recurs. If there are persistent indicators of discomfort when particular topics are reintroduced into the conversation, one may assume a stronger possibility of lying.

The bottom-line, however, is that, even for the trained expert, it is often very difficult to detect lying. There are video-tapes of famous spies lying; of murderers who pretend to be victims appealing for help; of politicians telling bare-faced lies in video close-ups, and they suc-ceed in fooling hundreds of people. Even the mechanical lie-detector can be relatively easily fooled. Studies using it have shown that when misdiagnosis occurs it is much more likely that an innocent person is judged to be guilty than the other way round. So beware the person who claims to be good at spotting liars at interview. It could be true ... or itself a self-delusional porkie!

But experts caution against feeling confident, particularly in the hard job of distinguishing between "disbelieving-the-truth" or "believing a lie". Clearly, the absence of a sign of deceit is not evidence of the truth. One problem, as noted above, is ever-present idiosyncratic individual differences. See the comments by Ekman (2001) in the box below.

It is not deviousness that causes some people to be judged lying when they are truthful but a quirk in their behavior, an idiosyncracy in their expressive style. What for most people might be a clue to deceit is not for such a person. Some people:

- Are indirect and circumlocutious in their speech;
- Speak with many or short or long pauses between words;
- Make many speech errors;
- Use few illustrators;
- Make many body manipulators;
- Often show signs of fear, distress, or anger in their facial expres-sions, regardless of how they actually feel;
- Show asymmetrical facial expressions.

There are enormous differences among individuals in all of these behaviors; and these differences produce not only disbelieving-the-truth but also believing-a-lie mistakes. Calling the truthful person who characteristically speaks indirectly a liar is a disbelieving-the-truth mistake; calling the lying smooth-talker truthful is a believing-a-lie mistake. Even though such a talker's speech when lying may become more indirect and have more errors, it may escape notice because it still is so much smoother than speech usually is for most people. (Ekman, 2001, p. 166)

How easy is it to determine whether somebody is lying? Which factors make it easier for the liar to avoid detection, and which make it easier for the detective to catch the liar? Essentially, the hardest lies to tell are those when the liar has to try to conceal many strong emotions while telling the lie. Table 5.2 supplies a checklist for the detection of lying.

Some researchers and practitioners have begun to look carefully at the structured interview and a careful analysis of the content and qualities of statements. These are called criteria-based content analyzes and look systematically at things like the structure of the logic, the quantity of details, reproduction of conversations, information about the mental state of the different parties involved, admitting to lack of memory and so on. They often look for inappropriateness of language and knowledge, inconsistency in statements and so on.

CONCLUSION

Training and experience do help in the business of lie detection, but even then it is by no means simple or foolproof. Because we are all used to lying, it is an everyday occurrence and to a large extent socially acceptable. People have quite different beliefs about when one can, should and should not lie. And they have considerable personal experience of catching out liars. However, many people are not well informed and, as we have seen, either look for or misinterpret the lies (or truth) they observe. Hence the ability of many liars to get away with it!

There is considerable consistency and overlap between reviewers' and researchers' conclusions in this area. They show that many "lay theses" – that is, the theories of ordinary people – are wrong: almost dramatically opposed to popular belief. They also admit that it is not an easy business. Those who have made it a lifetime research project to study the nature of lying admit that even they can often get it wrong. But they also offer good advice.

TABLE 5.2 Checklist to detect lying

Questions about the lie	For the lie-catcher to detect	
	Hard	Easy
1. Can the liar anticipate exactly when he or she has to lie?	YES: line prepared and rehearsed.	NO: line not prepared
2. Does the lie involve concealment only, without any need to falsify?	YES	NO
3. Does the lie involve emotions felt at the time?	NO	YES: specially difficult if: negative emotions such as anger, fear or distress must be concealed or falsified. Liar must appear emotionless and cannot use another emotion to mask felt emotions that have to be concealed.
4. Would there be an amnesty if the liar confesses to lying?	NO: enhances liar's motive to succeed.	YES: chance to induce confession.
5. Are the stakes in terms of either rewards or punishments very high?	Difficult to predict; while high stakes may increase detection apprehension, it should also motivate the liar to try harder.	
6. Are there severe punishments for being caught lying?	NO: low detection apprehension; but may produce carelessness.	YES: enhances detection apprehension, but may also fear being disbelieved, producing false positive errors.
7. Are there severe punishments for the very act of having lied apart from the losses incurred from the deceit failing?	NO	YES: enhances detection apprehension: person may be dissuaded from embarking on lie if she or he knows that punishment for attempting to lie will be worse than the loss incurred by not lying.

Continued on next page

TABLE 5.2 (Continued)

	For the lie-catcher to detect	
	Hard	Easy
8. Does the target suffer no loss or even benefit from the lie? Is the lie altruistic; not benefiting the liar?	YES: less deception guilt if liar believes this to be so.	NO: increases deception guilt.
9. Is it a situation in which the target is likely to trust the liar, not suspecting that he or she may be misled?	YES	NO
10. Has the liar successfully deceived the target before?	YES: decreases detection apprehension; and if target would be ashamed or otherwise suffer by having to acknowledge having been fooled, he or she may become a willing victim.	NO
11. Do liar and target share values?	NO: decreases deception guilt	YES: increases deception guilt.
12. Is the lie authorized?	YES: decreases deception guilt	NO: increases deception guilt
13. Is the target anonymous?	YES: decreases deception guilt.	NO
14. Are target and liar personally acquainted?	NO	YES: lie-catcher will be more able to avoid errors caused by individual differences.
15. Must lie-catcher conceal his/her suspicions from the liar?	YES: lie-catcher may become enmeshed in his/her own need to conceal and fail to be as alert to the liar's behavior	NO
16. Does lie-catcher have information that only a guilty person and not an innocent one would know?	NO	YES: can try to use the guilty knowledge test if the suspect can be interrogated.

No.	Question		
17.	Is there an audience who knows or suspects that the target is being deceived?	NO	YES: may enhance duping delight, detection apprehension, or deception guilt.
18.	Do liar and lie-catcher come from similar language, national and cultural backgrounds?	NO: more errors in judging clues to deceit.	YES: better able to interpret clues to deceit.

Questions about the liar

No.	Question		
19.	Is the liar practised in lying?	YES: especially if practised in this type of lie.	NO
20.	Is the liar inventive and clever in fabricating?	YES	NO
21.	Does the liar have a good memory?	YES	NO
22.	Is the liar a smooth talker with a convincing manner?	YES	NO
23.	Does the liar use the reliable facial muscles as conversational emphasizers?	YES: better able to conceal or falsify facial expressions.	NO
24.	Is the liar skilled as an actor, able to use the Stanislavski method?	YES	NO
25.	Is the liar likely to convince him/herself of his/her lie, believing that what s/he says is true?	YES	NO
26.	Is s/he a "natural liar" or psychopath?	YES	NO
27.	Does the liar's personality make him/her vulnerable either to fear, guilt or duping delight?	NO	YES
28.	Is the liar ashamed of what s/he is concealing?	Difficult to predict: while shame works to prevent confession, leakage of that shame may betray the lie.	
29.	Might the suspected liar feel fear, guilt, shame or duping delight even if the suspect is innocent and not lying, or lying about something else?	YES: can't interpret emotion clues.	NO: signs of these emotions are clues to deceit.

Continued on next page

TABLE 5.2 (Continued)

Questions about the lie-catcher	For the lie-catcher to detect	
	Hard	Easy
30. Does the lie-catcher have a reputation of being tough to mislead?	NO: if the liar has in the past been successful in fooling the lie-catcher.	YES: increases detection apprehension may also increase duping delight.
31. Does the lie-catcher have a reputation of being distrustful?	Difficult to predict: such a reputation might decrease deception guilt, but might also increase detection apprehension.	
32. Does the lie-catcher have a reputation for being fair-minded?	NO: liar less likely to feel guilt about deceiving the lie-catcher.	YES: increases deception guilt.
33. Is the lie-catcher someone who avoids problems, and tends to always think the best of people?	YES: will probably overlook clues to deceit; vulnerable to false negative errors.	NO
34. Is the lie-catcher unusually able to interpret accurately expressive behaviors?	NO	YES
35. Does the lie-catcher have preconceptions which bias the lie-catcher against the liar?	NO	YES: while the lie-catcher will be alert to clues to deceit, s/he will be liable to false positive errors.
36. Does the lie-catcher gain any benefits from not detecting the lie?	YES: the lie-catcher will ignore, deliberately or unwittingly, clues to deceit.	NO
37. Is the lie-catcher unable to tolerate uncertainty about whether s/he is being deceived?	Difficult to predict: may cause either false positive or false negative errors	
38. Does the lie-catcher have a strong emotional drive to catch the liar out ?	NO	YES: liars will be caught, but innocents will be judged to be lying (false positive error).

132

Ekman (2001) offered nine specific suggestions that help people who are trying to detect lies to do a better and more reliable job. These are:

1. Once the suspicion is raised, try to think of logical explanations for your intuitive feelings. Consider which nonverbal clues influenced your judgment. By recognizing and working on your errors, you will be able to avoid overly confident decisions.
2. There are two different types of mistakes: "disbelieving-the-truth (judging a truthful person to be lying) and believing-a-lie (judging a liar to be truthful)". You need to anticipate the implications of making either of these.
3. Truth does not equate with the "the absence of a sign of deceit". Remember than people differ in their ability to "truthfully lie". The reverse is, however, also true: some people have a lower affective threshold and experience stress even when telling the truth. That is why establishing the base line is paramount.
4. Analyze your own judgment. Is there any preconceived bias? Also, avoid making a judgment on the spur of the moment. Sometimes assuming that someone is lying is the easiest option, but the wrong one, especially if there are no other possible explanations for the situation.
5. Acknowledge the fact that sometimes emotional leakage is a sign of "how a truthful person feels about being suspected of lying". Reduce the weight of this evidence if the emotional signs could be explained by the personality of the person in question, the nature of your relationship, or suspected person's expectations.
6. Remember that some clues are associated with more than one emotion. Again, these should not be taken too much into consideration.
7. Does the person know they are suspected of lying? What do they achieve or lose if discovered?
8. Create and use a Guilty Knowledge Test if you are aware of some information the suspect could only know if s/he were lying.
9. Do not make the ultimate judgment of untruthfulness based only on nonverbal signals. These should activate alarm bells and encourage extra research rather than form the basis for the final conclusion.

6

APPLYING THE THEORY: WORK CONTEXTS

A great amount of any person's business is involved with communication. Managers have to persuade and delegate, negotiate and motivate, buy and sell. They have to make presentations to the board, chair small committee meetings and counsel individuals. Others have to "delight" customers, get on with colleagues and set a good example.

But business is about more than putting across one's message skilfully and sensitively. It is also about reading the signals of others. Negotiators, like poker players, have to try to distinguish bluff, bravado and bravura from the true position of their "opponents". Small nuances and subtle changes over time are eagerly scanned for evidence of a change in position. Understanding how an employee is reacting to a negative appraisal can be helped greatly by body language. As, of course, is the watching for signals in a potential buyer an important part of the successful salesperson's job.

Equally vital is that organizations realise that the physical environment can have an important impact on communication patterns – and ultimately on the productivity – of employees. Being seated at a square, oval or a round table inevitable affects eye-contact patterns. Having meetings standing up gives clues about posture. And where meetings are held – that is, on whose territory – can make participants feel less or more confident. Communicating by letter or e-mail has different consequences from making telephone calls, and these are different again from those of face-to-face teleconferencing.

The practical application of a thorough "scientific" knowledge of body communication is supposedly that various techniques can be learnt to read others' "secret" thoughts and motives, and hence to have some control over them. Some people believe that salespeople are trained in these techniques to enable them in some way to manipulate a possible customer into buying a product against his/her better judgment. This is simply not true. Salespeople are taught various techniques, but these are aimed more at relaxing potential customers and playing down anxieties. However, there is some limited evidence that salespeople's ability to "read" their customers' body language correlates with the number of sales they make.

COMMUNICATING DOMINANCE, IDENTITY AND STATUS NONVERBALLY

We send messages about our status and power all the time. People can have status with power (for example, a constitutional monarch) as well as influence without either (through the person's skills, contacts, insight). People can be domineering, and certain acts interpreted as dominant. Acquiring and maintaining dominance may involve different behavior.

While there are many suggestions offered by magazines regarding how to be or to appear dominant (the firm handshake, the physical stance and so on), work in this area has shown some pretty obvious findings. Those who *are, wish to be seen as* or *are judged as being* more dominant display the following behaviors:

- Initiate speech more in groups
- Are last to break the mutual gaze in conversations
- Smile less and touch more
- Gaze and glare more
- Stand more erect and closer to others
- Pay less attention to the other person
- Speak more loudly but in a more relaxed way
- Have more facial expressiveness.

However, and inevitably, these observations need to be qualified by various issues, particularly the context in which the behavior is occurring and the nature of the relationship between the people involved. Nevertheless, we need to recognize status in a group. Leaders need, on occasion, to be able and willing to send messages reminding of their dominance.

We also assert out identity nonverbally. Through appearance and mannerism, speech style and demeanour we hope to convey messages about our personal, but also our social, identity. The latter refers to the social group we belong to, or aspire to belong to. In every society there are gender roles comprising attitudes and behaviors that are deemed acceptable, desirable, even demanded, of the two sexes. Stereotypically, men are viewed as being more autonomous, assertive, dominant and task-orientated, while women are more empathic, gentle, warm and socio-emotionally orientated. In the process of growing up we learn various nonverbal behaviors that confirm our sex roles. Thus men, compared to women overall, smile, look and laugh less, have less expressive faces and gestures, and seem less attentive to visual and vocal cues from others. They remain at greater distances from others, and tend to be far less skilled at giving and receiving nonverbal emotional cues. Men also touch less.

These typical gender differences seem more common during adolescence, yet it remains debatable as to what extent these behaviors have important evolutionary significance, or whether they merely reflect highly changeable socially constructed stereotypes. Indeed, this soon became a "hot" topic between nature versus nurture supporters, as well as those who were politically on the left or right wing. What of the nonverbal behaviors of androgynous people, or those with same-sex orientation? What happens when people undergo a sex change?

Certainly, watching skilful actors play different roles gives a clue as to how they signal personal and social identity nonverbally. With keen observations and consummate skills they are able, with the subtlest of gestures, gaze patterns or vocal inflections, to convey a wealth of meanings.

BUSINESS TALKS

Senior managers often have to give talks and conduct interviews. They may have to address a shareholders' meeting, and the annual conference. They have to talk to their department regularly and may have to attend and speak at many conferences. Hence the commonness of presentation skills courses, which are almost all about nonverbal behavior.

Often politicians and top business people have their speeches written for them, but the skill is in the delivery. Both writer and speaker need to know about the "P-words" – *Pitch, Poetry, Pause* and *Pace*. They need to understand metaphor and repetition.

A speech is a talking show. Speech-writing is an art, but more so is speech delivery. The speakers need the "C words" – *Confidence, Cadence, Conviction* and *Color*. Speech-making is visible thought: it is performance, and the performer needs to be overflowing with zeal and exuberance.

Speech-making is often pure theatre. The orator has to be at once proud and humble, powerful and powerless. The speech needs to be both visceral and intellectual. Most of all it needs to be personal and emotional, exclamatory and climactic. And the speaker needs to *show* all these emotions.

Clever speakers practice their gestures, their eye contact and all their movements. Many "psych" themselves up before a great speech so that they come across well.

Television has changed oratory. By and large, it has been made more difficult. Close-ups mean that every small eye movement, every drop of sweat, every wrinkle is seen and commented upon. The orator is up-close, intimate, just feet away from the viewer. Further, sound-bites dictate the ultra importance of catchphrases. Speeches are rehearsed and timed: the gestures, the voice, and the pauses. Speech writers revise right up to the last moment.

There are often "plants" among the audience, clap, yelp and shriek at the right time, accompanied by euphoric, orchestrated hand-clapping. The camera operators follow the speakers' moves; gestures have been synchronized with speech. Cuts to crowd shots are pre-planned by the camera crew.

The paradox is that authenticity and naturalness cannot easily be taught. Speeches have to be clear, simple and genuine, but that is often the problem. It takes a lot of "effort" to be natural!

What are speeches for? Their primary function is to inspire action, often just to encourage people to vote. Sometimes the objective is also to feel good about the leader, the cause and those listening. Speeches are about articulating dreams. They are not full of numbers, but of passionate conviction. Leaders need to be "one of us" to all their listeners. They must understand inclusivity and they need to gesture it and show it with their "sweeps" of the audience.

Great oratory is poetry. The writer must understand alliteration and imagery. It is important to use and understand symbolism and meter. No wonder so many great speech-givers have often been classically trained. They have to articulate with clarity.

Good speeches should be, and often are, spell-binding, mesmeric, hypnotic. Adolf Hitler knew the secret of oration before scriptwriters and make-up artists. He wasn't young, but nor was Winston Churchill. John F. Kennedy and Nelson Mandela were young when their greatest and most memorable speeches were given. Youth is energy, hope, the future. Youth is passion, optimism and idealism. Hence the importance of the pace of speaking and movement.

Great speeches are about journeys. They need to capture a sense of destiny and destination. They create tension by specifying a challenging problem *but* then they offer a solution. They must inspire trust. Many speakers make recognizable gestures like "hand on heart" or "praying hands".

Many researchers have studied great orators and indeed great speeches. Hitler and Kennedy, Churchill and Mandela were as famous for what they said as how they said it. Equally, famous people who have to give speeches but who are poor orators are often teased for their inadequacies. Because speaking to great crowds is often highly anxiety-provoking, the nonverbal behaviors contrast with the verbal. This includes sweating, self-touching (particularly around the mouth), and clearly faked and rehearsed smiles. Indeed, anxiety management is one of the most important tasks for business speakers and others.

Presentation techniques

Giving a presentation is one of the most daunting prospects for many. According to some often quoted popular research, a large percentage of UK citizens would rather have their leg cut off than speak in public. Public speaking is inherently different from social conversations. There is no turn-taking, often no verbal feedback, and no safety net. The speaker feels vulnerable, tense and lonely standing in front of a potentially malicious audience. One starts to wonder how people do it so well (or not, as the case might be).

There are two components to a successful presentation: content of the speech and its delivery. Both *what* you've got to say and *how* you say it are important. Speech-writers, for example, confess that they compose addresses not using what they would have said, but thinking of what their "character" would. And playing the part of the character is paramount to be believed and listened to. The word "naturally", as used by British Prime Minister Gordon Brown and US President Barack Obama are different, as are their intonations, and their scriptwriters know this.

Of course, such acting skills might not be as necessary to report your company's third quarter performance figures. But they do help if for no other reason than to gather confidence and lose inhibitions. On the other hand, it is words that paint pictures, not gestures or facial expressions, so make sure you've got ideas worth listening to.

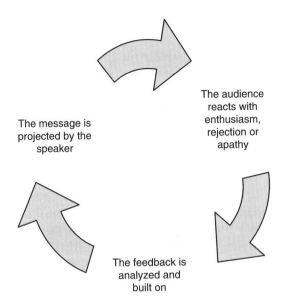

The message is
projected by the
speaker

The audience
reacts with
enthusiasm,
rejection or
apathy

The feedback is
analyzed and
built on

Figure 6.1 **Verbal communication in front of others is a circular process**

Verbal communication in front of others is a circular process. The message is put across to be received, the audience reacts with approval, disapproval or indifference; the feedback is gathered and analyzed by the speaker, who either tries to ride a wave, improve his/her delivery or liven up the atmosphere. This relationship is represented by the diagram in Figure 6.1.

Public speaking is a two-way activity with the audience. It usually involves both the speaker and his/her listeners. However, because of the stage lighting, some speakers may not be able to see their audiences very well, or, if the audience is large, only see the faces of the people in the first few rows. In this sense, visual information is restricted, though speakers often develop acute hearing as a feedback mechanism.

The nature of public communication is very different from other forms of speaking. It is not a conversation where an array of signs and cues, easily picked up by almost everyone, guide the communication. There is no turn-taking, where, while one speaks, the other listens. Public speaking and presentation-giving is a monologue, well practised, often manically rehearsed, and logically organized. Because one party to the communication process (the audience) has to remain silent for prolonged periods of time, the other one has to ensure it keeps the interaction engaging or worthy of attention.

Types of speakers

So what can we learn from successful speakers? What techniques do they use? What tricks do they employ, both verbally and nonverbally?

Many businesses employ motivational speakers. Many countries have organizations (speakers' bureaus) with dozens of speakers "on their books". They tend to be academics, media stars, politicians and successful business people who are paid handsomely for relatively short after-dinner or conference speeches. In one sense, there is nothing new about the concept of a motivational speaker. Our parents had Billy Graham, Lord Soper and, of course, Churchill. In those days, such speakers were almost always found in religious, political or military contexts. They had the ability to uplift the heart; to perk up the dispirited; to energize the weary and to convert the indecisive.

So how do motivational speakers perform and what can we learn from them?

There are several versions of the genre: *the manic evangelist*; *the sincere believer*; and *the serious comic*. Curiously, they are very different in style but similar in content. The manic evangelist is really an American export. Such speakers require plenty of audience participation. One is required to jump, clap, scream, sing and perform other crypto-cheerleader activities during the course of the meeting. The speech of these evangelists is often musical and full of rhythm. The sincere believer is the street corner preacher who tells his moving tale with timing, passion and anecdote. The serious comic is a night club act that is full of riotous humour but interspersed with a serious message, which may be delivered in a quite different tone. There are various others whose job is speaking: barristers, teachers, media people and lecturers.

Churchill had a curious approach to speech-giving. He would put much preparation into his speeches and did not like giving them spontaneously. He would revise and rehearse extensively beforehand. One of his tricks was to dictate speeches to secretaries rather than to write them himself. That allowed him to listen to the speech as it would be delivered and polish the words "on the go". His notes were also remarkable: each page would only have a single paragraph, similar to what we know as bullet points now. The diligence in speech preparation has clearly paid off for the former prime minister. His speeches are among the most cited and best remembered. It comes as no surprise, then, that Members of Parliament in the UK touch the foot of Churchill's statue for luck before giving a speech in the House of Commons.

TABLE 6.1 **Features that make a message outstanding**

Message quality	Description	Example
Novel	Nobody had said it quite like that before	"The lady is not for turning." Margaret Thatcher
Timely	Associated with historical events	"Ich bin ein Berliner." John F. Kennedy
Important	Capture and reflect back the "zeitgeist"	"I have a dream." Martin L. King
Passionate	The speaker him/herself believes in the righteousness of the message	"We shall fight on the beaches." Winston Churchill

Other famous historical speakers include Elizabeth I, who wrote poetry and was familiar with teachings of rhetoric through her classical schooling; and Shakespeare, who while he might not have delivered any great speeches himself, wrote one of the most influential ones in his play, *Julius Caesar*.

Hitler exploited the power of oratory. All the details of his performances were carefully rehearsed (he would practice exaggerated moves and gestures in front of the mirror) and staged. During his rallies, sound amplifying devices were planted around the stadiums to enhance the perceptual effect of his speeches. His lack of inhibition while speaking was also particularly convincing.

By analyzing celebrated speeches and performances, it is also possible to consider the distinguishing characteristics of the messages that became memorable (see Table 6.1).

Great speeches meet these conditions precisely. The result is audiences who are inspired and moved, and almost a purifying, cathartic experience for the listeners.

ARE ALL SUBJECTS MADE EQUAL?

Next is the issue of the subject. For a psychologist, it might be more interesting to teach "The origin and treatment of sexual perversion" rather than "Advanced multivariate statistics". Equally, those studying English may find "Turning novels into movie scripts" easier than "Irony in Restoration comedies".

On the other hand, it is believed that all topics and subjects can be made equally appealing. Videos, visiting celebrities and field trips all help in learning settings. Using many didactic methods to bring the material alive is the stuff of teaching. Note how people on television have made archaeology, geology and (even) cookery exciting and popular.

The other factor is, of course, the presenter's ability and personality. Enthusiasm, energy and commitment go a long way. Complex issues need to be illustrated with examples. Giving clear explanations, and being open to suggestions, count. The lecturer needs to be stimulating, inspirational and influential: in short, charismatic. But charisma cannot compensate for not being organized, knowledgeable or up-to-date.

Content and style of talks

To "deconstruct" a talk is an interesting challenge. There are similar metaphors and techniques in all motivational talks. There is a lot of "I believe" talk and repetition. Phrases that "taste good" in some way are often repeated; for example, "Talent is not enough".

But most of all one notices the *metaphors* in the story. People seem best attuned to stories. From early childhood we learn about this world and its rules through stories that have structure, believable characters and often a moral. The plot includes a journey or, often, a race. This emphasizes both the past and the future. It is about having goals and the journey to reach them. Human beings are designed, it seems, to take in information via stories. All good stories have structure: a beginning, middle and end. They can contain puzzles and dilemmas. But they need resolution: ideally, a victory for the truth, the right and the virtuous. The story itself is a journey and tales often tell of travels and pilgrimages.

The stories are also, of necessity, about fortitude, tenacity and endurance in the face of setbacks. What is inspiring is how obstacles were overcome; how the failure turned into success; how overcoming disappointment was the key factor. It's the solution to the problem of evil in theology: evil is there to teach us a lesson.

Another theme is the *fall of the proud*: how cockiness and egotism lead to failure. There is a lot of talk about the best/worst experience of one's life, and how learning life's lessons enabled one later to be a success. Parents and friends sometimes appear in the talk. This is the social support/teamwork bit that managers like their staff to hear. So there is reference to synergy, interdependence and the necessity of give and take in teams. Nearly all stories have happy endings. Nearly all business books are upbeat, positive, moral tales. They are full of homilies, heart-warming stories of "little people" whose simplicity, essential goodness and wisdom won the day. They call for acting: to get the voice, the gesture and the posture match the themes in the story.

In case of motivational talks, they are deeply anti-fatalist in the sense that *we make our destiny*. We make our beds and we lie in them. We are, and can be, captains of our fate and masters of our ship. And at the heart of everything is the C-word uttered so often everywhere nowadays: *change*, or better, *progress*. The theme is how, if you change your goals, change your strategy, change your lifestyle, change your foolish ways you too can win an Olympic gold medal, become the top salesman and so on. Life is not a dress rehearsal. Unlike shopping at Marks & Spencer, you can't get a refund. With only the talent that you have, plus enthusiasm, determination and a good team, you can WIN BIG.

Great orators never ignore "pitch, pace and pause". Hit the right notes; vary speed: pause for effect. Learn rhetorical devices, such as the power of repetition, the magic number three, the influence of body language to punctuate and emphasize. Get the pace and timing right, tickle the heartstrings with stories of joy and sadness, and have a happy ending ... and you too could be a motivational speaker.

Speech-giving and emotions

Giving speeches and presentations is stressful for most people. As noted earlier, it is the most common of all phobias. People vary in their reaction to the prospect of public speaking. It ranges from the "buzz", nervousness and anxiety right up to utter panic. However, often the tension is good. Atkinson (2004) mentions some cases where experienced presenters deliberately create the conditions of apprehension before and during the performance (for example, former British MP and noted orator, Enoch Powell, would not visit the toilet before giving speeches).

Physiologically, public speaking causes rising blood pressure, increased rate of heartbeat, and sweating. Adrenalin rushes through the body. Muscles in the neck and chest constrict, sometimes affecting the voice and causing it to tremble. Relaxing breathing exercises should take away this tension, and generally, taking a few deep breaths could also do the job.

Mouth movements should be wider than usual, as this technique helps to eliminate monotony from the way the speaker sounds. Those who don't do this when speaking (the Queen, Prince Charles, former UK Prime Minister John Major) sound flat and unexciting.

Emotions influence the rate of speech. Some people "belt through" the speech to get it over with, but speed of delivery is very important. To communicate effectively you need to slow down substantially, from the conversational rate of 170–180 words per minute to 120–130. That might feel too slow in the beginning, but it makes your message digestible to your listeners.

Fear of the audience is usually (but not always) irrational. It stems from the phobia of being ridiculed or intimidated by one's listeners, thus creating a "me against them" confrontational attitude. Generally, however, listeners do not want you to make a fool of yourself in front of them so that they can laugh. More often than not, if you are speaking, you've got something useful or interesting to say and people want to hear it. Audiences also do not comprise a "collective mind". Atkinson (2004) suggests thinking of public speaking as "a number of one-to-one encounters that happen to be taking place at the same time", rather like a group conversation.

Good public speaking needs to be *melodic, like singing*. Our brain seems "wired" in the way that any novel stimulus – auditory, visual or kinesthetic – gradually dissolves into the surrounding noise at some point after the initial exposure. Thus a motionless speaker and monotonous speech lose the audience's attention very fast. To keep your audience interested you need to alternate between tones, swing the notes and switch tempo. In other words, you need to conduct your speech as if you are telling a story or singing a song, building up the suspense and intriguing the listener. To do that, exaggerate your pitch and create an exciting sequence.

The more senior you become in business, the more often you have to speak in public, to both friends and foes, colleagues and shareholders, local and international media. It has been said that a company owner or a shareholder could – by their performance alone – influence the company's share price. A conspicuously calm, clear and confident speaker can allay the fears of investors. Equally, a bumbling, nervous, rattled speaker can lose the trust of everybody.

Studies of the great orators of the world should give clues about how to give a speech. However brilliant the words, they are not enough on their own: witness world famous speeches given by the inexperienced. Speech-giving is a skill. It is the art of presenting yourself, your agenda and your case. It is about looking and sounding right; about controlling your emotions while "manipulating" those of the audiences.

It is about using well-known rhetorical devices matched to theatrical prowess.

Body language of the speaker

The presenter needs to be engaging and entertaining: he or she has to both lead and be led by the audience. Gestures, movements, facial expressions and eye gaze patterns are the most common nonverbal signals during speeches. Nonverbal signs in speech-making and presentations can be broadly divided in two categories: *affirmative* and *negative*. Affirmative gestures emphasize, stress and highlight the verbal message; they engage the audience, keep it focused and interested. Negative signs are those associated with tension, anxiety and nervousness; they are distractive, unnecessary and generally best avoided at any time.

Positive body language signs are either *explanatory* or *evaluative*. Explanatory gestures clarify the meaning of what is being said, accentuate viewpoints, and call attention to the message. They can also serve the purpose of sustaining the audience's attention or to help the speaker to elucidate the verbal communication. Evaluative gestures and facial expressions comprise those types of nonverbal cues that are being exhibited by the audience. Public speaking is a credibility exercise; it takes both guts and ability. It is an art and science, a performance and a lecture.

Atkinson (2004), an expert researcher in public speaking, suggests some nonverbal tips:

1. The speaker has to display open body language signals. This projects both the confidence of the speaker and the trustworthiness of the message. Folded arms and associated closed, hunched posture will influence the quality and the projection of your voice and articulation by making your chest constrict. An open posture also communicates honesty and sincerity of the speaker and their message. One of the first things speakers have to learn is to open up and be less rigid on stage.
2. The public tends to interpret folded arms gestures as:
   - Defensiveness;
   - Comfort;
   - Missing armrests; or
   - Feeling cold.
   Consequently, Atkinson advises speakers not to fold their arms when speaking, whether in an interview or a talk. That is because

of a widespread (but erroneous) belief made popular by the mass media and the like that it signals defensiveness and hostility. Keep your arms open and you are much more likely to create a favorable impression.

3. Anxious nonverbal body language not only distracts the speaker from the delivery, but also diverts the audience from attending to the message. Again, such speakers are judged as lacking ability and for that reason cannot keep their audience's attention. Nonverbal cues that communicate anxiety are:
   - Fiddling with objects/hair;
   - Nervous pacing;
   - "White-knuckle syndrome" – clenching fists or gripping objects too hard; and
   - Self-touching.

4. Some gestures can potentially be distracting, while others are good for capturing and sustaining attention, such as sudden pointing, a sharp raising of the arm and so on. These show excitement and energy, and break the routine. Repetitive movements – swinging, swaying, pacing up and down – on the other hand, can be annoying to the listener.

5. While gestures are natural to conversations and can be used for various reasons, conscious inhibition of movements is likely to interfere with the flow of speech. If you would like either to use or not use a particular gesture or facial expression while speaking in public, you could try practising speaking in front of a mirror. This would allow you to discover when you use this particular gesture, and how desirable/undesirable it is. It is good to seek the opinion of close, truthful friends. Then rehearse the speech with movements until the new pattern becomes literally second nature. Otherwise, allow the original gesture to remain as it is, because conscious monitoring would only impair your performance.

6. The larger the audience, the more you should exaggerate gesticulation. Theatre actors know well the power of dramatizing one's message. The same clearly goes for voice: the larger the room and the more people who are listening, the louder the volume should be.

Body language of the audience

Audiences have the upper hand during speech-giving. They are on the receiving end, usually (though not always) sitting cosily and comfortable. Their job is to analyze and evaluate the speaker while she/he sweats, blushes and considers taking tranquilizers. The audience is being entertained; the performance has been tailored for their eyes and ears. "Bread and theatre!", they used to demand in ancient Rome, and now, as ever, audiences need to be fought over, persuaded and cajoled.

Comedians know about the audience's advantage and are always keen to turn the tables. They start picking on members of the audience or ask latecomers questions, making fun at the expense of someone's embarrassment. But usually audiences have an easy ride with being mere listeners. However, they have the power to help the speaker or distract them. They can show their support in the form of clapping or nodding, or express disagreement by booing, hissing or vigorously shaking their heads from side to side. The frequency and strength of these signals can be used to gauge the degree of liking or disliking of the message.

Interestingly, Atkinson (2004), in his study of speech-making, found that audiences seem to know implicitly the rules of when, how often, and how much to clap. His comparisons of different recordings of political speeches, including some from non-English-speaking countries, showed a striking similarity in the duration of general spontaneous clapping: this would last around eight (plus or minus one) seconds. He also found that some types of messages such as boasts about "us", insults about "them", speech introductions and "clap trap" techniques produce the greatest response from the audience. Consequently, Atkinson proposed there is a shared knowledge of an "unwritten rule" regarding how much applause is necessary to acknowledge and support the speaker.

TRAINING SPEAKERS

The power of audiences is striking. Consider one of the favorite pastimes of many psychology undergraduates, involving classical conditioning and public speaking. Imagine a tutor giving a lecture in a medium-sized auditorium. It is early morning and the attention levels of the audience are understandably low. The lecturer walks nervously from one side of the room to the other; lecturing is not his favorite activity and they would rather finish it off quickly. Suddenly, the speaker notices how attentively some students on one side of the room are listening. They nod vigorously in agreement, smile at the occasional jokes, and take dutiful notes of the material. Gradually, after several minutes, the lecturer starts talking only to that side of the class. His body is orientated to one side and his gestures are selective in that direction. The canny psychology undergraduates in the audience had conditioned the speaker to talk to them exclusively through positive nonverbal reinforcement of his behavior.

The body language of the audiences can:

1. Allow the speaker to learn about the listeners' agreement/disagreement with the speaker's message.
2. Provide the speaker with the feedback necessary to improve the quality of his/her speech (for example, to speak more loudly).
3. Let speakers know if they have been understood (correctly).
4. Act as a confidence boost. Signals of liking, such as laughter, cheering or smiling reinforce the esteem of the speaker and his/her ability to convey the message.
5. Tell you about who is who in the audiences. Proximity to the stage can reflect status, purchasing power, personality or motivation.

Speakers also evaluate their audiences. They can see who is attentive and who is not. Who yawns, who slouches, who glances away. If you, on the other hand, want, as a member of the audience, to attract the speaker's attention and create a favorable impression about yourself, show, or even better, *do* more active listening.

Speech-giving paraphernalia

Dress

Appearance, as we saw earlier, matters a great deal. The key to successful dressing for speech giving is, however, suitability and comfort. There is definitely no one grand rule for how to achieve a winning look. It depends on the context and the environment where the speech is taking place. Obviously, formal business events, such as conferences or meetings, should be attended in formal business dress, but more relaxed settings allow for a looser dress code.

It is, indeed, credibility and confidence that counts in speech-giving, not the latest designer fashion craze. Nowadays, popular public speech-giving is followed by close-up shots of what the speakers were wearing or forgot to put on, so perhaps special attention should be paid to dress if one expects to be filmed or photographed at the venue. Discreetly check your appearance moments before you are called on stage, to avoid embarrassment or untidiness.

Authority can be projected by wearing formal suits or dresses in darker colors. Consider the significance of the tie in creating an impression of power. It is, in fact, most noticed when wearers takes their ties off: their whole look suddenly becomes much more friendly and relaxed.

In most cases, dress sense should be synonymous with common sense. If, however you are in doubt about your look, ask family or (real) friends for advice. Remember that some clothes might be fashion statements, but not everyone is aware of which colors are "in" this season.

Tables and lecterns

Tables and lecterns are commonly used during presentations. Sometimes for no specific purpose apart from being there. Atkinson (2004), however, advises against using them, as audiences usually perceive them as barriers impeding rapport building. However, some speakers might choose to stay behind a table or a lectern because of their fear of speech-giving. Physical objects of a large size located between the speaker and the audience demarcate the border between the listener and the talker. They may in some cases communicate defensiveness and distance.

On the other hand, speakers generally find tables quite useful. They are convenient, practical tools to help in speech-giving. Lecterns are particular good for resting notes on, and tables are well suited for setting up your laptop, resting a briefcase, or putting up a projector.

Given this contradiction, should one stand behind tables and lecterns, or move about? The answer is simple and obvious: use them purposefully, but do not hide yourself behind them all the time. Aggressive, nervous gripping on to lecterns or tables can sometimes result in the "white knuckle syndrome" that is an easily detectable giveaway of anxiety and stiffness. Both excessive movement or complete absence of any at all send a negative impression to the audience. The former movement pattern conveys restlessness and unease, while the latter is most likely to be seen as a manifestation of fear.

Good advice includes:

1. Check if the technology allows you to move about freely, and think of a strategy to overcome any limitations, perhaps by asking

for another type of microphone or switching off unpleasant stage lighting.

2. Also, ensure your microphone is in working order and, most important, do not forget to switch it off once you have finished speaking. We have all heard of those people who used the restroom facility while still having their microphone switched on.

The setting of the speech should also reflect its nature, add some value to it (artistic or political) but not distract from the performance. At some poetry readings or in some plays the set is, indeed, minimal: it does not detract from the message in any way. Set designers know how to match the set to the play. Contemporary popular music, for example, capitalizes on tricks and gimmicks such as special lighting and fireworks to create an unforgettable show. The same is often true at conferences, especially those of political parties. The logo, the colors, the motto all ensure maximum visibility and provide perfect photo opportunities for message promotion.

NEGOTIATION SKILLS AND STYLES

In short, negotiating is about reaching a mutually acceptable agreement. Sometimes negotiation is a relatively straightforward process, but at other times it takes months, or, in some extreme cases even years. One example to illustrate this: investment banks first analyze the market, then approach and persuade a client whom they think can benefit from an acquisition of another company, and negotiate the terms of the takeover or merger. It is therefore evident that negotiations in such a case can be extremely laborious, slow and painstaking, and involve business acumen, tact, determination and patience.

Business negotiations involve many steps and issues on which common grounds need to be found: from financial terms to 'late completion' agreement, from employment matters to contingent liability. Each party has its own agenda, plans and conditions. Negotiating is therefore about needs and wants. Needs are the requirements of the offer, while the wants are the extra "icing on the cake". Negotiation is thus about research, planning and strategic thinking. Homework about the other party, the potential reaction to your offer, and the other party's current and future needs would be of great benefit before and during the negotiation process.

Negotiation is both a skill (to get more of what you want while giving up less of what you have) and an art (doing the deal diplomatically and quickly). It shares some of its style with poker and some of its substance with chess. Notice how many idioms frequently used in "business speak" have come from card games such as poker:

- An ace in the hole/Have an ace up one's sleeve/To hold all the aces.
- To come/turn up trumps.
- To deal someone in.
- To follow suit.
- To force someone's hand.
- To play one's cards close to one's chest/To play one's cards right.

Negotiation is reminiscent of poker in the way that players try to deceive or trick each other, and thus raise the stakes to achieve the maximum payout. This is not to say that deception is an asset in negotiations. On the contrary, successful negotiations leading on to prosperous business deals have to be open, fair and honest. However, a degree of competition seems always to be present. To put it differently, full honesty and transparency is not expected. Further, in poker, as in any negotiation, the game unfolds gradually, stage-by-stage, card-by-card. Thus the players need to stay alert and agile, to decide when it is best to raise or to fold.

Negotiations remind many of chess, with its elaborate give and take dance. Some of the moves are deliberately capitulating, to enable a later advantage to be established. Chess, like negotiations, rely on a detailed, forward-projected strategy. In chess, as in negotiations, it is necessary to calculate the odds and re-evaluate tactics at every step of the game.

What does research on body language say about the process of negotiation? First, it emphasizes the dynamics of group processes. Whether it is a one-to-one transaction or involves several teammates matters a great deal to the negotiation strategy. Dyads reach agreement faster, especially if the two people have worked together before. Larger groups need to assign roles and responsibilities to each person, to avoid confusion and set the chain of command prior to the beginning of the negotiation. Nonverbal signs of status, assertiveness and dominance indicate who is in charge of the group, who makes the ultimate decisions, or who is the right hand of the leader.

Second, because of its subtlety, nonverbal communication can be a powerful tool in negotiation. Whereas words and verbal statements are usually taken as a binding promise of action or intention, nonverbal

TABLE 6.2 **Nonverbal signs in negotiations**

Category	Examples	Relevance
1. Alliance	Closer interpersonal distance, mimicry	Identify key players and decision-makers; can be used to establish rapport and intimacy
2. Cooperation	Nodding, smiling, open body posture	
3. Antagonism	Folded arms, little eye contact	Recognize who has not been persuaded by your deal terms; who needs to be persuaded further
4. Doubt	Hand over mouth gestures, nose rubbing, scratching of eyebrows, ear touching	

statement of agreement, allegiance, or rejection are not. They hint or "nudge" the other party towards a plan of action rather than state them explicitly.

Negotiation is a process of message exchange. Apart from the substance of the negotiation (what the negotiation is about), there is also the issue of strategy (for example, concession-making) and the behavior of the negotiating agents. The nonverbal component of communication is connected to the behavioral aspects, but this chapter will also consider stages in the negotiation process and the relevant nonverbal behaviors.

Nonverbal signals can point to friends and foes among the other negotiating party members (see Table 6.2). Alliance and cooperation can be conveyed through closer interpersonal distance, while antagonism and doubt would result in parties seating further away from each other. Nodding and smiling are universal signs of agreement, though the frequency of display might be prescribed by cultural etiquette. Postural echo is a phenomenon characterizing a friendly or intimate relationship, and this usually happens without any awareness or intent. Thus, a lack of such echoing would signal that there was little understanding or a low intimacy level among the negotiating parties. Signals of distress and doubt tell of confusion or hesitation. There are classic signs of uncertainty such as hand over mouth gestures ("speak no evil"), little eye contact ("see no evil") and touching one's ears ("hear no evil").

It is nevertheless hard to devise a definitive description of even the most common nonverbal signals used in negotiations. This is because such behaviors vary across contexts, agendas and times. Also because negotiations are complex, multistage processes which unfold over several phases of negotiation. Hendon and Hendon (1989), in their book *How to Negotiate Worldwide*, list six typical stages of business negotiations. Below is a brief description of what sorts of actions and preparations are involved in each of them. Some involve relevant nonverbal behaviors, while others entail reasoning, planning and superior verbal skills.

Pre-negotiation

Pre-negotiation includes two stages.

First, it is the time for a simple cost–benefit analysis. Is the deal and the effort one needs to put in the negotiation worth the trouble? What are the prospects, the opportunities and the problems of the scenario?

Second, if the decision is affirmative and the negotiations are to go ahead, do your groundwork. The trick is to gather enough knowledge about the other party, and knowing your own standing. Set your objectives, take the market and the environment into account, consider the difficulties and the threats of changing circumstances. Make a list of your significant and marginal concerns. Do the same for the other company. Most importantly, decide on the acceptable trade-offs. What are you prepared to give up, and what would you like to get in return for that? What is going to be your opening offer? What sort of reaction would that evoke in the other camp? What is your back-up? Who are you going to take with you? Who is the best person to negotiate or deal with the client?

Entry

At this stage you will need to pitch and sell your presentation to the client. We have described in the previous sections the nonverbal aspect of sales and presentations. To reiterate: be friendly and project sincerity through open body language such as relaxed but elevated posture; smile and nod in agreement to send out signals of receptiveness and attention; give a firm, steady handshake when greeting and saying goodbye; make sure that, if the sale were to fall through, it would not be because of a personal dislike, but because the terms of the deal were not satisfactory for both parties.

The last recommendation is probably even more relevant to negotiations. Some of them do not reach closure because the parties cannot agree on some specific clauses of the business contract, but once the setting changes, negotiations re-open. Make sure the clients still want to do business with you.

Establishing effective relationships

Here is where body language has a definite role to play. To achieve effective working relationships, one needs to establish rapport and gain the trust of the other party. Subtle matching of your client's body language can sometimes do the trick, but more often, that is not enough. In private life, trust is built up gradually, by allowing another person into more delicate and personal spheres of one's life. In business it is more complicated: when money is involved, everyone looks out for their own interests. Trust in business means knowing that the other party will play fair, will abide by the rules, will not take advantage. This is the message your body language should be sending alongside your verbal utterances.

And look out for those signs of reassurance in the person with whom you are negotiating. Are there contradictions between what a person is saying and what his or her body is showing? If yes, what are the possible reasons for this? Do not assume falsehood or faking immediately, but get to know the other party. Observe his/her interactions within the team, the telephone mannerisms, and conduct outside the boardroom to determine a *baseline behavior pattern*. If you are still unsure, ask questions directly and make a mental note of the person's reaction. The preceding chapter offers a comprehensive review of the psychology of lying and its nonverbal components.

The overall purpose of this stage is to learn more about the other party. Consider cultural variations in friend- and acquaintance-making. In the West, for example, personal matters are disregarded, while the organization and the effectiveness of the transaction are of major importance. Time is money, and money doesn't wait. Other cultures (the Middle East, South America, South Asia, for example) place the emphasis on relationship development. They tend to spend longer at this stage getting to know the people with whom they are dealing. They value patience, respect and long-term vision as alternatives to efficiency and time-saving methods.

Hendon and Hendon (1989) also point out that at this stage of nego-tiations both parties learn about the *actual* needs and goals of the other party. The initial entry pitch is usually based on a (sometimes inaccurate) perception of these, thus the aims need to be refined by a further exchange of ideas and information. Trust and assurance are critical to win over the other party and facilitate the flow of discussion and disclosure.

Reformulating your strategy in light of the new knowledge

Mistakes and errors have to be corrected; and assumptions re-evaluated. The aim of this stage is to be better able ultimately to meet the needs of your client. Casual interactions are an important part of the deal-making process too. Do not miss an opportunity to connect with the other party in a more relaxed atmosphere, such as after-work drinks or dinner. As far as nonverbal behaviors are concerned, calm, stable, open and trustworthy individuals (or simply people who project these qualities) leave better impressions, which are incredibly long-lasting.

Bargaining and concession-making

The most energetic part of the negotiation is the bargaining stage. This is where your skills at give-and-take are put to the ultimate test. Remember your bottom line and be aware of not pushing the other party too close to theirs at the very beginning. Hendon and Hendon (1989) give the following recommendations to achieve success at bargaining:

1. *Separate the people from the problems*
   People problems are the ones concerned with misperception and miscommunication. They stem from emotional charges and perception errors. They are psychological problems and thus need to be addressed correspondingly, and not by business concessions.
2. *Focus on interests, not positions*
   Interests are wants and needs, while positions are courses of action. Positions are limiting (a customer wanting to buy a lipstick without a make-up bag), while interests are the essence of the request (to make them look and feel better by purchasing that lipstick). Thus, make

sure you concentrate on the underlying needs and desires and not situational positions. Positions are usually negotiable and subject to a better alternative, while interests are the bottom-line needs at the heart of the negotiation.

3. *Devise options for mutual gain*

Promote shared interests and options for mutual profit. This not only shows consideration of the other party's interests but also facilitates the progress of the deal.

4. *Use objective measures*

In case of a dispute, or simply in order to avoid one, seek out independent, bias-free advice and specialist opinion on the subject matter of the negotiation, such as the value of goods or products.

Concession-making is a separate issue. In short, a concession is something you are prepared to sacrifice to get something in return. Concessions tend to be mutual: if one party gives way, the other is expected to follow. Thus concessions rely on the most basic building block of human relationships – reciprocity.

Hendon and Hendon (1989) conducted a simple but insightful study into the concession patterns of negotiators. They studied the concession preferences of executives from fifteen different cultural backgrounds, resulting in a list of seven possible concession strategies. In the exercise participants were asked to imagine themselves in negotiation situation, where they were able to concede $100 dollars off the asking price. They were then presented with alternative concession strategies and asked to rate them on effectiveness and how much or little they liked them. Table 6.3 describes these patterns of concession. It is clear from the table that there are quite a few strategies for concession-making. Concessions can be evenly (Strategy 1) or unevenly (Strategy 5, 6) spread out across time periods. They can be upfront (Strategy 4) or held on to until the very last moment in the negotiation (Strategy 3). They can even be intentionally deceiving by giving out slightly more than the total concession budget (Strategy 7).

The first strategy is obviously too consistent and thus can easily be exposed by the other party. The danger is that your opponent may soon realize how much money you are willing to give away and use this knowledge to his/her advantage.

The second strategy shows your generosity from the very start. While it may be beneficial in some situations, it may also jeopardize your later efforts to bargain and ask for a reciprocal concession from your partner.

TABLE 6.3 **Patterns of concession between negotiators**

	Time periods			
	1	**2**	**3**	**4**
Strategy 1	25	25	25	25
Strategy 2	50	50	0	0
Strategy 3	0	0	0	100
Strategy 4	100	0	0	0
Strategy 5	10	20	30	40
Strategy 6	40	30	20	10
Strategy 7	50	30	25	−5
				(take $5 back)

The third strategy is called "hard-nosed". You are only willing to concede at the very end of the negotiation if all else fails and no compromise or alternative has been found.

The fourth strategy is described as "naïve". You reveal your sine qua non, your indispensable condition, at the very start of bargaining, which does not leave you much room for further maneuvering. Such a tactic can be advantageous if the other party also sticks to the same approach or, as Hendon and Hendon (1989) point out, if "both sides are long time negotiating partners and have achieved over the years a high level of trust" (p. 28). Otherwise it might expose you excessively and make you particularly vulnerable in further bargaining.

The fifth strategy is "escalating." An astute negotiator will soon realize that concessions turn out to be in their favor as the bargaining progresses and will try to extend the negotiations.

The sixth pattern is "de-escalating" making it clear to the other party that, despite initial generosity, your willingness to concede is gradually shrinking. That puts the pressure on your negotiating partner to get as much out of you in the beginning as possible.

The seventh pattern of concession is similar to the "de-escalating" strategy, but by demanding some money back at the very end you could put pressure on your negotiating partner. Your action clearly signals that, while you have given away too much, your big-heartedness has not been reciprocated. You can indicate to your negotiation partner that your expectations of their concessions have not materialized and that you are disappointed.

So which of the tactics did the executives like the most? The answers were split into three groups, according to the cultural preferences for, and expectations of, how business should be conducted. The USA's, Brazil's and South Africa's managers preferred the hard-nosed strategy; Canadians, Australians, New Zealanders, Taiwanese and Thai executives chose the de-escalating pattern as their favorite; and those from Hong Kong, Singapore, Malaysia, Indonesia, the Philippines, India and Kenya gave the thumbs-up to the escalating strategy.

As for the most disliked strategy, all executives apart from Singaporeans, Indonesians, Indians and Brazilians selected the "naïve" strategy as their least preferred one. Thus, authors speculate whether such unanimous choice points to a universal agreement across cultures that such a degree of honesty is considered to be imprudent and hasty in negotiations.

Managers from the other four countries voted the seventh strategy as their most disliked, while eight other nations (the USA, Canada, Australia, New Zealand, Hong Kong, Taiwan, Malaysia and the Philippines) rated it their second most disliked one. This tactic involved asking for a part of the earlier concession back in order to manipulate the other party into conceding even more. Hendon and Hendon (1989) hypothesize that this choice among Asian nationals can be explained by their concern about losing face. Similarly, in the West, while face-saving might not be an overwhelming anxiety, revisiting an earlier agreed decision is considered unacceptable in business where, as Hendon and Hendon put it, "a deal is a deal".

Reaching agreement

The final round is reached when both parties have settled all the terms of the future business contract. Note that some cultures place much importance on the honor of verbal agreements, and while a written contract inevitably has to be signed, rushing it might come across as insulting. Explore and research the practices of the local culture: how is agreement usually expressed? Cultural variations are the subject matter of a section on cross-cultural differences in body language (see Chapter 4).

COMMUNICATION IN SALES

Perhaps more than anywhere else, nonverbal behavior plays a part in sales. Consider the car showroom and what salesmen have been trained to do. Most showrooms have three different areas: the reception desk, the car display and the relaxation (soft) area. The customer meets the sales person behind the desk. This is a formal area where particulars may be obtained. Soon, however, customers are encouraged to inspect the vehicle. Salespeople encourage the customer to sit in the driving seat. But they leave the door open, go around to the other side of the car and crouch at the same height talking through the open door. Thus, both front doors are open. Experience has shown that customers, especially women, can take fright if the doors are closed. It has also shown that talking to people from a similar height position makes people more collaborative and questioning.

Salespeople rarely show customers the engine by opening the hood because this serves mainly to frighten and confuse, and remind customers of what can go wrong. Salespeople are trained to watch eye movements carefully to see what customers are "really" interested in – boot space, baby seats, wheel trims. Customers are encouraged to touch and later to drive the car: to mark it as theirs.

The third phase often takes place in the lounge area, where sofas are arranged in a semi-circle or at right angles. It is here that other discussions take place, covering any remaining questions the customer might have. The final signing, however, takes place at the desk.

Salespeople know not to touch customers, but encourage them to touch the product. They know the importance of the "new car smell" and of interpreting the customers' movements and glances. They have to know when "No" means "Yes" and vice versa; when one customer needs to be sold the product on its technical specifications and another on its family-friendliness.

In his popular, influential and comprehensive book on the science of influence, Cialdini (2007) set out six well-known and often used methods of persuasion. These have been documented by psychologists and are familiar to all sales people. These persuasion techniques are types of heuristics and are concerned with influencing the decision-making of the other party.

There have been many studies about how people make up their minds. *First*, we make judgments rapidly and in a context of constant mental overload. *Second*, purchases might also be of high or low involvement. Thus a computer or a washing machine would be a high involvement sale, while a chocolate bar or a washing powder would be a low involvement one. The consequence of this differentiation is how much mental effort people are willing to go through before they are ready to buy. Low involvement purchases (fast-moving consumer goods, in particular) are usually mindlessly bought. Nobody spends a half an hour at a shop determining which brand of chewing gum to buy. Even with expensive, durable goods there is only a certain amount of time you are willing to spend researching the product category before you choose the best option. Hence, *time* is a crucial ingredient in sales and one of the most powerful leverages of a salesperson. *Third*, these heuristics, or mental shortcuts, represent instant patterns of thinking. Their main appeal is in saving the most valuable commodity we have – time. Therefore, when salespeople give arguments in favor of their product or brand, they try to press these cognitive buttons by boasting the properties processed heuristically.

Below is a brief overview of these influencing strategies:

1. *Commitment and consistency*: people do not like to change their mind once a decision has been made. We have an internal story or script about who we are, how we ought to behave, and what we represent in life. Thus, people would go to great lengths to keep their word or stand by their position, especially if that position had been announced publicly. Changing one's mind too often is usually seen as indecisive or lacking in ability or vision, and thus must be avoided at all costs. A great way to use this tactic is to ask for a small favor, and once that has been agreed, to solicit a much bigger request. The purpose of the small demand is not profit, but *commitment*. This can be shown nonverbally.
2. *Reciprocation*: we are social animals that have survived the gene race through our ability to cooperate and share. Teamwork or cooperation depends on all members of the group assisting and backing each other up. Thus, if someone shares his or her food with you, or pays a restaurant bill, you feel obliged to return the favor. In sales, making a small, but conspicuous, concession or giving a discount will most definitely work to your advantage, as your client will feel a compulsion to *reciprocate*.
3. *Social proof*: we often look to others to decide what to do, especially in ambiguous and novel situations. That is why advertising claims such as "That is why moms go to Iceland" or "On average, 236 eHarmony members marry every day in the United States" appeal so much. Consider which café you would prefer to eat at while on a trip to a foreign country: one buzzing with people, or an empty one? The former is the visual, social proof of quality.
4. *Authority*: an infamous experiment carried out by psychologist Stanley Milgram in the early 1960s demonstrated the power of authority. Participants were willing to knowingly give electric shocks to another person when told to do so by a powerful and

demanding doctor, even up to lethal levels. While this would be an extreme example of authority abuse, it shows how much blind trust we put in credentials and expertise. The implication of this research is obvious: look appropriate and suitable for the occasion.

5. *Liking*: we are more willing to part with our hard-earned cash if we like the cause, the product or the salesperson. Most of all, we like people who are similar to us, as it reinforces our own self-image. Liking is also easy to increase through body language. Note how friends and family members often sit in similar positions or adopt similar postures. The process of mirroring often happens unconsciously, but relentlessly. Thus, subtly matching your nonverbal behavior to that of your customer will increase liking and, ultimately, sales.

6. *Scarcity*: scarcity creates desire and value. Think antiques, think collectables. This is perhaps one of the most frequently used strategies in business: "limited offer", "two items only per person", "three days of sales only". Make sure your client knows what they are *missing* if they do not agree to the deal or make a purchase on the spot.

More important, these strategies of influence each have a relevant nonverbal component. They are summarized in Table 6.4. below. Of course, the given examples cannot work in all situations at all times and should be used when appropriate, with good judgment.

TABLE 6.4 **Strategies of influence and their relevant nonverbal components**

Strategy of influence	Nonverbal component
Commitment and consistency	A *handshake* is one of the best commitment strategies, and in many cultures all that is needed to be able to proceed with the deal
Reciprocation	"I'll scratch your back if you scratch mine." Sending *signals of openness and cooperation* through your body language increases the chances of the other party's compliance
Social proof	Make sure your clients know about your *previous successes and your track record*. Affiliations, name dropping, and a list of successful deals help to create an aura of professionalism and expertise
Authority	Abide by *the dress code*. Invest in suits, coats and all the paraphernalia associated with the image you are attempting to project
Liking	*Mirror and match* the body language of your client/customer
Scarcity	Create *time scarcity* by, for example, glancing at your watch; or *attention scarcity* by facing not your ultimate customer but someone else

Neuro-linguistic programming (NLP) experts propose sales techniques based on clients' preferred sensory modality. While NLP is not by any means a science, research seems to support that the idea of different people have different preferences when processing information. In brief, people's processing styles tend to be more:

- Visual;
- Auditory; or
- Kinaesthetic.

However, it would be erroneous to conclude that once a customer's preferred channel of communication has been established, the salesperson should concentrate on it exclusively. A much better approach would be to include information influencing all the modalities simultaneously, regardless of the apparent favorite.

This idea of concurrent influence fits well with research on body language. As we have already mentioned in this book, nonverbal behaviors rarely happen in isolation from each other. On the contrary, it is the clusters of several behaviors that let us attribute mental states to physical body changes. Thus a happy person not only smiles, but also speaks cheerfully and loudly, gesticulates a lot and adopts an open, upright posture. In a similar fashion, a customer with a visual preference choosing a car (if we stick with the automotive examples) would most certainly appreciate the clarity of your purchase rates graphs and the visual impact of the car's interior design. However, they would be just as likely to want to touch its leather finish, or hear its engine running.

Another area of applied body language research concentrates on rejection signs and signals. People who are not convinced by the salesperson's arguments would exhibit, among other nonverbal behaviors, a shifty gaze pattern. They would cover their mouths with their hands or fingers, or clench their hands in front of their face. Some suggest that an easy strategy to "unlock" the person is to give them something to hold: a drink, a booklet, a pen. But is this really true?

This tactic works on the assumption that a physical change in the person's position is likely to lead to a change in mental attitude. Interestingly, it is backed up by experimental investigations. In one of these, participants were asked to rate their mood at the beginning of the study. Then one group was asked to hold a pencil between their teeth (creating a movement of facial muscles approximating a smile), the other was instructed to suck on the tip of the pencil (thus generating a simplified version of a frown); the third group had no manipulation. After doing as asked, all the participants indicated their mood again. Not surprisingly, more people in the "smile" condition felt happier, and more people in the "frown" condition felt sadder compared to the control group.

Another curious observation has been made about the temperature of the drink offered. An experiment was carried out to check whether people's feelings about their encounter with a stranger might vary as a function of an offered drink's temperature. Participants were met by a confederate in the hall and taken to the laboratory. While in the elevator, they were asked to hold a plastic cup of either an ice-cold cola drink or a hot coffee for a few seconds. They then proceeded to talk with another researcher in the lab and, before they left, filled in a questionnaire indicating how much they had liked their chat. Astonishing as it sounds, participants exposed to the warm drink gave much higher liking ratings. One of the speculations explaining the reason for such a result links physical warmth with emotions of affection and love. It is suggested that such an association is an unconscious response to a basic stimulus that we learn in very early childhood.

The lesson is simple. Nonverbal clues, processed both consciously and unconsciously, influence our decision-making.

INTERVIEWS

A great deal of nonsense is spoken about interviews. But one, somewhat disarming, "factoid" has proven to be half true. The surprise is not so much that people make up their minds about candidates in the first 10 seconds after meeting them, but rather that their estimation can be quite accurate in that short time.

In research terms this is called *"the validity of thin slices of behavior"*. Early researchers were impressed by very trivial features of a person leading to erroneous judgments. For example, a celebrated study conducted in the early 1970s demonstrated that interviewees who were seen wearing spectacles in a 15-second video clip were judged to be significantly more intelligent than those without glasses. However, if the tape clip was extended to five minutes, this effect (fortunately) disappeared.

Various studies have examined the ratings of strangers with "zero acquaintance" of others to see how accurate they are. This is the procedure. Certain individuals are targeted as "experimental stimuli". They are tested so that their ability level and personality test scores are known. In the best of these studies the test scores are validated by people who know them well. These typical targeted individuals may also rate themselves; for example, on a 10-point introversion–extroversion scale, or the extent to which they worry or are stress-prone.

Thus, the researchers know if their targets are bright extroverts, average neurotics, conscientious dullards or whatever. Then a video-tape is made of them. Most often they are giving a talk, reading from a test card or just answering interview questions. The video may last up to 10 minutes and, from that, typical or interesting, 10-, 15- or 20-second segments are extracted.

A group of people who have never met the video-taped person and know nothing about them are then shown the short clips. The question is *how accurate* the viewers' opinions are. Do they rate extroverts as introverts, dim impression managers as being bright, and quite conscientious people as inadequate? Do the self-ratings of the video-taped people concur with those who have seen them only for a matter of seconds?

The first serious study in this area was undertaken in 1966. It showed, as have many others with different groups in different countries since then, that there is a surprising and significant amount of agreement between observer ratings and target self-ratings, and between these ratings and test scores. In one study, people rated either a photograph, heard a short audio recording, watching a silent video clip or watched a clip with sound. Naturally, they were most accurate with the latter, but surprisingly, they could quite accurately rate extroversion, agreeableness and conscientiousness from simple photographs.

Clearly, some attributes are more observable than others. Also, some people are more perceptive than others; and some tasks are more revealing than others. So telling a joke, talking about hobbies and inventing a neologism seem to yield richer data than doing a role play or describing how one overcame a frustrating problem.

But there are some worrying implications. One study looked at the correlation between students' ratings based on "thin slice" video exposure of one of their lecturers, and the average rating of the lecturer after the full course involving many lectures, seminars and so on. They saw first a 10-second clip and rated the lecturer on such attributes as "accepting", "competent" and "enthusiastic". If they were shown a 30-second clip the correlation was very high indeed ($r = 0.89$).

So students' ratings *before* the course, based on first impressions, were virtually identical to those elicited after a long, thorough and revealing set of lectures which presented many different features of teaching quality.

These researchers then showed, amazingly, that after being shown only a 6-second, silent clip of the lecturer, the rating correlated highly with post-course ratings.

What are the implications of this? You learn everything you want to know about a teacher in six seconds? Or, in the jargon: there is high validity of the inferences people make about complex performances based on minimal, thin-slice data? Or could it be that students' ratings are based on superficial, possibly trivial, criteria? Do bouncy extroverts do the best even if they are poorly prepared, badly organized and moderately incompetent?

So, what is the moral of the story? Speedy judgments of others based on very short meetings can be surprisingly accurate, though the accuracy depends somewhat on what those being judged are asked to do, and the criteria used. What you see is what you get!

The average interview may easily reveal social skills, self-confidence and articulation. However, it says little of job attitude, technical skills and specific abilities. Those, alas, takes a little longer to understand.

MEETINGS

Meetings frequently do, as the old adage has it, "take minutes and waste hours". Fully three-quarters or more of a senior manager's day may be taken up with meetings. However, despite deep cynicism about their productivity and usefulness, they remain sacrosanct. Many a caller has been fobbed off with the simple phrase "He's in a meeting".

Most of us know that meetings have little or nothing to do with the quality of decision-making or the communication of information. Their two major functions are, quite simply, first, the *diffusion of responsibility*, and second, *decision acceptance*. That is, they are there to ensure that all present take equal blame and responsibility for the decision taken (particularly if it goes wrong).

Frustration with the time-and-effort-wastefulness of meetings has led various organizations to attempt to implement certain strategies to improve them. Some follow a *structure*. Thus all meetings begin with *expectations* and end with *benefits and concerns*. Some try to shock with efficiency by calculating a return on investment on meetings by working out the real cost (in money) of holding a meeting. This involves calculating the salaries of the people present per hour and totalling it all up.

A recent fad is to *color code* meetings beforehand to indicate the type and amount of acceptable and unacceptable verbal and nonverbal behavior at the meeting. Some like to follow the black to red alert categories used by police and security services. Others like a simple traffic light system. But the trouble with both of these arrangements is that they bring conceptual associations. So a simple one-to-five with varied colors works best.

The system starts with some criterion such as level of contribution or level of support. The color or number chosen for the meeting indicate the desired behavior. Thus a high number might indicate the expectation that everyone will "chip in" regularly. A low number means the meeting is more about receiving information.

This system is usually used for three types of issues. The first is about *process*, not *content*. That is, how attendees treat each other. In brainstorming, there are very clear rules about not criticising others' ideas; about valuing quantity over quality; about acceptable piggy-backing on somebody else's ideas. The same applies here.

Some process prescriptions are about politeness, while others are about simple things such as for how long one may speak, or indeed how to get the floor in the first place. So a green meeting may indicate that what is required is short, crisp interjections. A blue meeting might indicate that it is acceptable to develop an idea.

Some meetings may prescribe while others proscribe *humour* – always a dangerous issue. Jokes can lighten the mood, but can also offend. They may introduce inappropriate levity where seriousness is required. One useful rule is about criticism. A blue meeting may indicate no criticism; green, a criticism of certain features; yellow, that no criticism is allowed *unless* a feasible alternative is apparent; and red, anything can be said.

But, more important, the system can be applied to content. Thus the rule may be about rule-breaking – about really thinking outside the box; about radical reformation, not just adaptation. The color-indicated rules might put certain things out of bounds. One of the advantages of the system is that it sets expectations beforehand. It's a bit like a dress code – black tie, smart casual, dress-down. The rule says a lot about how the meeting is expected to go, and therefore also its outcome.

The nonverbal behaviors at meetings are particularly important. These are often a function of the physical features of the meeting room and space. Is the meeting conducted standing up or sitting down; is there a table; can the participants all see each other; what are the ranks of people present; what topics are being discussed; what are the hidden agendas and so on? Behaviors are most interesting when they change, and indices of anxiety are also attention-grabbing. First there is *eye contact:* who looks at whom the most and the most frequently, and when do parties avoid eye contact. This is usually an index of discomfort. Next there is *posture*, reflecting how tense or relaxed people are. Third, meetings can show a lot of *displacement fidgeting* such as foot tapping, hair touching and so on when people are bored, frustrated or trying (unsuccessfully) to look relaxed and as if they are concentrating. Also look out for displacement yawns. It is known that people, faced with a tedious task, often yawn or suddenly feel extremely tired or sleepy. Desmond Morris (1982) reports on a curious case of soldiers feeling a tremendous urge to sleep immediately after they were told to go into an attack. He explains that this behavior was not a product of physical weariness but rather a displacement response to a threatening situation.

Orientation can change during meetings when people push back their chairs or turn them to face one person while turning their backs on someone else. Make sure you chose your seat strategically when trying to push your agenda across in a meeting. We know that sitting opposite the other party implies competition and antagonism. Cooperation can, conversely, be instilled by physical proximity and seating side by side. The person who is being persuaded in a meeting is more likely to agree if s/he is physically surrounded by the members of the other "camp". Certainly, while literally pushing your case through, you should be aware of the other party's behavior. If the other party is growing uncomfortable with the setting, an attempt would be made to move away from it.

The use of *gestures* may be particularly telling where speakers use repetitive, inappropriate or clumsy gestures to indicate signs of agreement. Some signals can also be in conflict with each other. For example, smiling – a general sign of joy and accord – that is accompanied by the aversion of the head and a pushing away of the, let's say, report on the desk, sends a mixed message. We know that people who agree display a cluster of certain gestures to indicate their community, and each of the behaviors from this cluster reinforces the same message. If there is a sign that does not fit the general pattern, it might signal ambivalence or, in fact, inner contradiction to what is being said.

As well as nonverbal gestures, we get a lot of information from vocal cues: changes in voice quality or accent, or coughing. A change to a shrill voice may indicate frustrated attempts to persuade, while the use of a low-register, warm voice attempts to seduce.

ADVERTISING AND POLITICAL MESSAGES

The amount spent on a 30-second commercial appearing halfway through a 30-minute TV programme may well "consume" the same budget as the programme itself. Television as well as magazine advertising is essentially nonverbal – that is, visual. Some advertisements may have as little as three phrases in them, often not even mentioning the product.

Equally, politicians and political parties spend billons on advertising and conference design, not to mention the cost of training politicians to be better communicators: all to put across their message.

Advertising, from soap powder to political parties, wants us to notice, remember but most important of all, to act on our awareness by buying the product or voting for the candidate.

Consider the task of selling a new chocolate bar, or a financial product or a holiday destination. The questions are endless: should one use actors, and if so, male or female; young or mature, black or white, "posh or common"? Should one use children or animals, or both or neither? Should one confirm or disconfirm stereotypes – the male scientist/expert, the female homemaker? Should one use humour or sex to attract attention? Should there be music or not, and if so which, why and when? What should the location of the advertisement be? And what are the effects of close-ups?

The party-political advertiser wants to know how to make its candidate maximally appealing and believable. How to portray energy and ability as well as confidence and approachability, and more important, sincerity. It is an amusing oxymoron that politicians have to learn to *fake sincerity*. They are trained in how to sit and stand, point and smile. Researchers have been able to infer the training leaders and lawmakers have had by playing back video clips of their behavior over the years. It is startling to see how some nonverbal behaviors have been accentuated or "removed", how gaze patterns and smiling have changed, and how quirky mannerisms have been adopted or erased.

The clothes they wear, their preferred hairstyles and even how closely they shave are all considered in detail to understand the message they send. Speeches are carefully scripted but also regularly rehearsed, and they are choreographed to reduce less favorable camera angles and accentuate open gestures.

A candidate can be "destroyed" in a television interview by looking down or away; freezing or hesitating and making rapid, jerky, nervous movements all convey negative messages. Make-up artists know candidates with "mature" faces are preferred over those with "baby faces". The size of the eyes and hips also give clues to maturity. However, older candidates need to have a youthful and healthy look.

Compared to the average of many of their age, politicians are less often bald or balding; wear glasses less often; are taller, slimmer and appear fitter. They tend to try to epitomize and accentuate the values of their society. This is, of course, less important in non-democratic countries where people are unelected to political positions.

OBSERVATION AND IDENTIFICATION

Could you accurately identify the person who sold you a newspaper this morning? Are you sure you would pick the right person in a classic identity parade? How many people languish in prison because of confident, but wrong, identification just because they looked like "a criminal type"? And how many people escape punishment for serious crimes because they were not identified by one or more witnesses?

The psychology of eyewitness identification is one of the most important areas of applied psychology. It bridges the intersection of psychology and the law. We know that jurors overestimate the importance of eyewitness reports: conviction rates rise from 20 percent to 70 percent with just one witness testimony. However, most people are unaware of how many different factors can falsely influence our recollection of events. Poor viewing conditions, brief exposure and situational stress are all established and well-researched factors, yet expectations, biases, personal stereotypes and leading questions can all intervene to create erroneous reports. The question here is, how does the body language of people influence recall? How does the memory connect to the system of nonverbal communication? The answer has to consider several factors.

First, several variables affect the formation and successful retrieval of any memory. These issues can be broadly divided into four categories: individual, contextual, social and interrogational. Table 6.5 provides examples for each of the categories.

TABLE 6.5 **Factors affecting the formation and successful retrieval of memories**

Individual factors	Contextual factors	Social factors	Interrogational factors
Sex	Type of crime	Expectations	Identity parade
Age	Complexity	Cultural biases	Photofit
Race	Duration	Latent prejudice	Sketch
Personality	Involvement in the event	Political beliefs	Influence of line-up administrator
Education	Light (illumination)	Emotionality of the language used	Order of line-up (simultaneous or sequential)
Training and experience in observation	Time of day Number of other people present		Error feedback

Witnesses vary in their ability to recall an event correctly. Women notice different things than men. Older people may have both worse sight and memory, while young adults perform best at this task. People tend to be better at identifying people from their own racial group. This may be because of the amount of exposure we have to different racial groups, or to racist attitudes.

The *situation* also influences one's recall and recognition faculty. The more stressed the eyewitness, the less they recall accurately. One experiment showed that stressed witnesses made around two in three false identifications while unstressed witnesses only made only one in ten errors. Also, there is an established "weapon-focus effect", so that if a gun or knife is involved in an incident, this seems to command a lot of attention and the chances of an accurate eyewitness identification decline.

Next, there are the *social* factors associated with the very particular constraints and regulations of the courtroom and the social status of the interrogator. The language used in court can have a powerful effect. In a famous study (Loftus & Palmer, 1974), different words were used to describe a car accident: bump, collide, contact, hit and smash. The choice of words influenced later recall. Thus, if the word "smash" was used, people were more like to say erroneous that they saw broken glass than when the word "bumped" was used.

There are also a host of important factors associated with the *interrogational* methods and tools. These have also been called "police procedures" or system variables. Consider something as simple but important as the "line up". Should the suspected culprit be in the line up or not? We know from evidence that when the actual perpetuator of the crime is not present, a suspect has a significantly higher chance of being incorrectly identified. If the witness is told the guilty person *may or may not* be present, the likelihood of a mistake sharply decreases compared to the situation when the witness assumes the guilty person must be there. The "line-up administrator" may easily "leak" information and influence the witness, – by perhaps lingering for longer near the criminal, or has a different pattern of gestures or eye contact when looking at the suspect. This is often done unconsciously by the administrator but picked up by the identifier. To avoid such "leaks', it is recommended that the procedure is carried out by someone not connected to, or ignorant about, the case.

Feedback on witnesses' errors aid the identification, especially if they choose "known innocents". Errors are more likely to occur if people are shown the full line-up (all the people are seen at the same time) rather than the people being seen one at a time. A sequential parade reduces problems of relative as opposed to absolute judgments.

What does this information tell us about the influence of body language on memory? First, identification happens on the basis of salient physical features. The descriptive reports of fugitives always involve details of their height, weight, hair color, skin tone, facial features and clothing.

Memory is, however, fallible, flexible and fragile. It is fragile in the sense that we do not remember everything that happens to us: sometime it is just the details that escape, while at other times we lose the memory gradually by not refreshing it often enough. It is flexible in the sense that it is changeable. Indeed, even fake memories can be created and planted in our minds. Memory is fallible in the sense that it is prone to all types of errors. Indeed, things that we remember do not always reflect the truth.

Memory can, for example, easily be influenced by the type of question asked. One example of early experimental work showed participants a clip of a car crash and then asked them to estimate the speed of the vehicles when they either "contacted" or "smashed" into each other. The estimation people gave was directly related to the force implied by the verb used, ranging from 32 mph to 41 mph. Leading questions have had many replicable findings with just a subtle change to the wording leading to a dramatic effect on testimony; "Did you see *a* ..." compared to "Did you see *the* ..." being just one example of how changing one seemingly insignificant word can influence respondents' answers.

Jurors, like other people, may be unaware of the factors that can interfere with eyewitness perception, such as the weapons focus effect, or factors that interfere with memory storage, such as the effect of prior exposures on suspect identification. This may explain why a review of 205 cases of wrongful arrest found that 52 percent of these cases were associated with mistaken eyewitness testimony.

Thus, lawyers and jurors are often encouraged to consider a range of issues before giving much attention to an eyewitness testimony. These include:

- Did the witness get a *good opportunity* to observe the person (for how long, at what distance and angle, and in what light)?
- Was the witness's capacity hindered by alcohol, drugs or injury?
- Do the witness and accused know each other?
- Are they of the same race?
- How long ago did the event happen?
- How was the accused identified (photographs, line up)?
- How confident was the witness at the initial identification?

It is been established that any testimony given in an assertive and positive matter is considered to be more accurate and truthful. We know the longer ago an event happened, the less we remember. We also know that scenes that are vivid, striking or novel are always better recalled than the mundane. Thus various techniques such as the cognitive interview have been formulated to improve eyewitness recall. This encourages various specific acts: recount the story both forward and backward, and from different points of view; reporting all remembered details, however trivial.

BODY LANGUAGE AND MEMORY

Memory for names

If you struggle with putting a name to a face, there is a technique that can ease the process of name recall. The tip is simple: you either associate the name with a particular facial feature of the person that is most striking (Mark has a beauty spot or mole or freckles, Jane has a big jaw and so on). However, it is obvious this approach would not work all the time, since some names are more popular than others and their frequency in the population varies. Alternatively, one could draw in their "mind's eye" the first letter of a person's name over their face. Connect the facial features – eyebrows, eyes, nose, chin, cheekbones – into the letter and keep the image as interactive as possible. This method of memorization relies on a well-known technique of mnemonics. It links two or more pieces of unrelated information into one whole, builds an associative bridge between them which is at the heart of successful learning.

The role of gesture in speech

Speech memory also seems to be connected to gestures. Patients with speech impairments, for example, gesticulate more when they cannot retrieve the right word to express their thought. Further, fluency of speech seems to worsen if people are not allowed to use their hands to gesture. Consider the tip-of-the-tongue phenomenon: there is evidence supporting the fact that gesticulation helps in successful information retrieval.

Gesturing while learning new information aids recall, perhaps by utilizing and forming another link between the environment, experience and the learning material. As noted earlier, one piece of advice frequently dispensed by speech-giving experts is to rehearse the speech with the gestures one will be using. Not only does it make the flow of presentation more natural, but also helps the recall of speech contents that need to be mentioned by creating kinaesthetic markers and engaging procedural memory.

What type of nonverbal body language do we remember the best?

Some research point out to the significance of eyes and eyebrows in the formation of memories of faces. Their uniqueness aids memory formation and subsequent retrieval. Shape of the jaw and the size of mouth also influence how well the face is remembered. Memory for a person's identity is affected by their facial expression, with happy faces being better remembered and better recalled. Smiling faces are also better remembered, even if the attention is not directed explicitly to the target's emotional state. This is backed up not only by experimental work, but also by neurological research, with FMRi (functional magnetic resonance imaging): studies showing the brain areas responsible for rewarding behavior light up whenever names of smiling people are memorized.

This finding has a clear implication at work. Joyful, cheery faces are easier to recall, since we want to remember people who are nice to us and are nice people in general. It could make all the difference for that promotion or career move opportunity.

Remembering what you read, hear and see

Imagine the following scenario. A large group of people with very similar backgrounds is randomly divided into three smaller groups. One group watches a 15-minute television programme (say a news broadcast); another listens to the identical programme, but without the benefit of pictures; while the third group has 15 minutes to read through the news broadcaster's script. They all get the same information: the television group gets visual, vocal and verbal (audio-visual) data, the radio group gets vocal and verbal (audio-only) data; and the print group gets verbal (script-only) data. Shortly after the exposure, members of each group are asked questions testing their free recall of all they can remember, and their recall of answers to specific questions. Which group remembers the most and is most accurate? In short, who shows better recall? Many studies have shown, to people's surprise, that the print group (those who read) remembered most, and the television group (those who watched) remembered the least. Put another way, having additional body-language information leads, paradoxically, to poorer memory. We are constantly told of the "power of television" and yet studies are fairly consistent on the point that we remember least of what we see, and more of what we read. What is the explanation for this somewhat paradoxical finding?

- *Depth of processing*
  Reading requires more mental effort, and more processing of material. Reading the words, and when appropriate conjuring up mental images, involves more concentration, which can and does result in better memory. Looking at the television is associated with relaxation rather than learning, even when we are told to concentrate.
- *Speed of reading*
  While radio and television presenters are taught to read at a particular pace and in a style that is maximally intelligible, not all people like this pace. When reading one's own material, one can select the pace. Difficult material, unfamiliar jargon or reading in a second language all demand a slower pace to make the text comprehensible.

- *Visual interference*
  Except in some advertisements, it is often the case that the pictures and the storyline are not perfectly synchronized. This is often the case with the news, but occurs very frequently in television as a whole. Particularly when the pictures involve violence or emotional anxiety, people pay little attention to the storyline! Thus while they may remember a great deal about the color of the newsreader's tie, or the images of people tending graves, they do not recall salient features of the story.
- *Paragraphing and textual chunking*
  Newspaper and magazine editors are very concerned with layout because they know this helps to present information in easily comprehensible "bites". However, this chunking of stories is more difficult on radio and television.

The lesson to be learnt is this; when meeting people face-to-face we are privileged to obtain verbal (what they say), vocal (how they say it) and visual cues (what they look like). But paying close attention to foot-tapping or changes in the pace or tone of voice can mean that we pay less attention to equally interesting and important material – what is being said. Conjurors know the importance of distracting attention. Being over-sensitive to nonverbal behavior also has its drawbacks – not remembering very well what was said.

CONCLUSION

Various work contexts present a rich, fertile ground for the application of knowledge on body language. Nonverbal information about the dynamics of the situation or the attitudes or intentions of other people inescapably feeds into the decision-making in business. Indeed, it seems that there is no getaway from nonverbal communication at work.

This is especially true of novel or threatening situations where we are very likely to resort to over-trusting nonverbal information. Salespeople, for example, have to be adept at dealing with many different people every day and try to appear to each of them as personable and likable. Since one of the factors that affect likability is the degree of similiarity, faking or unconsciously imitating the other party's body language seems to give leverage to these commission-paid professionals and often be a part of their work repertoire. Successful politicians and their PR teams are also renowned for their ability to take advantage of the nonverbal channel of influence over their constituents. Further, job interviews are often designed to put hopeful applicants under pressure: what stress signs do they exhibit, how do they handle challenging questions, what is their strategy to cope with excessive praise or sneer?

The next chapter will look more closely at emotions and their nonverbal components at work. Since emotions underlie most if not all body language expressions, we think it is useful to consider a number of significant and curious areas of work contexts where emotions run high, or indeed, low. We will scrutinise the body language of the bully; the victim, the frustrated, the stressed, the in-love, the winner; the follower and the gossiper. Hopefully, it will make you more aware of the hidden and often heated emotions at work.

7

APPLYING THE THEORY:
EMOTIONS AT WORK

BODY LANGUAGE AND BULLYING AT WORK

It seems from reports that physical, emotional and verbal bullying is
on the increase at work. This may be simply because of over-reporting
by incompetent, lazy, vengeful staff eager to punish their bosses and
sue their organizations, but it could also be because of the stress and
complexity of modern business life. The demanding environment produces stressed figures of authority who then bully, harass and victimize
innocent and vulnerable workers.

Bullying is usually defined in terms of the duration, frequency and
intentionality by people in positions of power to unduly accuse, crit-
icize or humiliate others. For most adults, bullying is a *psychological*
rather than a *physical* process, though of course it can be both. In
essence, work bullying is the product of power abuse, rooted in power
inequality, though victims can also be bullied by peers and subordinates. Customers can also be bullies, but they vie for a different type
of power. Bullying often involves anger, frustration and fear, all self-
evidently strong, negative emotions. Thus the nonverbal expression of
bullying is triggered and explained though this emotional connection.

Explanations for bullying

The central question for those interested in the issue of bullying at work
is whether can or should be explained by organizational, personality or
social factors. One hypothesis suggests that it is the structure of organizations that should be held responsible, arguing that certain business
models seem to condone or even promote bullying as a management

technique. The individualistic explanation runs along the lines of the "deadly attraction" premise, which suggests that the make-up (personality, intelligence, social skills) of both bullies *and* their victims leads them to seek each other out for their bizarre and beastly rituals. Further, the social theory seeks to understand the issue of bullying by studying the "people" factors at work (that is, competition between groups, power struggles, the dynamics of interaction) which lead to, or equally prevent, bullying. Imagine a line-up of working people. How easily could one correctly identify the bullies and the bullied? Do they look different? Do they behave differently?

Certainly, bullying is more likely to occur in some environments than others; where there is role conflict or ambiguity; where there is acute or chronic work overload; where workers have little autonomy; where there is an atmosphere of fear of redundancy or dismissal, or whole organization collapse. In these circumstances, bullying is more likely to happen. Whenever there is *win–lose* rather than *win–win* as a philosophy, there is conflict and, often, in the shadows, lurks bullying.

Further, some organizations have a history of autocratic leaders whose style becomes not only acceptable but required. They eschew consultative, democratic management and favor an authoritarian approach. Authoritarians demand rigid adherence to rules, an uncritical acceptance of authority, and a strong, open, aggressive condemnation of the weak, the outsider or those who do not obey the rules. Many project their inner emotions and impulses on to others and have a sort of free-floating, generalized feeling of anger and hostility. Authoritarian leaders admire power and toughness. They have a preoccupation with dominance over others.

Next, is the question of the personality make-up of both bullies and their victims. Various groups do not want this to be discussed or researched because it might do two things they do not want. First, it might indicate that the bullied, as well as the bully, is to blame for the situation. Second, it might imply that very little can be done to remedy bullying, because personality is difficult to change.

There has been a lot of research, both in schools and the workplace, on the *vulnerable* personality, who is likely to be bullied, and the *provocative* personality, who is likely to end up being a bully. The investigations seem to be conclusive. Bullied people tend to be less emotionally stable – more anxious and depressed. They also tend to have low emotional intelligence and few social skills, which means they find it harder to make and keep friends. They tend always to avoid conflict, to be submissive and to be passive. They appear to have poor coping skills, which exacerbates the problem further: they are both supersensitive to any sort of bullying and unable to cope adequately when bullied. They look sacred and nervous. They avoid eye contact, they slouch and they move away from other people.

And, yes, bullies are everywhere – in the playground, on the shop-floor and in the boardroom: aggressive, competitive and impulsive. Note that it is aggressiveness rather than assertiveness that under-lies the issue. What is more, lack of self-confidence is attributable to both bullies and the bullied. Bullies are hostile, the bullied are passive; neither seem very assertive.

Does the bullying experience change the individual? Is the neurosis of the bullied a consequence rather than a cause of bullying? Does this personality research amount to blaming the victim and condoning the perpetrator? While it is true that the victims of bullying do appear to share various personality traits, there are differences between them. As for the cause-and-effect relationship, only longitudinal studies can determine the direction of the link and there have not been any such studies as far as we are aware.

Everyone agrees with three issues. *First*, bullying is a serious problem that blights people's lives and affects workplace efficiency. *Second*, there are many things we can do to prevent it, though one must point out the difficulties associated with competing solutions: some just mask the problem, others might actually increase it, and some genuinely help. *Third*, it is a problem with multiple causes. Bullying is likely to arise from various factors arising at the same time, thus interventions also have to reflect that.

The body language of the bully and the bullied

What is the body language of the bully and the bullied? Can subtle, nonverbal clues give early warnings of a likely victim and the potential aggressor? One needs to distinguish between the nonverbal behaviors displayed as a warning of future conflict and those taking place during the bullying itself (see Table 7.1).

Bullying can be verbal; however, there is a powerful nonverbal com-ponent to it as well. Obscene gestures, exclusion from the group's social activities or damage to the victim's possessions convey the message of threat and attack very clearly. At work, such undercover bullying is more likely to take place than overt confrontation.

TABLE 7.1 **Body language of the bully**

Type of behavior	Area	Example	Function
Intimidation	Face	1. Deliberately widened or narrowed eyes	To intimidate with the "I am watching you" look
		2. "Fake" smile or sneer	To convey superiority and power imbalance
		3. Reduced or no eye contact	To exclude from the social interaction
	Arms	4. Crossed arms	To show disinterest or disregard
		5. Obscene gestures such as showing the middle finger or temple screw	To insult and offend
	Torso	6. Turned away, deliberately not facing someone	To keep the bullied out, to show lack of respect
Aggression	Hands	1. Aggressive gestures: punching the palm of the hand, fists display, stabbing the air	To display an indirect threat. A sure sign of immediate danger
	Torso	2. Showing off the physique or muscle flexing	To frighten

TABLE 7.2 **Body language of the bullied**

Type of behavior	Area	Example	Function
Discomfort	Face	1. Higher rate of blinking	Shows confusion and anxiety
		2. Downward gaze, avoidance of eye contact	Since the amount of eye contact is a function of dominance, victims look at their attackers less
		3. Sad facial expression, lack of smiling	
Defence	Hands	1. Self-hugging	Shows insecurity, the need to be comforted
	Torso	2. Raised shoulders	To protect the neck
		3. Lowered posture	To avoid being seen

The body language of the bullied is that of a distressed person: confused (why me?); angry (how dare they?); powerless (I can't do anything about it). The victim would, for example, slouch to make themselves less visible to the assailant, or avoid eye contact (see Table 7.2).

Nonverbal behaviors of a bully vary between the stages of intimidation and aggression. Similarly, the victim can show either discomfort or defence through their body language. Note the pairing of threats and responses to them: excessive staring on the part of the bully is usually met with reduced eye contact from the victim's side; rude gestures result in a distressed facial expression and so on.

But there is another party in the bully – bullied interaction that has been omitted so far: that is, the bystander. Because bullying usually takes place in the presence of other people, the bully relies on the "silent" agreement of the crowd, if not reinforcement. The behavior of the group witnessing the aggression largely determines its outcome. Equally, support for the bullied can be especially invaluable at the earlier stages of conflict. It is thus easier to prevent bullying and aggression at work than to deal with the consequences of employees' disengagement.

THE BODY LANGUAGE OF FRUSTRATING AND FRUSTRATED CUSTOMERS

If one had to rank-order daily hassles, then certainly high on the list would be such things as queuing. Everyone is becoming more and more time-conscious and time-urgent, so we seem to have to wait longer for service: at the bank, at the supermarket, at the airport, at the post office, and at the doctor's surgery.

Managers in banks and supermarkets struggle with this problem. Serving staff are expensive: demand is variable. Managers know that if you really want to annoy cash-rich-time-poor professionals you force them to wait in line with no alternative for something they want quickly: they want it now, if not sooner.

Road rage, air rage, hospital rage are triggered by the frustration of waiting. Such anger is exacerbated by drinking alcohol, childlike impulsivity and other factors. How does one spot the angry, time-conscious customer? It isn't difficult: the scowl, the finger tapping, the constant checking of the time.

Waiting is an essential ingredient of most service experiences. Time is a resource. It adds to the cost. However what is a long, unacceptable wait: the point at which customers will walk away?

Service providers have various options. The most expensive and possibly the most unreliable is to utilize *more service personnel*. The favored option is time-saving technology such as *self-ticketing*, but that has its limits. Next, customer service managers turned their attention to ways of making the wait seem less unpleasant. There are a whole range of these:

- Give people explanations for why they are waiting.
- Provide them with information about the anticipated length of wait.
- Keep them distracted with music, television and so on.

It is said there are four popular ways of helping the waiting process:

- Animate: television distractions, mirrors in elevators, playing recorded music.
- Discriminate: frequent-customer (Goldcard) treatment.
- Automate: use computer scripts to address 75 percent of questions.
- Obfuscate: fudge the cause and the solution.

There are some principles of waiting:

- Unoccupied time feels longer.
- Pre-process/post-process waiting feels longer than in-process.
- Anxiety makes waiting seem longer.
- Uncertain waiting feels longer than known, finite waiting.
- Unexplained waiting seems longer.
- Unfair waiting seems longer than equitable waiting.
- People will wait longer for more valuable services.
- Waiting alone feels longer than in groups.
- Physically uncomfortable waiting feels longer.
- Waiting seems longer to new or occasional participants.

Take one of these hypotheses: *Uncertain waiting feels longer than known waiting.* Here, the anxiety and frustration of waiting is compounded by not knowing how long the wait will be. The suggestion posits that it is not the delay and waiting per se, but rather the uncertainty and ambiguity that evoke anger and stress. Thus, if you give people a "reasonable" estimate of waiting time, they will calm down, experience less tension, and accept events as inevitable. Yet, experimental studies testing this theory showed that giving waiting-time estimates caused more, rather than less, negative affective reactions among customers. They were more, not less, angry, possibly because it was yet more evidence of the incompetence of the organization.

It may well be that waiting-time estimates help organizations with a good time-keeping record, while they just confirm the reputation of a bad one. Results show the effects of being given waiting-time information are quite modest but nevertheless significant.

What of the benefits of providing an explanation (often seen more as an excuse)? As we have all learnt at airports, explanations offered serve best to push the blame down the line. That is, it is not the fault of the service provider standing in front of you.

There are three options to appease frustrated waiting customers. The order of their effectiveness is: explanation without blame; no explanation; explanation as a personal fault.

Watch queues at airports, banks and supermarket. Note what the restless, increasingly angry customer does. Note how s/he attempts to gain the support of those around them, which can be done in two ways. One is to solicit the backing of other unfortunate bystanders, while the other vents the frustration on the service staff.

It is thus clear that front-line customer service staff have a tough job on their hands. Even before any verbal interaction they can spot customers' frustration by observing their body language. Calm, relaxed people tend to project non-confrontational, composed body language, whereas frustrated, rushed customers exhibit nonverbal signs of impatience and irritation (see Table 7.3). The challenge for the employees here is to deal effectively with the query in a reassuring and soothing manner.

Frustration and anger only escalate if both the customer and the service representative are on the defensive. On the other hand, professional, calm, reassuring body language can help to deal with the customer's dissatisfaction. A calm but firm tone of voice sends a message of support. Open body posture and steady eye contact project authority, competence and appreciation of the customer's difficulty. Empathy is the key emotion to deal successfully with frustration: let your customer know they are valued, let them feel taken care of and listened to.

TABLE 7.3 **Body language of frustrated people and how to deal with it**

Body language of the frustrated person	Body language used to deal with the frustrated person
Hands on hips	Neutrality of facial expression
Growling, angry tone of voice, higher pitch	Open, relaxed body posture
Neck rub – literally "a pain in the neck"	Good eye contact
Drumming the fingers, tapping the foot, signs of impatience	Emphatic voice and verbal message

RECOGNIZING STRESS AT WORK

The word "stress" is derived from the Latin word stringere, which means "to draw tight".

Some believe that stress can and should be defined *subjectively* (that is, what one says about how one feels); others consider that an *objective* definition is needed (perhaps physical measures of saliva, blood or heart rate). Some researchers insist that a *global* definition is more appropriate (that is, there is one general thing called stress); while others emphasize that stress is *multidimensional* (it is made up of very different features) Also, it can be defined by the outside stimulus factors that *cause* it or rather how people *respond* to it. That is, if a person does not experience an event or situation as stressful, can it really be called a stressor?

There are various models or theories that attempt to describe and understand stress. The simplest perhaps is the *demand-control* theory, which looks at the various psychological and physical demands put on a person to behave in a particular way, and the control or decision latitude they then have in delivery. High-demand, low-control situations are the worst. Another way of describing this is challenge and support:

- *Much support, little challenge*: People in this role are in the fortunate position of having good technical and social support, but because they are under-challenged it probably means that they under-perform. They may actually be stressed by boredom and monotony. Such employees are likely to appear listless or even depressed.
- *Much support, much challenge*: This combination tends to get the most out of people as they are challenged by superiors, subordinates, shareholders and customers to "work smarter", but are given appropriate support to enable them to succeed. Theoretically, this category of workers should be and look the most happy and satisfied at work.
- *Little support, much challenge*: This unfortunate, but very common, situation is a major cause of stress for any employee, because s/he is challenged to work consistently hard but is offered only minimal emotional, informational (feedback) and physical (equipment) support. This is the typical stress response that will be considered below.
- *Little support, little challenge*: People in some bureaucracies lead a quiet and unstressed life because they are neither challenged nor supported, which usually means neither they nor their organization benefits.

184

Stress is caused by a range of things peculiar to the *make-up of the individual*, such as their personality, ability and life history. There are also specific features about the *environment* (job, family, organization), usually but not exclusively considered in terms of the work setting. Consequently, the combination of the two produces an assorted cluster of even more complex stress factors; that is, how individuals and their immediate social environment perceive, define but more importantly try to *cope* with stress, strain and pressure.

The individual

First, there are the anxious worriers, more commonly known by the name of *neurotics*. They are the people with "negative affectivity", which is a mix of anxiety, irritability, neuroticism and self-deprecation. They tend to be less productive, have less job satisfaction and be more prone to absenteeism.

Other people can be labelled *fatalists*. This category of employees believes that the events occurring in their lives are a function of luck, chance, fate, God, powerful others or powers beyond their control, comprehension or manipulation. Not surprisingly, they are much more stressed at work compared to those who believe it is in their power to influence the outcomes of events through their behavior and/or ability, personality and effort.

Competitive, frantic individuals with spirited drive and an enhanced sense of time urgency also tend to experience more stress. They may have an intense, sustained desire to achieve, an eagerness to compete, a persistent drive for recognition, a continuous involvement in deadline activities, a habitual propensity to accelerate mental and physical functions, and consistent alertness.

The job (organization) or social environment

Some jobs are more stressful than others. Usually, the greater the extent to which the job requires such activities as making decisions, constant monitoring of machines or materials, repeated exchange of information with others, unpleasant physical conditions, and performing unstructured rather than structured tasks, the more stressful the job tends to be.

Further, some people have to engage in role juggling: switching rapidly from one role and one type of activity to another (from boss to friend, teacher to partner, law enforcer to father confessor). Stress can also result from role ambiguity. This can occur when people are uncertain of the scope of their responsibilities, what is expected of them, and how to divide their time between various duties.

Over- and under-load stress stems from having too little or too much to do. Responsibility for others also often leads to stress. Many people are (or should be) responsible for their subordinates: they have to motivate them, reward and punish them, as well as communicate and listen to them. Lack of social support can also be a powerful stress trigger developing from being socially isolated or ignored. Having friends and supporters in times of difficulty helps managers to see hectic events as being less threatening and more controllable than if they had to deal with them on their own or with little support. Lack of participation in decisions also causes stress by inducing feelings of helplessness and alienation. Stressful organizations are plain to see: the way people walk, talk and interact shows how brittle, tough and trained they are.

Coping

People differ in their typical, habitual ways of coping with the stressful situations in their lives. These coping strategies vary in their effectiveness. One distinction that has been made is between *problem*-focused coping (aimed at problem-solving or doing something to alter the source of stress) and *emotion*-focused coping (aimed at reducing or managing the emotional distress associated with, or cued by, a particular set of circumstances). Some emotion-focused responses involve denial, others involve a positive reinterpretation of events, and still others involve seeking social support. Similarly, problem-focused coping can potentially involve several distinct activities, such as planning, taking direct action, seeking assistance, screening out particular activities, and sometimes stopping the action for an extended period.

Consequences of stress

These include a noticeable decline in the physical state of the person, such as:

- Physical appearance;
- Chronic fatigue and tiredness;
- Frequent infections, especially respiratory infections;

- Health complaints, such as headaches, backaches, stomach and skin problems;
- Signs of depression; and
- Change in weight or eating habits.

Second, there are emotional symptoms of stress too. These are:

- Boredom or apathy: lack of affect and hopelessness;
- Cynicism and resentfulness;
- Depressed appearance, sad expression, slumped posture; and
- Expressions of anxiety, frustration, tearfulness.

The third cluster of stress reactions are behavioral symptoms. These include:

- Absenteeism and accidents;
- Increase in alcohol or caffeine consumptions;
- Increase in smoking;
- Obsessive exercising or eating;
- Irrationally quick to fly off the handle, lose temper; and
- Reduced productivity: inability to concentrate on or complete a task.

The body language of stress is most noticeable. Here are some nonverbal behaviors associated with the experience of stress:

- Pale complexion;
- Thin appearance;
- Less smiling;
- Struggling to hold the posture;
- Appears shaky;
- Slouching; and
- Lacking energy in gait and overall body movement.

By recognizing and acting on the early warning signs of stress, one could take preventing steps to reduce or cancel out detrimental health consequences associated with it.

OFFICE POLITICS

Politics is a bad word. In polls of public opinion, politicians come between used car dealers and estate agents in terms of their trustworthiness – or indeed untrustworthiness. A heady mix of hypocrisy, spin and hubris means that many people have lost faith in their elected representatives' ability to do much for them. Everywhere, except where it is compulsory, the tendency is to reduce, or even to stop, voting for our politicians.

Nevertheless, along with national and local politics, there are also office or workplace politics. This phenomenon is about individual influence, about group conflict and about power struggles. We hear people say things like: "He plays politics all the time"; "Office politics caused the failure"; "She was only promoted because of office politics". It seems that everyone is engaged in some or form or another of extending their immediate job responsibility.

What are the key features of the concept? *First*, perhaps is the secrecy, the covert agendas, the underhandedness of it all. Politics conducted in smoky rooms, behind closed doors, in private clubs, on the golf course. There are the insiders and the outsiders; the players and the pawns; those in the know and those in the dark. Politics are exclusionary. Office politics are about processes, procedures and decisions that are not meant to be scrutinized. Politics are about opaqueness not transparency.

Second, there is impression management. Another word for this may be hypocrisy. Office politicians (all unelected) "speak with forked tongue". The clever ones understand the difference between sins of omission and commission. The others just dissimulate. What you see, hear and read is *not* what you get. Internal communications (except those carefully encrypted) are half truths, little more than management propaganda. Office politics are about censorship; about disguise.

Third, office politics are about self-interest. They are concerned with power and all the trappings such as money and prestige; about select groups high-jacking activities, processes and procedures to secure their (and only their interests). Covert groupings of individuals based on clan, ideology or simply greed, cooperate with each other to obtain an unfair share of the resources of an organization. In this sense, office politics act against long-term organizational interests, at least from a shareholder perspective.

The negative view is clear. Office politics cause distrust, conflict and lowered productivity. People do not openly share; they are guarded. They spend too much time and energy ingratiating themselves with the in-group and trying to work the system. And the in-group are as much concerned with increasing or holding on to power as steering the company. The opposition is internal, not external. Office politics are dysfunctional.

But there is another perspective and it's much more positive. Office politics are about building and strengthening networks and coalition. About getting together movers and shakers prepared to do the hardest thing of all – make change happen. About driving through necessary but unpopular strategies. About identifying those with energy and vision; those who command various constituencies.

Yes, politics are about power – the power to influence, persuade and cajole. Most organizations seek out and admire a chief executive officer (CEO) who is well-respected and well-connected. One who knows how to "play the game"; how to get people (investors, journalists, and "real" politicians) onside. In this sense, being political is about being shrewd, proactive and strategic.

CEOs have to present a positive picture of their organization. And they have to align, steer and change that organization. They often need help, and they turn to those who have a reputation for being helpful.

It's not possible to outlaw office politics. You might want to blame everything from personal failure to falling share price onthem. There is no doubt that some offices are dysfunctional places to be, but better to study and try to understand management power than to condemn it. Powerful people show off their power nonverbally. They display it, but only appropriately. Office politics is the subtle use of power: knowing how and when to flatter others; how to bargain; what to offer. Watch a prime minister or president in public and you will learn about office politics as well as national ones.

BODY LANGUAGE AND WORKPLACE
ROMANTIC RELATIONSHIPS

How should the corporation cope with corporate cupid? Is sex at work (attraction in organizations, office romances, intimacy at work, co-worker affairs) a matter for human resources (HR) policy? Can, or indeed should, one try to legislate on matters of the heart or hormones? Should romance or affairs be dealt with in an open, adult way or made taboo? How do secret lovers leak their relationship by their body language?

Workplace romances can and do have an impact on organizational dynamics, which in turn affect outcomes – productivity, morale and efficiency. Senior people can compromise their integrity. New channels of unofficial communication can be opened up and closed down depending on who is having what sort of relationship with whom.

The appointment of favored sexual partners can seriously affect how people perceive the transparency and justice of the selection or promotional system.

It is not easy to obtain evidence on the number of workplace romances within big and small organizations. Studies in large organizations in the USA and Europe found that two-thirds to three-fourths of employees admit to having (closely) observed a workplace romance in their organization. Only about 10 percent of people admit to having had such a romance, but a third of them later agreed that all their romantic relationships had been initiated in the office.

It is really no wonder that they happen. The best predictor of attraction is proximity. If one spends eight hours a day in the presence (or near presence) of others, it is no surprise that one begins to like and possibly feel attracted to them. One meets people of different ages and sexes that one otherwise might not encounter. Why should the office not be a good place to find a partner? People with similar levels of education, interests and values are recruited to organizations, so the process of assortative mating begins at corporate selection. People in unhappy relationships may be particularly attracted to their colleagues at work.

Workplace relationships can be grouped and categorized in various ways, but two dimensions seem most crucial. The first is whether the two people are at the same level on the corporate ladder or not: these are called lateral or hierarchical relationships. The second is whether the relationship is open (recognized, explicit) or closed (unacknowledged, secret). Thus we have four distinct groups, which are demonstrated in Table 7.4.

Open-lateral refers to, for example, two junior accountants, or nurses, or journalists, who begin to live together and (in time) announce their engagement. *Open-hierarchical* dimension describes the relationship of the head of marketing, say, who makes no secret of his affair with a new recruit from sales. Two divorced board members, who are romantically

TABLE 7.4 **Types of romantic workplace relationships**

	Lateral	Hierarchical
Open	Unconcealed, overt romance between two similarly-ranked employees	Publicly-known relationship between two people of asymmetrical standing
Closed	Secret attraction between two people of equal status	Secret relationship between employees holding different positions in the organization

linked but trying to keep it quiet, would be an example of a *closed-lateral* dimension. However, the case of the engineering director, say, who is secretly bedding his married secretary, would fall in the *closed-hierarchical* category.

A romance is different from an affair. The latter implies that one or both parties are married/committed to others, infusing the whole problem with an added moral dimension. A charge of *nepotism* can arise where people (say, husband and wife) are appointed together and acknowledge their relationship. Another concern – almost unspeakable – is whether couples are having a sexual relationship. The paradox is that the *more* intimacy they show at work (that is, physical touching, kissing and so on), the *less* likely they are to be "physical" outside work, and vice versa. Inevitably, employers who are themselves having a workplace relationship are more forgiving or even show a positive attitude towards them. Various studies have shown that female employees are significantly less favorably inclined towards office romance and sexual intimacy than males. It is assumed that they have more to lose, though of course the opposite case could be made.

There is also some evidence that when in *lateral* relationships, job performance goes *up*, but in *hierarchical* relationships, it goes *down*. It may be that work motivation improves because workplace romantics increase their enthusiasm for being at work. Equally, workplace relationships can increase employee motivation because the participants feel better about themselves and are willing to work longer shifts in order to extend their time together. They may even get more involved with their work, since their "partners" are part of the job. Also, the increase in positive affect experienced by people in a workplace relationship "spills over" to increase their general level of satisfaction.

The more popular lay belief is that workplace relationships have a detrimental or deleterious effect on the work of both parties. Energy is wasted in a closed relationship on the effort of keeping the whole thing a secret, and too much time is spent on irrelevancies.

However, there are three factors that determine whether such relationships help or hinder factors relevant to organizational outcomes. The *first* is how good is the relationship. A good, healthy relationship must boost general morale, energy and enthusiasm, and vice versa. Put pressure on a relationship and you stress individuals.

Second, there are the corporate cultural values regarding relationships. These are different from corporate policy, HR recommendations, or professional guidelines. The more that relationships are counter-cultural to the organization, the more it is a problem, and vice versa.

Third, there is the resentment among the employees not in relationships, who feel, rightly or wrongly, that favoritism occurs. This therefore means that, while the happy pairs might increase their productivity and morale, these factors decrease for the majority not in a relationship. If nepotism leads to positive discrimination, it can also lead to a lot of people becoming alienated and disengaged. Some couples go to great lengths to show that their relationship does not compromise their decision-making abilities.

The body language question is, what are the behaviors of attraction? How does one "know" two people are attracted to one another? What are the separate, perhaps evolutionary, markers of physical and sexual attraction?

To answer these questions, one needs to distinguish between the stages of a couple's relationship development. Body language of a duo at the courtship or flirting stage differs from the one displayed by an established couple. In line with life wisdom, intimates in an established close relationships show less liking signals since their relationship are already formed and their association is already revealed to others.

The beginning of a romantic relationship is, however, marked by playful signals of availability and attraction. Knapp and Hall (2009) cite three types of gazing that is most typical of flirting: (i) a broad look encircling the whole room; (ii) short, quick glances at a specific person; and (iii) longer glances continuing for at least three seconds. Females also often play with their hair, fiddle with their clothes and accessories, and laugh in response to the comments made by their potential "lovers".

Clothes and make-up also play a part in attracting the mate. A recent study suggests that women who expose 40 percent of their body get the most attention from the opposite sex. In fact, the findings state that women revealing 40 percent of their body attracted twice as many males in a nightclub as those women who carefully covered up. The experimenters counted bare flesh on different parts of the body as worthy of different percentages or, put simply, of different attraction power. Arms counted towards 10 percent, legs 15 percent and torso 50 percent. While the percentage assignment is quite vague (how do you assign a definite number to different depths of cleavage?), this research raises a number of important points. Showing some skin has the undeniable power of gaining instant attraction, hence societies have always prescribed rules over what is an acceptable amount of skin exposure, and situations and places in which it can be shown. Next, from the evolutionary point of view, both mates have to be certain of each other's fidelity for the attraction to persist and develop. Thus revealing too much usually turns out to be a failing strategy. Finally, it underscores the significance of the issue of dress code and formal attire in the workplace. Changes in the style of dress or excessive body revelation may therefore be attributed to some external influences such as romantic involvement.

It should be pointed out that most research on courtship has been done in the physical environments typical of dating, such as clubs and bars. Studies looking at the nonverbal signals of flirting in more formal contexts (libraries and meetings, for example) reported much less of such amorous behavior. Following the same logic, workplace romantic couples would exhibit less overt flirtation, especially if one is hiding the feelings or relationship, but there would be more discreet, tender signal exchange. The office does not provide extensive opportunities for courtship, while informal outings and after-hours drinks do.

Overall, nonverbal behaviors indicative of attraction or greater liking come in clusters. Albert Mehrabian, a famous body language researcher, correlated the rate of occurrence of certain nonverbal signals and the degree of liking between two people. He found that the frequency of positive signal displays is related to the intimacy between the couple. He labelled this type of closeness behavior *"immediacy"*. Below is the list of the behavioral clusters he studied:

- Lean towards/ away from the person;
- Proximity or further distance;
- Regularity of looking at the person of interest;
- Openness or defensiveness of body and arm gestures;
- Body orientation (facing or turned away from the other person);
- How relaxed or rigid the posture; and
- Facial and vocal expressions (negative/positive).

However, in more established couples these behaviors are not as evident. Intimacy is usually conveyed by the quality rather than the quantity of positive nonverbal signals. Timing, scale and genuineness of immediacy behaviors become much more important the further the relationship progresses. Situational factors also affect the nonverbal display of greater liking in close couples. Partners would, for example, look for, and display more of, immediacy signals in situations threatening to their relationship, perhaps for reassurance. Also, couples tend to acquire more idiosyncratic signals to indicate their allegiance to each other. Nevertheless they would resort to immediacy behaviors to send an explicit message about their level of closeness to new acquaintances, who are not familiar with the couple's bond.

Interestingly, research points to the dominance of women in early attraction signalling. They select an appealing mate and send signs of openness for contact. Men, however, can also gain an advantage over their competitors to attract females by sending more of particular nonverbal messages. Research shows that men who engage in more glancing at their object of interest, display more body openness, and boost their status by friendly, but unrequited, touching of other males are given more female attention. These findings are perhaps not that surprising when one considers other species' mating behavior. It is usually the male of the species, who develops specific "attraction" markers such as brighter coloring or bigger body parts. It is also usually the male who performs a mating dance or a song routine. All there is left for females to do is to select the most powerful, skilled or attractive partner and signal their readiness to mate or form a bond.

Workplace romances happen for different reasons, can have different impacts on work productivity, and are displayed differently according to the stage of the relationship. It is both reasonable, if not trivial, to state that romantic attraction clearly has no boundaries. On the contrary, work structure seems to increase the power of romance by creating greater opportunities to interact within a more intimate space over prolonged time periods.

MIND CONTROL

How do leaders use nonverbal behavior to help them organize and manage groups? The study of cults and their leaders is particularly interesting from a nonverbal perspective. They often behave in heavily prescribed ways: the group members have to dress alike and address each other in a very particular way.

There is a great deal of interest in "cults", which can take many forms: they may be religious or racial, political or mystical, self-help or pseudo-psychological, but they all have half a dozen recognizable characteristics:

- Powerful and exclusive dedication/devotion to an explicit person or creed.
- They use of "thought-reform" programmes to integrate, socialize, persuade, and therefore control, members.

- A well thought through recruitment, selection and socialization process.
- Attempts to maintain psychological and physical dependency among cult members.
- Cults insist on reprogramming the way people see the world.
- Consistent exploitation of group members specifically to advance the leaders' goals.
- Cults nearly always opt for milieu control signals: a different, unfamiliar setting with different rules, terms and behavior patterns.
- Ultimately causing psychological and physical harm to cult members, their friends and relatives, and possibly the community as a whole.

Most cults start their inductions by trying to stop both individualistic and critical thinking. Like the army, their job is first to break the new recruit than remake him or her as one of them. This involves the introduction of a "sacred creed" that members have to live by. Through open confession and subordination of the individual to the doctrine, the cult ensures control and "purity". Nearly all nonverbal behaviors, such as how people walk or gesture, are very clearly prescribed. Cults deliberately induce powerful emotions like fear and guilt, but also pride. They tend to develop their own language, dress and signals, which shows their exclusivity. They rejoice in their uniform, and their uniformity of speech, dress and behavior. They are encouraged to look, think and speak alike.

By why do people join cults? Could working for certain organizations be seen as cult following? Some organizations induct people and make behavior requirements of them that are essentially similar to the techniques used by cults.

All too often, we explain strange, unexpected behaviors (such as joining a cult) in terms of the dispositions (personality) of others; they (the poor, gullible, naïve, indoctrinated members) have quite defective personalities. But we explain more common behaviors in terms of the appeal of an accepted group's philosophy, leaders or benefits. Thus, sad "inadequates" join cults; but altruistic, caring people become churchgoers.

Rather than trying immediately to blame extremists for being different, it is equally important to try to understand the psychological appeal of cults, extremist groups and political cells, as well as some business organizations. Any analysis of the make-up of individuals in cult groups shows a surprising large diversity in terms of age, career,

education, ideology and ability level. They can attract postgradu-
ates and illiterates; teenagers and "senior citizens"; the solidly middle
class and those on the fringes of society. It is not so much people's
demography that is important as their psychological needs.

Studies of those who have signed up for all sorts of cults and extremist
groups have, however, shown that all cults have similar and sophisticated recruitment promises, induction techniques and agendas of
social influence. They use methods of "indoctrination" and "mind-
control" no different from many respectable groups, though these may
be applied much more intensely. The mind-controlling techniques of
extremist groups are little different form those of the army, religious
organizations and prisons. These techniques are in fact well known;
demanding total, consistent compliance and conformity; using heavy
persuasive techniques; creating dissonance; and involving emotional
manipulation. These techniques can easily be observed in the nonverbal behaviors of people "signing up" to cults. They differ only in
intensity and duration, and thus in effectiveness.

What do all groups (cult and non-cult) and organizations offer to a
potential recruit? The answer is friendship, identity, respect and security. Organizations also offer money, security and something to do.
And they offer a world-view: a way of discerning right from wrong;
good from bad. Hence all the talk of *vision* and *mission*, both of which
are essentially cult words. These are powerful incentives for all people,
whatever their background. They offer more: a structured lifestyle and
the ability to acquire new skills. Through their (very different) ideolo-
gies, and products and processes, they also offer moral explanations of
how the world works, what is important, and what is desirable.

Essentially, five aspects make extreme groups dangerous to their
members:

- *First*, they demand that group members sever all ties with other
  people (family, friends) and organizations (schools, churches). This
  naturally makes them more dependent on the cult itself and helps
  to create the person's new identity. They start again, wipe the slate
  clean. This rule is also found in extreme Christian monastic orders.
- *Second*, the members are required to show immediate and unques-
  tioning obedience to rules and regulations which may be arbitrary,
  petty or pointless, and many of which are body language rules. The
  idea of this is to ensure allegiance and obedience. This strategy is
  used to "break-in" army recruits. It is the very stuff of boot camps.

196

- *Third*, group members often have to do long hours of tedious work. It may be drilling, begging for money or cooking, followed by compulsory reading, chanting or mediating. Recruits usually become physically, emotionally and mentally exhausted. Sleep deprivation is a good start. It's all part of the induction process.
- *Fourth*, all groups need money to exist. Some are very much into money, both as an end and as a means. This may therefore quickly involve recruits getting involved in illegal or semi-legal activities. Groups that are state supported or those with a long history of operation may, however, be different. Members need to understand how, when and why money is required, and to set about getting it quickly.
- *Fifth*, groups make "exit costs" very high. Leaving is associated with failure, persecution and isolation. It is more than just a waste of time and effort. They make the member feel as if nothing will ever be the same and s/he will be an outcast. Leaving the cult is made to sound a very unattractive, indeed impossible, option.

But it is true that certain individuals are more receptive to the message of cults than others? Recruiters know that what they appear to have in common is they are at some transitional phase in their life: something has gone and not been replaced. The person might have moved location, or given up work or education. They may have just left the bosom of their family because of age or poverty or divorce. They may have drifted away from their religion or ideological roots. They are dislodged from their social group ... and looking for another.

In short, such people often feel alienated; they experience all the meaninglessness, powerlessness and helplessness that goes with the state. They can feel increasingly isolated from the commercial, political and technical world that offers little to them. Disaffected, often angry and resentful, they can seek each other out.

Enter the group recruiter. S/he is introduced into a group with simple (but "sensible") answers. Simple rules and a simple lifestyle and social support are offered. Most recruits are happy to trade off their liberty (and assets such as they have) for the (illusory) glory, power and security of that group. The group (cult) appears to offer all the recruits what they need and want.

Rather shy, unassertive people who seem inhibited and awkward in social situations are particularly attracted to groups with formulaic interaction patterns, with their predictability and rule following.

People who join extreme groups are not strange, disturbed, sheep-like idiots. We are all social animals and members of many groups. But the more secretive the group, the more we are likely to label it a cult. The more zealous the members, the more likely we are to call them deviants. And if they are involved in quasi-military activity, they are labelled terrorists.

No one sees themselves as a cult member. Indeed, even members of fairly extreme groups such as Trappist monks or Amish farmers would never think of themselves as cult members. But they owe their survival to many of the principles outlined above.

WINNING AND LOSING AT WORK

It is clear why ceremonies are so important to us. Ceremonies celebrate history, link the past with the present, the exerted effort with the obtained result. They honor and promote perseverance, ambition and hard work. They create milestones and cherish collective memories.

Business ceremonies have similar functions too. Some celebrate the day of the company's establishment, some its quarterly and yearly performance, and some lucrative deal-clinching. Such gatherings often boost employees' morale and motivation; they bring teams together in a (hopefully) joyful and relaxed atmosphere; they reward commitment and loyalty.

There is always a certain amount of symbolism in any kind of ceremony. Whether it is a wedding, a funeral, an inauguration, or an awards ceremony, there are traditions and rules associated with each of them. These rules vary from culture to culture, but are always deeply prescribed. The Japanese tea ceremony, for example, can last up to four hours and includes details not only on technical aspects of the ritual, such as the temperature of the water and the type of kettle to be used, but also social and aesthetic rules such as what clothes are to be worn by the host and how flowers are to be arranged in the room.

Celebratory body language is almost always associated with a body lift. It can mean raising your arms above your head, elevating your posture or jumping up and down in an erratic fashion. These nonverbal behaviors are especially vivid in sport, such as at Olympic award ceremonies. There three winners stand on a pedestal in an obvious hierarchical order, with the gold medal winner being raised above the other two contestants. Football players celebrating a decisive goal leap into the air, extending their arms and even their forefingers, as if to show they are the number one now.

Politicians have also adopted raised gestures. One arm lifted or two palms together raised above the head are commonly found among leaders celebrating their victory. Their supporters copy the stance of the leader, often unintentionally. Consider the behavior of the crowd rejoicing in the good news. Flags or other objects of group significance are waved in the air. Sometimes even the person being celebrated is taken by the group and carried around or thrown in the air. Nowadays these practices are observed at many events, from rock concerts to stag nights.

The prizes themselves are worth a mention. The trophies received as part of the completion of a successful business deal always carry the logos or the brand names of the parties involved. Thus the miniature statues serve as a reminder of success, and they build and maintain authority. They allow your guests to pick up on your track record without you saying a word. They are easy tools for discreet impression management. Educational diplomas work in a similar fashion too. A degree awarded by a good university speaks volumes, not only about your education, but also about your abilities, background and social connections.

Both the quality and quantity of the prize matter. Some try to impress with the color or the size of the trophy, while others value understatement and quiet taste. When did more become less, and where did this obsession with "the bigger, the better" start? People from all cultures seem to interpret size symbolically. The great Egyptian pyramids and the ambitiousness of the buildings in modern-day Dubai both come across as symbols of the power and success of the society, even if only temporarily. Religions have always employed the power of size and beauty to capture the hearts and minds of people, as illustrated by the magnificent grandeur of the Vatican. Political aspirations also shape and reflect the scale of design, such as, for example, Stalinist architecture or the Ryugyong Hotel in Pyongyang, North Korea, better known as the world's ugliest building, but which is nevertheless one of its tallest skyscrapers.

Thus, size matters: it intimidates and astounds. It is no wonder then, that winners raise their chins and glasses, while losers slouch and slump. A graceful winner, or a graceful loser, however, displays their joy or disappointment tactfully, to avoid hurting the feelings of the other party, though it is understandably hard to hide discontent at losing, especially if the competition was fierce or the outcome close.

TABLE 7.5 **Nonverbal behaviors of winners and losers in the Western world**

Winners' nonverbal behaviors	Losers' nonverbal behaviors
Dominant, high-status posture	A smile, which is rarely genuine
Head is raised	Head is lowered
One arm or both arms lifted with an open palm facing the others or with clenched fist punching the air	Arms-akimbo posture telling of irritation
V-for-victory signal with the fingers	Covering of the face or mouth
Slight bow in acceptance of the praise	A facial expression of disbelief and displeasure

Table 7.5 gives a list of celebratory and commiserative nonverbal behaviors common in the Western world.

It has already been stated that in business it pays to look the part. Thus by displaying the body language of a winner, such as straightening the back or raising the head, a more favorable impression might be created by an individual.

The other apparent recommendation is to display the physical signs of success. If all else is equal or unknown, which psychologist would you rather have examine or counsel you: one whose door sign reads PhD, or the one with no qualification mentioned at all? In an ambiguous situation, especially if time is tight, humans look for telltale signs, and, what is more, first impressions are extremely pervasive. It is also an acknowledged fact that the best predictor of future behavior is past behavior. It never hurts to restate your achievements.

It also used to be said that if you want to become something, you simply need to be it. By fooling yourself into believing you are something you are currently not, you modify your behavior in line with your perception of that other person's image. That tricks others around you into thinking you or something about you has changed. This triggers them to treat you differently, which reinforces and strengthens your chosen line of new behavior. Bear in mind, though, that this pattern is applicable to both the virtuous and the vicious cycle, and can only work to your advantage if you truly believe in yourself. If, on the other hand, you lack this crucial ingredient, *self-efficacy*, you are more likely to end up experiencing anxiety or, even worse, depression.

CONCLUSION

Look around you. Some people you know are more dominant, more forceful, and more persuasive than others. Some are lazy, grumpy and constantly irritable. It is one of the axioms of psychology that people are all shaped by the same personality dimensions; are all influenced by the rules of the immediate group they live in, dictated by the immediate culture; and subject to the same evolutionary pressures to adapt to the ever-changing environment. Yet, through the mixing and stirring of these three levels, each person becomes unique and inimitable.

Nevertheless, a certain mix of individual differences seems to equate with life success. Theory tells us that extroverted, stable, conscientious, empathic, intelligent and attractive individuals have been dealt the best hand for their future. They excel at tasks at hand; find healthy ways of coping with stress at work and life adversaries; build prosperous careers; and lead healthier lifestyles. Why, one might ask, should such unfairness exist? To answer this question we need to jump from the level of uniqueness to the level of the mechanism of global evolution. Both individuals and groups need to adapt to their environment or face extinction. Groups, however, rely on the prowess of their leaders to select the best way forward, to innovate and to inspire collective action. Since a larger part of intelligence and personality appears to be heritable, those blessed with the "best recipe" are not only better-equipped to lead and are selected as leaders more often, but also, in consequence, are continually reproduced in the population.

In this book, we attempted to give an accessible, comprehensive review of the psychology of body language. We noted how signs of assertiveness and power are transmitted nonverbally; how status is inferred from "silent" cues; and how liking and alliances can be signalled through movements of the body. Since this is a business-orientated book, we also considered the influence of nonverbal communication in and across work situations. Great speech-giving is, for example, unimaginable without subtle, timely and appropriate gesturing. In fact, this statement can easily be tested empirically by anyone: tie your hands behind your back the next time you need to give a presentation, or even engage in a social conversation, and you will find speaking rather hard, if not impossible.

There are some nonverbal signals that have evolutionary significance, such as proximity, matching and elevated position. They are also better researched, most frequently used, and are applicable across contexts. Other signs are much more idiosyncratic, individual or situation-bound, and should be interpreted with care and attention, if at all. Cultural interpretations of the meanings of gestures are, for example, incredibly diverse, with identical gestures changing the connotation from praise to insult as you cross a border.

While we state explicitly that body language should not be regarded as a philosopher's stone capable of giving access to the secrets of human behavior and motivation, we certainly agree with its profound and pervasive influence on our lives. We know that emotions can be detected unmistakably from facial expressions. We also know that it is possible for us to form accurate impressions of other people's personalities and intentions during extremely brief exposures. Further, we know that body language is the product of physiological changes in the nervous system which are activated by situational and emotional cues, and hence can sometimes be a true reflection of our inner state at that point in time.

However, that is where the danger lies. Since some truth about an individual's condition can be surmised via reading his or her body language, it is a natural tendency to generalize and to apply the standards across contexts. This in turn leads to popular claims and misconceptions blown out of proportion by various media and self-help counsellors hungry for the next headline or sale. We hope we have done our part in refuting some of those myths.

What sort of conclusion does this book reach? Well, if you take one thing from this book, we would like it to be this:

The power of body language lies in its subtlety, in its promise of an action rather than the action itself. Body language hints towards a certain disposition or behavior rather than identifies or determines it.

Verbal statements of allegiance, attraction and friendship are explicit commitments that are in some countries are even legally binding. Oral declarations of status, dominance and aggressiveness are likely to be met with hostility and aversion. In contrast, body language is understood momentarily and acceptingly. It does not have to be processed consciously to be appreciated or to elicit action. That is why body language is so important in business. In negotiations, for example, where the stakes are high and the disclosure of interests is often only partial, the acceptance of the deal relies heavily on the sincerity of the spoken word, or to put it simply, on how trustworthy is the other party. Trustworthiness can certainly be signalled verbally (and most job interviewees would have attempted to do just that) but has to be matched by the sincerity of the message expressed. As none of us have the ability to see too far into the future, one has to trust that the option or action selected in the present will effect the desired outcomes over the next few days, months or years. Thus, nonverbal communication plays a crucial role in our perception of the other party, by enhancing, or indeed, contradicting the verbal declaration.

The other way of looking at this would be to turn the situation around and ask: if body language is not that important and should be disregarded as an irritating "noise" in the system, why do we still have the ability to use it? One could explain the phenomenon by pointing to the evolutionary advantages this system of communication brought to our ancestors and its similarity to those of other, especially closely related, species. In line with this argument is the notion of *how* we process incoming information. The amount of information we are bombarded with every day is extraordinary. Twenty-four-hour news reports, advertising messages, and pressure from work and home life add to the complexity of the urban lifestyle of modern men and women. No wonder that cognitive filters processing the information sift most of it away (as they have always done), apart from the details considered to be the most relevant and significant. Nonverbal signals often act as clues to behaviors and intentions that do not need to be processed consciously in order to be understood, and thus reduce the cognitive load from our busy minds and facilitate complex daily interaction.

The reading of body language is a system of communication that is advantageous to us, and the absence of it is usually detrimental to individuals' social skills, as evident, for example, in Asperger's or Down's disorder sufferers, who have difficulties learning the clues about appropriate behavior for different situations. In short, body language helps us quickly to sort out friends from foes, good from bad, and sincere from dishonest words.

However, it is also necessary to discuss the implications of knowing too much about body language. Nonverbal communication is an incredibly popular topic, with hundreds of books and papers being written about it. Yet, once a trait or a behavioral pattern is labelled as being socially desirable, people will inevitably fake "good" or overinterpret what they see. One example of this tendency is the modern obsession with beauty which, exacerbated by the advances of science and media reach, has resulted in a huge increase in the number of plastic surgery interventions and eating disorders. This degree of recognition of the body language topic, in essence, may result in copy-cat behavior by some. This, of course, carries the risk of this channel of communication being abused for dishonest purposes. It was Bernard Madoff's excellent reputation in high-class circles that clouded the perception of investors and let him continue with one of the largest Ponzi schemes for years.

But how far can body language faking take you? Is it really as easy as it sounds to be? First, it is a question of *ability*. One has to not only know how to fake, but also be a good actor to perform a behavior that is not in one's natural repertoire. Think of the case of Frank Abagnale, Jr., on whose life was based the script of a famous movie, *Catch Me If You Can*. In the movie, a juvenile delinquent manages to pose successfully as a number of highly qualified professionals. With the necessary paper-work in place, he fakes being a pilot, a doctor and a lawyer. Of course, this incredible ability to fake is not something everyone possesses, but it shows that it is, indeed, possible. Con artists and impostors are often highly skilled in body language reading and portrayal.

Body language faking is, perhaps, more possible for short durations of time, but it is unlikely that one is capable of a sustained change in behavior. Most of it happens without awareness, and no degree of self-control would let, for example, an anxious individual maintain relaxed body language across various business contexts. Coupled with our implicit, unconscious trust in bodily communication and heuristic information processing (if it looks good, it must be good), it opens up the possibility of influence, as demonstrated vividly by modern staged political debates and the advertising industry. One simple piece of advice is offered to curb faking in business settings: *trust but test*. Important decisions, such as hiring or firing, should always be reached through extensive background research, not simply intuition. On the other hand, the good news for business is that nonverbal communication can be used to "nudge" employees, colleagues and consumers towards a desirable course of action.

Finally, we need to discuss issues of modernity and the effect of technology on human communication. More and more of our life is spent in digital reality communicating via telephones, text messages, e-mails, voice calls over the Internet and instant chats, and the trend is expected to steadily increase. How do these new media affect the communication process if all the usual connotations provided by body language are stripped away? The answer is threefold.

First, it does indeed create a challenge for message interpretation. What is missing from this type of communication is the immediate feedback mechanism that is typical of face-to-face interactions. Emotional cues, such as humour, sarcasm or positive affect become harder to read and understand. The information decoded in digital messages is deprived of the sensory tinge; instead, it relegates the essence of communication to the bare, plain, verbal facts. By doing so, it does not allow the sender and the recipient to instantly clarify or confirm their understanding of the message.

Second, however, people are creative creatures. They overcome the shortcomings of new technologies by inventing or utilizing different nonverbal signs and signals. Emoticons, for example, elucidate the affective context of the message. People also start using such clues as response time, length of the answer, or quality of the writing to infer hidden meaning behind the communication. There is a popular anecdote in business that recommends setting a reply system for out-going e-mails which automatically sends them at a designated time during the night. The image such behavior creates is the impression that the sender is a hard-working individual committed to doing extra time in the organization. As for video conferencing, since the interaction involves visual information, some nonverbal clues come into play there. Eye gaze patterns, smiling and facial attraction are all going to be important signals contributing to inference of meaning.

Third, digital media, detached from the sometimes irrelevant and bias-creating information such as physical attractiveness, may in fact provide an unexpected advantage to human communication at work. By subtracting the clues unrelated to the message of communication, it makes sure the focus is, finally, on *what* is being said, not on how or by whom.

APPENDIX: OTHER LITERATURE ON THE TOPIC OF BODY LANGUAGE

Borg, J. (2008). *Body Language: 7 Easy Lessons to Master the Silent Language*. Harlow: Pearson Education. Well-written and informative, combines wit and wisdom; includes personal stories, Q&A section, famous quotations on the topic.

Boyes, C. (2005). *Need to Know? Body Language*. London: Collins. Good overview of available information in a very concise style. Material is broken down into numerous sections with lots of subheadings. It is also very descriptive, and photographs are included on every page.

Fast, J. (2002). *Body Language*. New York: Evans. Novel-like narration with lots of personal stories, observations and memories.

Hargrave, J. (2008). *Strictly Business: Body Language – Using Nonverbal Communication for Power and Success* (2nd edn). Dubuque, Ia: Kendall/Hunt. An informative collection of material on nonverbal communication in business. Good overview of the area, practical applications are provided; a range of business situations are covered.

James, J. (2008). *The Body Language Bible*. London: Vermilion. Material is accessible and clear, though sometimes repetitive. The book has got a separate section on nonverbal communication in business: a self-assessment guide to body language styles and advice on how to tune it effectively to your career goals.

Jaskolka, A. (2004). *How to Read and Use Body Language*. Slough: Foulsham. The style is clear and comprehensible, with reader-friendly layout and multiple subsections. Personal memories and experiences give it a pleasant touch.

Kuhnke, E. (2007). *Body Language for Dummies*. Chichester: John Wiley. A DIY book at its best, with bullet points, pictures, anecdotes and an impressive table of contents for quick reference.

Navarro, J. (with M. Karlins) (2008). *What Every Body Is Saying: An Ex-FBI Agent's Guide to Speed-Reading People*. New York: HarperCollins. By drawing on personal experience in the security service, the author does a good job of explaining both the basics and the applications of nonverbal communication. However, some of the conclusions he reaches seem hasty and unsubstantiated, and are almost encouraging the reading of too much into body language.

Pease, A. and Pease, B. (2006) *The Definitive Book of Body Language*. London: Orion. Entertaining and instructive, the book provides no-brainer tips and solutions on how to read, understand, interpret and improve one's body language.

REFERENCES

Argyle, M. (1975). *Bodily Communication*. London: Methuen.

Argyle, M. (1993). *Bodily Communication*, 2nd edn. London: Routledge.

Atkinson, M. (2004). *Lend Me Your Ears*. London: Vermillion.

Cialdini, R. (2007). *Yes! 50 Secrets from the Science of Persuasion*. London: Profile Books.

Collett, P. (1994). *Foreign Bodies: A Guide to European Mannerisms*. London: Simon & Schuster.

Collett, P. (2003). *The Book of Tells*. London: Doubleday.

Darwin, C. (1872/1998). *The Expression of the Emotions in Man and Animals*, 3rd edn. New York: Oxford University Press.

Eibl-Eibesfeldt, I. (1971). *Love and Hate: Natural History of Behaviour Patterns*. New York: Holt, Rinehart and Winston.

Ekman, P. (2001). *Telling Lies: Clues to Deceit in the Marketplace, Politics, and Marriage*, 3rd edn. New York: W. W. Norton.

Ekman, P. (2003). *Emotions Revealed: Recognizing Faces and Feelings to Improve Communication and Emotional Life*. New York: Times Books.

Ekman, P. and Friesen, W. (1972). Hand movements. *Journal of Communication*, 22, 253–374.

Floyd, K. (2006). An evolutionary approach to understanding nonverbal communication. In V. Manusov and M. L. Patterson (eds), *The SAGE Handbook of Nonverbal Communication*. London: Sage.

Fromkin, V. (2009) *Slips of the Tongue: Windows to the Mind*. Linguistic Society of America website. http://www.lsadc.org/info/ling-fields-slip.cfm. Accessed on 23 September 2009.

Furnham, A. (2000). *The Hopeless, Hapless and Helpless Manager*. London: Whurr Publishers.

Goleman, D. (1996). *Emotional Intelligence*. London: Bloomsbury.

Harzing, A. and Feely, J. (2008). The language barrier and its implications for HQ–subsidiary relationships. *Cross Cultural Management*, 15, 49–61.

Hendon, D. and Hendon, R. (1989). *How to Negotiate Worldwide: A Practical Handbook*. Aldershot: Gower.

Hochschild, A. (2003). *The Managed Heart: Commercialization of Human Feeling*, 2nd edn. Berkeley/Los Angeles/London: University of California Press.

Hofstede, G. and Hofstede, G. J. (2005). *Cultures and Organizations: Software of the Mind*, 2nd edn. New York: McGraw-Hill.

James, J. (2008). *The Body Language Bible*. London: Vermillion.

Knapp, M. and Hall, J. (2009). *Nonverbal Communication in Human Interaction*, 7th edn. Florence, KY: Wadsworth/Cengage Learning.

REFERENCES

Loftus, E.F. and Palmer, J.C. (1974) Reconstruction of auto-mobile destruction: An example of the interaction between language and memory. *Journal of Verbal Learning and Verbal Behaviour*, 13, 585–589.

Morgan, J. (1999). *Debrett's New Guide to Etiquette and Modern Manners*. London: Headline.

Morris, D. (1967). *The Naked Ape*. London: Cape.

Morris, D. (1982). *Manwatching: A Field Guide to Human Behaviour*. London: Granada.

Morris, D. (2002). *People Watching: The Desmond Morris Guide to Body Language*. London: Vintage.

Pease, A. (1990). *Body Language: How to Read Others' Thoughts by Their Gestures*. London: Sheldon Press.

Pease, A. and Pease, B. (2005). *The Definitive Book of Body Language*. London: Orion.

Sacks, O. (1986). *The Man Who Mistook His Wife for a Hat*, 13th edn. London: Picador.

Snyder, M. (1974). The self-monitoring of expressive behavior. *Journal of Personality and Social Psychology*, 30, 526–37.

Snyder, M. (1987). *Private Appearances and Private Realities*. New York: W. H. Freeman.

Swami, V., and Furnham, A. (2008). *Psychology of Physical Attraction*. London: Routledge.

Vrij, A. (2000). *Detecting Lies and Deceit*. Chichester: John Wiley.

INDEX